Lecture Notes in Computer Science   13045

More information about this series at https://link.springer.com/bookseries/558

David Clark · Hector Menendez ·
Ana Rosa Cavalli (Eds.)

Testing Software and Systems

33rd IFIP WG 6.1 International Conference, ICTSS 2021
London, UK, November 10–12, 2021
Proceedings

 Springer

Editors
David Clark ⓘ
University College London
London, UK

Hector Menendez ⓘ
Middlesex University
London, UK

Ana Rosa Cavalli
Telecom SudParis
Evry Cedex, France

ISSN 0302-9743   ISSN 1611-3349 (electronic)
Lecture Notes in Computer Science
ISBN 978-3-031-04672-8   ISBN 978-3-031-04673-5 (eBook)
https://doi.org/10.1007/978-3-031-04673-5

This Springer imprint is published by the registered company Springer Nature Switzerland AG
The registered company address is: Gewerbestrasse 11, 6330 Cham, Switzerland

Preface

This volume contains the proceedings of the 33rd IFIP International Conference on Testing Software Systems (ICTSS 2021). This event is a well-established conference of Working Group 6.1 of the International Federation for Information Processing (IFIP). The conference was organized at University College London in the UK but conducted online because of the prevalence of the Delta variant of the SARS-CoV-2 virus. The conference took place during November 10–11, 2021.

ICTSS addresses multiple topics related to software systems, ranging from theoretical concepts for testing to practical testing frameworks. These include communication protocols, services, distributed computing, embedded systems, cyber-physical systems, security, infrastructure evaluation, applications of artificial intelligence to testing, and more. The conference engages both academic researchers and industrial practitioners, providing a forum for reviews and discussions on new contributions to the testing field in the form of methodologies, theories, tools, and use cases.

This year, the conference received a total of 36 submissions consisting of regular papers, short papers, and project reports. From these submissions 10 were accepted as full papers, seven as short papers, and six as project reports. These papers cover multiple topics including artificial intelligence in testing, security of programs, monitoring and performance, and use cases. In this edition there is a strong emphasis on Finite State Machine (FSM)-based testing.

ICTSS 2021 created a forum to share experiences between existing research projects related to the conference topics. Projects from both academia and industry were represented and several European funded projects were brought to the discussion table, hopefully seeding future collaborations among the attendees. Reports from some of these are presented in the appendix.

We want to thank University College London for support in organizing the conference, the authors who submitted their insightful contributions, the reviewers who provided their time and expertise and helped to ensure the quality of the accepted papers, the session chairs who managed the sessions, the keynote speakers, Mohammad Reza Mousavi and Konstantin (Kostya) Serebryany, and, finally, the Program Committee for their participation and advice along with the local organization team for running the conference and handling every specific detail.

We would like to thank the ICTSS Steering Committee who gave support and advice when decisions were tricky. We especially thank Ilaria Pia de la Torre, Dan Blackwell, Dan Bruce, Afnan Alsubaihin, and Bill Langdon from the Organizing Committee who underpinned the conference organization and were always available to solve problems, whether of advertising, finance, the webpage, the online delivery platform, or technical support during the conference. In addition we would like to thank IFIP for their ongoing support for this and earlier conferences in the series, as well as our publishers, Springer.

On behalf of the ICTSS 2021 organizers, we hope that you find the conference proceedings useful, interesting, and challenging.

November 2021   David Clark
                                                Héctor D. Menéndez
                                                    Ana Cavalli

Organization

General Chair

David Clark   University College London, UK

Program Committee Chairs

Héctor D. Menéndez   Middlesex University London, UK
Ana Cavalli   Telecom SudParis, France

Steering Committee

Rob Hierons   University of Sheffield, UK
Ana Cavalli   Telecom SudParis, France
Andreas Ulrich   Siemens AG, Germany
Nikolai Kosmatov   CEA List, France
Christophe Gaston   CEA List, France
Pascale Le Gall   CentraleSupelec, France
Inmaculada Medina-Bulo University of Càdiz, Spain
Mercedes Merayo   Universidad Complutense de Madrid, Spain
Francisco Palomo-Lozano University of Càdiz, Spain
Valentina Casola   University of Napoli Federico II, Italy
Massimiliano Rak   Università della Campania Luigi Vanvitelli, Italy
Alessandra De Benedictis University of Napoli Federico II, Italy

Program Committee

Héctor D. Menéndez   Middlesex University London, UK
Antonio Pecchia   Università degli Studi del Sannio, Italy
Burkhart Wolff   Paris-Saclay University, France
Natalia Kushik   Telecom SudParis and Paris-Saclay University, France
Roland Groz   Grenoble INP - LIG, France
Jorge Lopez   Airbus Defence and Space, Spain
Antoine Rollet   University of Bordeaux, France
Ana Cavalli   Telecom SudParis, France
Porfirio Tramontana   University of Naples Federico II, Italy
David Clark   University College London, UK
Manuel Núñez   Universidad Complutense de Madrid, Spain
Nikolai Kosmatov   CEA List, France
Stephane Maag   Telecom SudParis, France
Christophe Gaston   CEA List, France
Alessandra De Benedictis University of Naples Federico II, Italy

Radu Mateescu	Inria, France
Roberto Natella	University of Naples Federico II, Italy
Wissam Mallouli	Montimage, France
Justyna Petke	University College London, UK
Roberto Pietrantuono	University of Naples Federico II, Italy
Sergio Segura	University of Seville, Spain
Hüsnü Yenigün	Sabanci University, Turkey
Antonia Bertolino	ISTI-CNR, Italy
Inmaculada Medina-Bulo	Universidad de Càdiz, Spain
Mercedes Merayo	Universidad Complutense de Madrid, Spain
Gunel Jahangirova	Università della Svizzera Italiana, Switzerland
Rob Hierons	University of Sheffield, UK
Teruo Higashino	Osaka University, Japan
Ferhat Khendek	Concordia University, Canada
Robert Feldt	Blekinge Institute of Technology, Sweden
Jan Peleska	Universität Bremen, Germany
Umberto Villano	University of Sannio, Italy
Delphine Longuet	Paris-Saclay University, France
Franz Wotawa	Technische Universitaet Graz, Austria
Thierry Jéron	Inria, France
Pedro Delgado-Pérez	Universidad de Càdiz, Spain
Valentina Casola	University of Naples Federico II, Italy
Moez Krichen	University of Sfax, Tunisia
Angelo Gargantini	University of Bergamo, Italy
Khaled El-Fakih	American University of Sharjah, UAE
Shin Yoo	Korea Advanced Institute of Science and Technology, South Korea
Mike Papadakis	University of Luxembourg, Luxembourg
Luis Llana	Universidad Complutense de Madrid, Spain
Juergen Grossmann	Fraunhofer FOKUS, Germany
Bernhard K. Aichernig	TU Graz, Austria
Sébastien Salva	LIMOS, France
Andreas Ulrich	Siemens AG, Germany
Kelly Androutsopoulos	Middlesex University London, UK

Additional Reviewers

Huu Nghia Nguyen
Daniel Blackwell
Ilaria La Torre
Renzo Degiovanni
Guillaume Haben
Vinh Hoa La

Contents

Finite State Machine-based Testing

libfsmtest
An Open Source Library
for FSM-Based Testing

Moritz Bergenthal[ID], Niklas Krafczyk[ID], Jan Peleska[✉][ID],
and Robert Sachtleben[ID]

Department of Mathematics and Computer Science,
University of Bremen, Bremen, Germany
{mbergent,niklas,peleska,rob_sac}@uni-bremen.de

Abstract. In this paper, the open source library `libfsmtest` is presented. It has been developed to support model-based testing with finite state machine (FSM) models. The library is provided as a collection of C^{++} classes, each class supporting specific aspects of FSM creation and transformation, and test generation from FSM models. Additionally, the library provides main programs for test generation with the methods realised in the library and for testing 'implementation FSMs' with suites generated from 'reference FSMs'. Moreover, a generic test harness is provided for running test suites against C^{++} libraries. We explain the unique selling points of this library and compare it to competing approaches.

1 Introduction

Model-Based Testing with FSMs. Model-based testing has become one of the most important testing methods: it has been thoroughly investigated in the research communities [17], and it has been successfully applied in industrial practise [16]. One of the most widely researched areas of model-based testing uses FSM models. Of particular interest for testing safety-critical systems are the so-called *complete* testing methods. These accept correct implementations (relative to a reference model and a given conformance relation) and reject faulty ones, provided the latter fulfil some hypothesis about the maximal number of states needed to model the implementation behaviour as an FSM. While complete methods were mostly of theoretical interest in the early years of FSM-based testing [3] and thought to be of infeasible size in practice, the interest in practical application of complete methods has grown more recently, due to their optimal test strength. It has been shown that more complex systems can be abstracted to FSMs using input equivalence class testing methods, and these result in complete test suites of manageable size [9,11].

Funded by the Deutsche Forschungsgemeinschaft (DFG) – project number 407708394.

D. Clark et al. (Eds.): ICTSS 2021, LNCS 13045, pp. 3–19, 2022.
https://doi.org/10.1007/978-3-031-04673-5_1

The Open Source Library libfsmtest and Its Main Contributions. The practical generation of complete test suites from FSM models requires recurring application of non-trivial standard transformation algorithms for FSMs. Moreover, the proper test case generation algorithms associated with the known complete methods are quite complex and leave room for optimisations regarding the creation of complete test suites with preferably low numbers of test cases. Therefore, an open source library providing standard algorithms for FSM transformations and reference implementations of complete testing methods is helpful for researchers trying to improve algorithms and experiment with novel FSM-based testing methods, as well as for tool builders and practitioners wishing to experiment with complete testing methods before integrating them in their verification and validation (V&V) processes.

We consider the following features of the libfsmtest[1] to be of particular value for researchers and practitioners. (1) The libfsmtest is a thorough re-design of its predecessor fsmlib-cpp.[2] This re-design is focused on user-friendly APIs and ease of extendability, allowing researchers to add their own algorithms. (2) The library contains several test methods that are not available elsewhere. These comprise variants of reduction testing and a method for property-oriented testing. (3) Conformance relations between FSMs can be checked by running associated test suites generated from a reference FSM against an implementation FSM. This results in a model checker for conformance relations. (4) A C++-code framework is provided to generate test harnesses for running test suites generated from FSM models against software (class) libraries programmed in C/C++.

Overview. In Sect. 2, basic definitions about FSMs are introduced, in order to make this paper self-contained. In Sect. 3, the main features of the libfsmtest are described. A comparison to other open-source libraries for FSM-based testing is given in Sect. 4. Section 5 contains a conclusion and describes future work.

2   Basic Facts About FSMs

An FSM is a 5-tuple $M = (S, s_0, \Sigma_I, \Sigma_O, h)$ with finite state space S, initial state $s_0 \in S$, finite input and output alphabets Σ_I, Σ_O, and transition relation $h \subseteq S \times \Sigma_I \times \Sigma_O \times S$. An FSM is *completely specified* if for every pair $(s, x) \in S \times \Sigma_I$, *at least* one output y and target state s' exist, such that $(s, x, y, s') \in h$. Otherwise, the FSM is called *partial*. An FSM is *deterministic* (abbreviated as DFSM), if for every pair $(s, x) \in S \times \Sigma_I$ *at most* one output y and target state s' satisfying $(s, x, y, s') \in h$ exist. Otherwise the FSM is *nondeterministic*. An FSM is *observable* if for every triple $(s, x, y) \in S \times \Sigma_I \times \Sigma_O$, at most one target states s' satisfying $(s, x, y, s') \in h$ exists. An FSM is *initially connected* if every state of it can be reached from the initial state via a sequence of successive transitions.

A *trace* of an FSM M is a finite sequence of input/output pairs, such that this sequence can be produced by M, starting in the initial state and successively

---

[1] Licensed according to MIT license https://opensource.org/licenses/MIT. Source code available under https://bitbucket.org/JanPeleska/libfsmtest.

[2] https://github.com/agbs-uni-bremen/fsmlib-cpp.git.

applying the transition relation. The *language* $L(M)$ of an FSM M is the set of its traces. Given an input sequence $\bar{x} = x_1 \ldots x_k$, we say that M produces trace $\tau = x_1/y_1 \ldots x_k/y_k$ as reaction to input sequence $\bar{x}$, if τ is in $L(M)$. For nondeterministic FSMs, M may produce several different traces in reaction to $\bar{x}$. An FSM M' defined over the same alphabets as M is *equivalent* to M if $L(M') = L(M)$ holds. An FSM is *minimal* of no equivalent FSM with fewer states exists. An observable, minimal FSM is called a *prime machine*. In [8], we have introduced a more relaxed equivalence relation for deterministic FSMs, where expected outputs may be replaced in the implementation by others that are considered to be *at least as safe* as the outputs specified in the reference model. This so-called *safety equivalence* may require considerably fewer test cases than the full language equivalence.

If $L(M') \subseteq L(M)$ is satisfied, M' is called a *reduction* of M. For partial FSMs, the reduction variant *quasi-reduction* has been introduced in [7]: FSM M' is a quasi-reduction of M, if, for all traces in $L(M') \cap L(M)$, M' accepts at least the inputs that are accepted by M, and the associated outputs produced by M' for these inputs can also be produced according to M. For inputs not defined for M, the FSM M' can exhibit arbitrary behaviour. The *strong reduction* relation [20] complements quasi-reduction in the following sense: In contrast to quasi-reduction, the implementation must always be a reduction of the reference model, and after having run through an input/output trace, the implementation is required to accept *exactly the same* inputs accepted by the reference model in the associated state. Quasi-reduction is the relation of choice when dealing with incomplete reference models. In contrast to this, strong reduction is the appropriate relation for systems whose inputs may be disabled or enabled, depending on the internal system state, such as graphical user interfaces or systems with interfaces that are mechanically enabled or disabled during system execution [20].

The variants of equivalence and reduction listed above are called *conformance relations* between FSMs. A *fault domain* $\mathcal{F}(m)$ for given input and output alphabets Σ_I, Σ_O is the set of all FSMs over the same alphabets that have at most m states. Depending on the test generation method, the fault domains are further restricted to deterministic, observable or completely specified FSMs. Given a reference FSM M and a conformance relation $\leq$, a test suite is *complete* with respect to $(M, \leq, \mathcal{F}(m))$ if and only if (a) every FSM M' satisfying $M' \leq M$ passes every test of the suite (soundness), and (b) every FSM M' violating the conformance relation will fail at least one test cases, provided that $M' \in \mathcal{F}(m)$ (exhaustiveness).

3   Library Overview

The `libfsmtest` is structured into a (1) class library, (2) two main programs for test generation and model checking, and (3) a model-based test execution framework for running tests generated from FSMs against software modules programmed in C/C^{++}.

3.1 The Class Library

The class library is structured as follows. (1) The core classes `Fsm`, `Ofsm`, and `Dfsm` for arbitrary, observable, and deterministic state machines, respectively. Machines are allowed to be partial and need not be initially connected. These classes contain test-independent essential operations for checking their properties, simulating their behaviour for given inputs and checking language containment for given I/O-traces. (2) Creator classes implement factory methods for creating FSMs from files, by transformation of existing FSMs (e.g. minimisation), or by random generation. (3) Test generation methods are implemented as visitors to the main classes. Therefore, new methods can be added without having to change the core classes, just by adding another visitor. A test generation framework is instantiated with a concrete generation visitor. This instance activates the generation process and stores the results in a test suite. (4) Auxiliary classes are used for representing states, transition, and test suites, and for storing FSMs in different formats (e.g. as GraphViz graphs).

The following test generation methods are provided in the current version of `libfsmtest`: T-Method [15], W-Method [3], Wp-Method [13], HSI-Method [18], H-Method [5], SPYH-Method [24], Safety-complete H-Method (SH-Method) [8] and support for property-oriented testing [10], State Counting Method for reduction testing [6], grey-box state counting method for Strong Reduction testing [20].

Listing 1.1 shows the application of the Wp-Method on an FSM which is instantiated from a CSV-file (transition table representation). Here, variable `numAddStates`, whose value is passed to the constructor of the WP-Method (line 14), is required to fix the fault domain. It specifies the maximal number of additional states that the prime machine representing the true behaviour of the system under test (SUT) might have, in comparison to the reference model's prime machine.

To the best of our knowledge, the SH-Method and the support for property-oriented testing, as well as the Strong Reduction test method have not been implemented in any open source library before. Therefore, more details will be given below for these strategies.

Property-Oriented Testing and the SH-Method. The Safety-complete H-Method (SH-Method) had originally been introduced as a new conformance testing strategy, where output faults can be tolerated as long as they are not safety-relevant [8]. It turns out, however, that this can be interpreted as a specific variant of property-oriented testing [14]. A more general approach to the latter which contains the SH-Method as a special case has been investigated in [10]. Therefore, we focus on property-oriented testing and its support in the `libfsmtest` in this section.

In the context of property-oriented testing, we are no longer focused on verifying a conformance relation between reference model and implementation. Instead, it has to be tested whether the SUT fulfils certain properties that are

Listing 1.1. Application of the Wp-Method to a deterministic FSM instance.

```
1  #include "..."
2  using namespace std;
3  ...
4  int main(int argc, char* argv[]) {
5      // Declare creator and instantiate fsm from csv-file
6      FsmFromCsvCreator creator(RESOURCEPATH+"garage-door-controller.csv");
7      unique_ptr<Fsm> fsm = creator.createFsm();
8
9      // Declare test generation frame
10     int numAddStates = 1;
11     TestGenerationFrame
12        genFrame("SUITE-GDC-WP", // Test suite name
13                 move(fsm), // Generate test cases from this FSM
14                 make_unique<WPMethod>(numAddStates) // Use Wp-Method visitor
15                 );
16     // Generate the tests and write the suite to file
17     genFrame.generateTestSuite();
18     genFrame.writeToFile();
19     return 0;
20  }
```

also fulfilled by the reference model. Properties are conditions about inputs, outputs, and their causal ordering. In practical applications, properties are often equivalent to, or derived from requirements to be fulfilled by the implementation. The most general way to specify properties is by means of a temporal logic such as LTL [19]. This, however, is currently not yet supported by libfsmtest.

A slightly less general, but still quite powerful way is to specify properties by means of *FSM abstractions*. The theory behind this has been investigated in [8,10]. Note that it is applicable to deterministic, completely specified FSMs only. We introduce the – quite intuitive – concept here by means of an example.

Example 1. Consider the completely specified DFSM $A = (S, s_0, \Sigma_I, \Sigma_O, h)$ shown in Fig. 1 with input alphabet $\Sigma_I = \{c_1, \ldots, c_6\}$ and output alphabet $\Sigma_O = \{d_0, \ldots, d_4\}$. Suppose we wish to test whether the implementation satisfies the following property which is obviously fulfilled by A.

Property 1. *If the inputs are always in range $\{c_1, c_2, c_3\}$ then the outputs will always be in range $\{d_0, d_1\}$.*   (*)

Expressed in LTL, this property is specified by $\mathbf{G}(c_1 \vee c_2 \vee c_3) \Rightarrow \mathbf{G}(d_0 \vee d_1)$, but we will not need this for the FSM abstraction approach. Instead, we specify an abstracted FSM $\alpha(A)$ as follows:

1. The input alphabet of $\alpha(A)$ equals that of A, that is, $\{c_1, \ldots, c_6\}$,
2. the output alphabet of $\alpha(A)$ is $\{e_0, e_1\}$, where e_0 stands for A"-output is in $\{d_0, d_1\}$" and e_1 stands for A"-output is not in $\{d_0, d_1\}$",
3. the states of $\alpha(A)$ and the initial state are the same as in A, and
4. the transition relation $\alpha(h_A)$ of $\alpha(A)$ is obtained from the transition relation h_A of A as

$$\alpha(h_A) = \{(s, x, e_0, s') \mid \exists y \in \{d_0, d_1\} . (s, x, y, s') \in h\} \cup$$
$$\{(s, x, e_1, s') \mid \exists y \in \{d_2, d_3, d_4\} . (s, x, y, s') \in h\}.$$

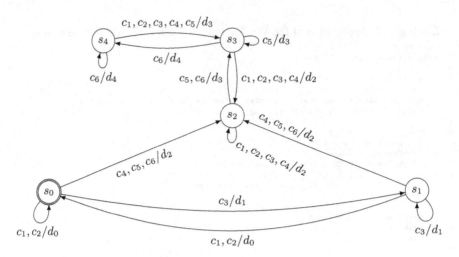

Fig. 1. FSM A with different regions: once state s_2 has been reached, the FSM will only visit states in $\{s_2, s_3, s_4\}$; it will never return to s_0 or s_1.

Intuitively speaking, $\alpha(A)$ has the same transition graph topology as A, and the transitions are labelled by the same inputs as in A. The outputs, however, are abstracted to the new values e_0, e_1, depending on whether the corresponding A-output is in $\{d_0, d_1\}$ or not.

Since the abstracted FSM has fewer outputs, it distinguishes fewer states than A: indeed, the minimised machine of $\alpha(A)$ only has two states, as shown in Fig. 2. Obviously, $\alpha(A)$ fulfils the **abstracted property**

> **Property 1a.** *If the inputs are always in range $\{c_1, c_2, c_3\}$ then the output will always be e_0.*   (**)

Now the theory developed in [8, 10] states that we can apply the generation algorithm of the SH-Method to derive an exhaustive test suite which is guaranteed to fail on an implementation violating property (*), because the abstraction FSM consistently abstracts this property to the one specified in (**). The SH-Method differs from the H-Method in the fact that distinguishing traces γ are appended to certain traces α, β already contained in the test suite only if the states reached by α and β, respectively, are also distinguishable in the abstracted FSM. The "normal" H method appends γ to α and β already if these reach states that are distinguishable in A^3.

As a consequence, the SH-Method may result in significantly fewer test cases than the H-Method. For the FSM example A discussed here, the SH-Method and the conventional H-Method produce the following numbers of test cases, depending on the maximal value a of additional states assumed for the implementation.

---

[3] States q, q' that are distinguishable in $\alpha(A)$ are by construction also distinguishable in A, but not every pair of states distinguishable in A is distinguishable in $\alpha(A)$.

	$a = 0$	$a = 1$	$a = 2$	$a = 3$
SH-method test suite size	21	126	756	4536
H-method test suite size	28	158	982	5888
Ratio	0.75	0.79	0.77	0.77

Further examples are presented in [8,10].

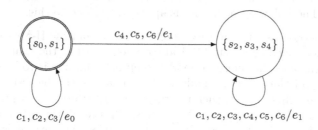

Fig. 2. Minimised FSM associated with $\alpha(A)$.

The abstraction concept described above is implemented by the SH-Method (class `SHMethod`). When using abstraction machines, the test generation frame is created with an additional parameter:

```
1  // ... read reference FSM and abstraction FSM ...
2  // referenceFsm is a unique pointer to the reference FSM.
3  // abstractionFsm is a unique pointer to the abstraction FSM.
4  TestGenerationFrame
5          genFrame("SAFETY-H-METHOD-FSBRTSX",
6                   move(referenceFsm),
7                   make_unique<SHMethod>(numAdditionalStates),
8                   move(abstractionFsm));
9
10 // Generate the test suite and write it to file
11 genFrame.generateTestSuite();
12 genFrame.writeToFile();
```

Observe that the SH-Method is exhaustive, but not sound. This means that an implementation can fail a test suite even though it correctly implements the property for which the abstraction FSM has been created. In this case, the test suite has uncovered a violation of language equivalence, which we consider as a good thing, because in principle, the SUT should really be equivalent to the reference model, though we are currently only interested in a certain property. Test suites generated by the SH-Method will never fail for implementations that are language equivalent to the reference model. In [10] it has been shown for a specific type of properties that it is possible to create complete (i.e. exhaustive and sound) test suites that only fail if the specified property is violated. This insight, however, is of theoretical value only, because these test suites may become *larger* than suites establishing language equivalence.

The fact that *two* FSMs are required for the SH-Method deserves an explanation. In principle, it would be possible to use the abstracted model itself as reference machine. However, the difference a between the potential number of states in the minimised DFSM representing the true implementation behaviour and the number of states in the minimised abstraction machine would be larger than this difference built with the original reference machine. The test suite size, however, grows exponentially in a. Therefore, it is better to use the original machine (A in the example above) with a smaller value of a.

Furthermore, note that it is not always the case that utilisation of an abstraction FSM will reduce the test suite size in comparison to testing for language equivalence. The following heuristics is applicable to decide this.

- The SH-Method never produces more test cases than the H-Method.
- If the prime machine of the FSM abstraction still has the same size as the prime machine of the reference model, then no reduction is to be expected.
- If all states of the reference model's prime machine can be distinguished by very few very short traces, then the test case reduction to be achieved by the SH-Method can be expected to be quite small, even if the prime machine of the FSM abstraction has fewer states than that of the reference model.
- If the reference FSM contains a region that is of no relevance for the property to be checked, and if this region can never be left once entered, the test suite size reduction achieved by the SH-Method grows with the size of this region.
- The ratio *"number of test cases generated by SH-Method/number of test cases generated by H-Method"* does not change significantly with the number a of potential additional states in the implementation.

In any case, the test suites can be calculated beforehand, and if their size is nearly identical, it is more advisable to test for language equivalence, since this guarantees that *all* properties fulfilled by the reference model are also fulfilled by the implementation.

Finally, note that the FSM abstraction and the resulting test suite created by the SH-Method are not only applicable to a single property, but to *all* properties captured by the same abstraction FSM. This fact is well-known from the field of model checking. If a Kripke structure has a labelling function L mapping concrete states s to sets $L(s) \subseteq \text{AP}$ of atomic propositions that are fulfilled in this state, then the resulting Kripke structure can be used for property checking of *all* temporal formulas (LTL, CTL, CTL*) over atomic propositions from AP [4].

Example 2. Consider the following property of A from Example 1 which is captured by the same FSM abstraction $\alpha(A)$.

Property 2. *After an output in $\{d_2, d_3, d_4\}$ has been produced, there will never be another output from $\{d_0, d_1\}$.*

Using LTL, this property would be expressed as $\mathbf{G}\big((d_2 \vee d_3 \vee d_4) \Rightarrow \mathbf{G}(\neg d_0 \wedge \neg d_1)\big)$. This property is encoded in $\alpha(A)$ as well, since it can be expressed by

Property 2a. *After output e_1 has been produced, there will never be another output e_0.*

The test suite created by the SH-Method for Property 1 from Example 1 is also exhaustive for Property 2.

Grey-Box Testing for the Strong Reduction Relation. As stated in Sect. 2, there are two complementary conformance relations for partial, potentially nondeterministic FSMs: quasi-reduction should be applied for reference models due to a lack of knowledge about the expected behaviour for certain (state, input) pairs, whereas strong reduction is the conformance relation of choice if missing (state, input) pairs indicates that this input is impossible in the specified state. This may happen in the case of graphical user interfaces, where an input widget is not displayed in a certain state, in the case of mechanical interfaces that may be physically blocked, or in case of communication protocols where certain communication endpoints do not yet or no longer exist in a specific state of the protocol execution.

The investigation of the strong reduction relation has only recently been started [20]. It requires a *grey-box* testing strategy: it is assumed that – apart from the SUT outputs produced in reaction to the inputs received – also the accepted inputs in each SUT state can be observed by the test environment. This assumption is frequently fulfilled: for testing graphical user interfaces, for example, it is possible to query the interface software whether certain widgets are visible or not. For mechanical interfaces, their blocked state might be detected by sensors or even by image recognition procedures (think of a credit card slot in an ATM which is mechanically blocked if one card has already been inserted). A communication socket could be checked by using the `ping` program checking its existence.

With this grey-box information at hand, a test oracle for strong reduction testing first checks in each state of the test execution whether the inputs accepted by the SUT coincide with the inputs to be accepted according to the reference model. If this condition is violated, the test execution is FAILED. Otherwise, inputs are passed to the SUT, and the associated outputs are checked against the reference model as in ordinary reduction testing. This alternating check of accepted inputs and produced outputs is performed by the test oracle throughout the entire test execution.

3.2   The Main Programs

The `libfsmtest` comes with two main programs: the `generator` produces test suites for given FSM model files, selected method, and fault domain (see Example 3 below), and `checker` performs FSM model checking by running a conformance test suite generated from a reference model against another FSM considered as implementation. Both main programs use the library classes to perform their services. Users only interested in test suite generation and FSM model checking can apply these programs, without having to build their own executables and associated library calls.

3.3   The Test Harness

A *test harness* is a program which exercises a given test suite on a software under test (SUT). The libfsmtest comes with a test harness, which allows to execute test suites generated by means of one of the FSM-based methods described above against a C/C^{++} library consisting of one or more operations to be tested. The re-usable test harness requires *input refinement* (each input alphabet value of the test case needs to be mapped to a concrete SUT operation call with input parameter values and presets of attributes) and *output abstraction* (the effect of each operation call on return value, reference parameters and attributes needs to be abstracted to the corresponding value of the reference FSM's output alphabet).

The connection between the predefined test harness and the SUT is established via an *SUT wrapper*, as shown in Fig. 3. This is a C^{++}-source frame to be completed for each test campaign, comprising three functions with fixed signatures to be accessed by the test harness. The first of the functions, void sut_init(), is called once by the test harness before the other functions and should initialise the state of the wrapper and the SUT. The second function, void sut_reset(), is called once before each test case and should reset the SUT into an initial state. Finally, function std::string sut(const std::string& x) is called by the test harness to apply a single input of a test case. The SUT wrapper then maps input string x, which represents a value of the input alphabet, to concrete input data (parameters and attributes) of the SUT and with this data calls the associated operation of the SUT. Thereafter, the SUT wrapper abstracts the observed response of the SUT to a value of the output alphabet, again represented as a string. Finally, this abstracted value is compared by the test harness to the expected response to the input as defined in the reference FSM. In order to obtain this expected response, the test harness simulates the test suite's reference FSM in back-to-back fashion during each test case. Since the test harness accesses the SUT via functions provided in the SUT wrapper only, it is the sole responsibility of the SUT wrapper to store and maintain any state data necessary to communicate with the SUT. Examples of these state data are session IDs, credentials, and message counters.

Example 3. To illustrate the preparation of an SUT wrapper and the usage of the test harness, we consider the specification of a *garage door controller (GDC)* which was originally introduced in [12]. This controller is a computer managing the up and down movement of a garage door via an electric motor. Its operational environment is shown in Fig. 4. The GDC transmits commands a1, a2, a3, a4 to a motor, which serve to initiate down movement, up movement, stop the motor, and reverse its down movement into up movement, respectively. Finally, the GDC receives inputs from several sources. First, command "button pressed" (e1) is received from a remote control device. Next, two events "door reaches position down" (e2) and "door reaches position up" (e3) are received from two door position sensors. Finally, a safety device is integrated by means of a light sensor which transmits an event "light beam crossed" (e4) when movement of an unexpected object is observed underneath the garage door while it is closing.

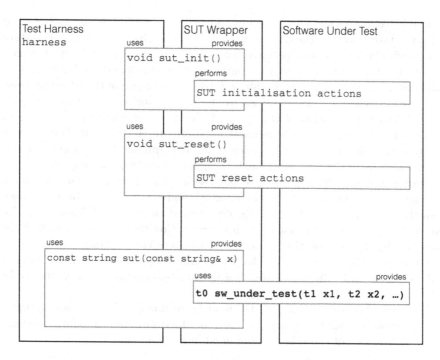

Fig. 3. Test harness, SUT wrapper, and software under test.

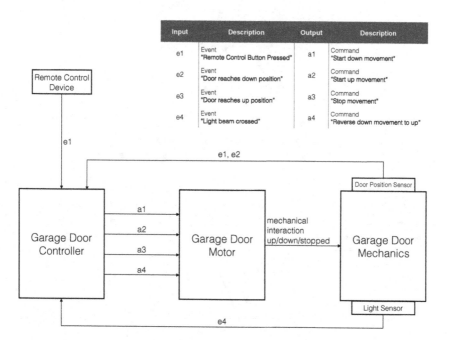

Fig. 4. Garage door controller and its operational environment.

The behaviour of the GDC can be modelled by the FSM shown in Fig. 5. In its initial state Door_Up, the door is expected to be in the UP position. The state is only left via the "button pressed" event e1 from the remote control, which triggers a "Start down movement" command a1 to the motor and a transit to state Door_closing. While in this state, a further occurrence of the e1-event leads to a "Stop movement" command a3 to the motor, and the controller transits to state Door_stopped_going_down, from which downward movement is resumed (output a1), after the next e1-command. Furthermore, in state state Door_closing an input e4 from the light sensor leads to an a4 command to the motor, which effects a reversal of the door movement, leading to state Door_opening. As soon as the door sensor signals that the door has reached the down position (via input e2), the motor is stopped with command a3 and state Door_down is reached. From this state, another e1-event triggers upward movement of the door analogous to the downward movement, with the exception that inputs from the light sensor are ignored during this movement. Note here that missing transitions in the states are interpreted as "self-loop-with null output" (null). For example, applying input e2 in the initial state results in response null and no change in state.

To create a test suite from the GDC model shown in Fig. 5, using, for example, the H method, we call the generator program of libfsmtest as follows (assume that a CSV model of the GDC is contained in file gdc.csv).

```
1    ./generator -h -a2 -cself "gdc-suite-h" gdc
```

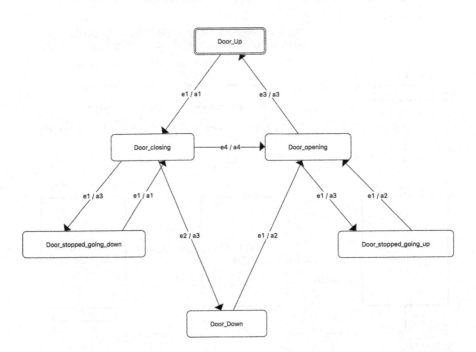

Fig. 5. Behaviour of the garage door controller, modelled by a DFSM.

Option -h selects the generation method, option -a2 indicates that the test suite shall be generated with the assumption that the DFSM representing the true SUT behaviour has at most two additional states in comparison to the minimised version of the GDC reference DFSM from Fig. 5. Option -cself indicates that missing transitions for certain inputs should always be treated as self loops with null output. The name of the test suite to be created shall be gdc-suite-h.txt.

Consider an SUT implementing the garage door controller using functions void gdc_reset() and gdc_outputs_t gdc(gdc_inputs_t x), the former resetting the SUT into an initial state and the latter realising the input-output behaviour of the GDC. Here types gdc_inputs_t and gdc_outputs_t are enumerations with values {e1, e2, e3, e4} and {nop, a1, a2, a3, a4}, respectively, corresponding to the inputs and outputs of the GDC as introduced above ("nop" corresponds to the null-output on implementation level). Assume that this implementation does not require any additional initialisation before calls to gdc_reset(). Then Listing 1.2 shows an example implementation of an SUT wrapper for this SUT. This wrapper is state-less: the transformation of FSM input events to SUT data only depends on the actual event, and not on the sequence of inputs processed so far. The same holds for outputs.

Finally, assume that the SUT accessed by this wrapper does not correctly implement the GDC by sending a stop command (a3) if a door down input (e2) is sent while the door is down, instead of the correct null. The test harness is created by compiling and linking the harness main-file together with the SUT wrapper and the SUT code. The resulting executable harness is called as follows (it is assumed that the test suite generated before is available in the working directory where the harness has been created).

```
1    ./harness gdc-suite-h gdc
```

For passed test cases, the I/O trace performed is documented by the harness. For failed test cases, the trace is documented up to its first output error. For the faulty implementation assumed here, this leads to result

```
1 PASS: e1/a1, e1/a3, e1/a1, e1/a3, e1/a1
2 PASS: e1/a1, e1/a3, e1/a1, e2/a3, e1/a2
3 ...
4 FAIL after I/O trace: e1/a1, e2/a3, e2/ <ERROR>a3
5 ... further test cases ...
```

Listing 1.2. An SUT wrapper for the garage door controller.

```
 1  #include <string>
 2  #include <map>
 3  using namespace std;
 4
 5  // Include header files of library to be tested
 6  #include "gdclib.hpp"
 7
 8  // map translating input strings to concrete inputs
 9  map<string,gdc_inputs_t> fsmIn2gdcIn = {
10      {"e1",e1}, {"e2",e2}, {"e3",e3}, {"e4",e4}
11  };
12  // map translating concrete outputs to output strings
13  map<gdc_outputs_t,string> gdcOut2fsmOut = {
14      {nop,"null"}, {a1,"a1"}, {a2,"a2"}, {a3,"a3"}, {a4,"a4"}
15  };
16
17  // initialise SUT
18  void sut_init() {
19      // Maps are already defined above; no further initialisation required
20  }
21
22  // reset SUT to initial state
23  void sut_reset() {
24      gdc_reset();
25  }
26
27  const string sut(const string& input) {
28      // empty string representing abstraction failure
29      string fsmOutputEvent;
30
31      // find the concrete input for the input string
32      map<string,gdc_inputs_t>::iterator inputIte = fsmIn2gdcIn.find(input);
33      if ( inputIte == fsmIn2gdcIn.end() ) return fsmOutputEvent;
34
35      // call the SUT with the concrete input
36      gdc_outputs_t y = gdc( inputIte->second );
37
38      // find the string representation of the observed output
39      map<gdc_outputs_t,string>::iterator outputIte = gdcOut2fsmOut.find(y);
40      if ( outputIte == gdcOut2fsmOut.end() ) return fsmOutputEvent;
41
42      // return the string representation of the observed output
43      return outputIte->second;
44  }
```

4   Related Work

We are aware of two libraries that are directly comparable to our libfsmtest:
the JPlavisFSM [1,22] and the FSMlib [23,25].

The JPlavisFSM [22] has been published as open source under the GNU
Public License GPL. It has been programmed in Java and supports test generation with methods W, UIO [2], HSI, and SPY. As a unique selling point,
the library also supports *mutation testing*: Given any test suite and a reference
model, JPlavisFSM can generate model mutants whose defects may or may not
be detected by the suite. For undetected errors, new test cases can be generated
to increase the fault coverage.

The FSMlib [23] has been programmed in C^{++} and is also distributed under GPL. It supports complete test generation methods for deterministic FSMs: W, Wp, HSI, H, SPY, SPYH [24] and a variety of lesser known methods. A special feature is that the author has set up a framework for supporting machine learning by testing [25].

A noteworthy, if not directly comparable, software program supporting FSM-based testing is the FSMTest tool [21]. It comes with a proprietary license (all rights reserved by Tomsk State University) and has been designed as a stand-alone tool programmed in C^{++}. The tool is also accessible (with restricted functionality) by means of a web interface.[4] Just like the libraries discussed above, FSMTest implements complete standard methods for test generation (W-Method, H-Method,...). As a unique selling point, the tool supports EFSM-based testing.

5 Conclusion

From the investigation of related libraries supporting FSM-based testing, we conclude that each has its unique selling points. The unique features of our libfsmtest are (a) the additional support of complete test suites for safety equivalence and varieties of reduction testing, (b) its user-friendly API and easy extendability by means of the visitor pattern, (c) the model checker for FSMs, and (d) the test harness framework for running tests against C/C^{++} software libraries. Finally, the very liberal MIT license under which libfsmtest is distributed facilitates its integration in commercial software.

For future enhancements, we plan to integrate property-based testing against LTL formulas and testing against the conformance relations quasi-equivalence and quasi-reduction according to the theory investigated in [7].

References

1. Ambrosio, A.M., Pinheiro, A.C., Simão, A.: FSM-based test case generation methods applied to test the communication software on board the ITASAT University satellite: a case study. J. Aerospace Technol. Manage. 6(4), 447–461 (2014). https://doi.org/10.5028/jatm.v6i4.369
2. Chen, W., Tang, C.Y., Vuong, S.T.: Improving the UIOV-method for protocol conformance testing. Comput. Commun. 18(9), 609–619 (1995). https://doi.org/10.1016/0140-3664(95)99804-L
3. Chow, T.S.: Testing software design modeled by finite-state machines. IEEE Trans. Softw. Eng. SE 4(3), 178–186 (1978)
4. Clarke, E.M., Grumberg, O., Peled, D.A.: Model Checking. The MIT Press, Cambridge (1999)
5. Dorofeeva, R., El-Fakih, K., Yevtushenko, N.: An improved conformance testing method. In: Wang, F. (ed.) FORTE 2005. LNCS, vol. 3731, pp. 204–218. Springer, Heidelberg (2005). https://doi.org/10.1007/11562436_16

---

[4] http://fsmtestonline.ru.

6. Hierons, R.M.: Testing from a nondeterministic finite state machine using adaptive state counting. IEEE Trans. Comput. **53**(10), 1330–1342 (2004). https://doi.org/10.1109/TC.2004.85, http://doi.ieeecomputersociety.org/10.1109/TC.2004.85

7. Hierons, R.M.: FSM quasi-equivalence testing via reduction and observing absences. Sci. Comput. Program. **177**, 1–18 (2019). https://doi.org/10.1016/j.scico.2019.03.004

8. Huang, W., Özoguz, S., Peleska, J.: Safety-complete test suites. Softw. Qual. J. **27**(2), 589–613 (2018). https://doi.org/10.1007/s11219-018-9421-y

9. Huang, W., Peleska, J.: Complete model-based equivalence class testing for nondeterministic systems. Formal Aspects Comput. **29**(2), 335–364 (2016). https://doi.org/10.1007/s00165-016-0402-2

10. Huang, W., Peleska, J.: Complete requirements-based testing with finite state machines. CoRR abs/2105.11786 (2021). https://arxiv.org/abs/2105.11786

11. Hübner, F., Huang, W., Peleska, J.: Experimental evaluation of a novel equivalence class partition testing strategy. Softw. Syst. Modeling **18**(1), 423–443 (2017). https://doi.org/10.1007/s10270-017-0595-8

12. Jorgensen, P.C.: The Craft of Model-Based Testing. CRC Press, Boca Raton (2017)

13. Luo, G., von Bochmann, G., Petrenko, A.: Test selection based on communicating nondeterministic finite-state machines using a generalized WP-method. IEEE Trans. Softw. Eng. **20**(2), 149–162 (1994). https://doi.org/10.1109/32.265636

14. Machado, P.D.L., Silva, D.A., Mota, A.C.: Towards property oriented testing. Electron. Notes Theoret. Comput. Sci. **184**(Suppl. C), 3–19 (2007). https://doi.org/10.1016/j.entcs.2007.06.001, http://www.sciencedirect.com/science/article/pii/S157106610700432X

15. Naito, S., Tsunoyama, M.: Fault detection for sequential machines by transition tours. In: Proceedings of IEEE Fault Tolerant Computing Conference, pp. 162–178 (1981)

16. Peleska, J.: Model-based avionic systems testing for the airbus family. In: 23rd IEEE European Test Symposium, ETS 2018, Bremen, Germany, May 28–June 1, 2018, pp. 1–10. IEEE (2018). https://doi.org/10.1109/ETS.2018.8400703, http://ieeexplore.ieee.org/xpl/mostRecentIssue.jsp?punumber=8392663

17. Petrenko, A., Simao, A., Maldonado, J.C.: Model-based testing of software and systems: recent advances and challenges. Int. J. Softw. Tools Technol. Transf. **14**(4), 383–386 (2012). https://doi.org/10.1007/s10009-012-0240-3

18. Petrenko, A., Yevtushenko, N., Lebedev, A., Das, A.: Nondeterministic state machines in protocol conformance testing. In: Rafiq, O. (ed.) Protocol Test Systems, VI, Proceedings of the IFIP TC6/WG6.1 Sixth International Workshop on Protocol Test systems, Pau, France, 28–30 September 1993. IFIP Transactions, vol. C-19, pp. 363–378. North-Holland (1993)

19. van de Pol, J., Meijer, J.: Synchronous or alternating? In: Margaria, T., Graf, S., Larsen, K.G. (eds.) Models, Mindsets, Meta: The What, the How, and the Why Not? LNCS, vol. 11200, pp. 417–430. Springer, Cham (2019). https://doi.org/10.1007/978-3-030-22348-9_24

20. Sachtleben, R., Peleska, J.: Effective grey-box testing with partial FSM models. CoRR abs/2106.14284 (2021). https://arxiv.org/abs/2106.14284

21. Shabaldina, N., Gromov, M.: Fsmtest-1.0: a manual for researches. In: 2015 IEEE East-West Design Test Symposium (EWDTS), pp. 1–4 (2015). https://doi.org/10.1109/EWDTS.2015.7493141

22. da Silva Simão, A.: Jplavisfsm (2021). https://github.com/adenilso/jplavisfsm. Accessed 27 Aug 2021

23. Soucha, M.: Fsmlib (2018). https://github.com/Soucha/FSMlib. Accessed 30 May 2021
24. Soucha, M., Bogdanov, K.: Spyh-method: An improvement in testing of finite-state machines. In: 2018 IEEE International Conference on Software Testing, Verification and Validation Workshops, ICST Workshops, Västerås, Sweden, 9–13 April 2018, pp. 194–203. IEEE Computer Society (2018). https://doi.org/10.1109/ICSTW. 2018.00050
25. Soucha, M., Bogdanov, K.: Observation tree approach: active learning relying on testing. Comput. J. **63**(9), 1298–1310 (2020). https://doi.org/10.1093/comjnl/ bxz056

Mining Precise Test Oracle Modelled by FSM

Omer Nguena Timo[(✉)]

Université du Québec en Outaouais,
Campus de Saint-Jérôme, Saint-Jérôme, QC, Canada
omer.nguena-timo@uqo.ca

Abstract. Precise test oracles for reactive systems such as critical control systems and communication protocols can be modelled with deterministic finite state machines (FSMs). Among other roles, they serve in evaluating the correctness of systems under test. A great number of candidate precise oracles (shortly, candidates) can be produced at the system design phase due to uncertainties, e.g., when interpreting their requirements expressed in ambiguous natural languages. Selecting the proper candidate becomes challenging for an expert. We propose a test-driven approach to assist experts in this selection task. The approach uses a non deterministic FSM to represent the candidates, includes the partitioning of the candidates into subsets of candidates via Boolean encodings and requires the intervention of experts to select subsets. We perform an empirical evaluation of the applicability of the proposed approach.

Keywords: Test oracle mining · Finite state machine · Uncertainty · Distinguishing test · Constraint solver

1 Introduction

Test oracles (simply called oracles) are usually used to evaluate the correctness of systems' responses to test data. In black-box testing approaches, test data are usually generated from machine-readable specifications which can also be used in automating the evaluation of responses and the production of verdicts on the presence of faults. In white-box testing approaches [8], test data serve to cover some artifacts during executions of a system and an expert which plays the role of the oracle evaluates the responses. Devising automated proper oracles is needed; however it is a tedious task which almost always requires the human expertise. Efforts are needed to facilitate this task [2,20] and to alleviate the intervention of experts in recurrent test activities.

Our work consider a typical conformance testing scenario [11], where an oracle is a deterministic finite state machine (DFSM). However, uncertainty can occur in devising oracles. E.g., it can be a consequence of misunderstanding or misinterpretation of requirements of systems often described with natural

© IFIP International Federation for Information Processing 2022
Published by Springer Nature Switzerland AG 2022
D. Clark et al. (Eds.): ICTSS 2021, LNCS 13045, pp. 20–36, 2022.
https://doi.org/10.1007/978-3-031-04673-5_2

languages [3,6,7]. As a result of the uncertainty, a set of candidate oracles can be proposed. For example, machine learning-based translation approaches [7,18] for reactive systems return the most likely DFSM, but the latter may be undesired due to decisions made by automated translation procedures. Instead, they could automatically return a set of candidate oracles of which the likelihood is above a certain threshold. On the other hand when a candidate oracle is available (e.g., it can be in the form of a Program under test), a set of its versions can be produced mutating it with operations mimicking the introduction or the correction of faults. Such a set can compactly be represented by a non deterministic finite state machine (NFSM) thus modelling an imprecise oracle. The candidate oracles are called precise in the opposite of the imprecise oracle defining them. Devising an oracle then consists in mining the proper candidate from the imprecise oracle.

In this paper we propose an approach to mining the proper oracle from an imprecise oracle represented with a NFSM. An expert can answer queries related to the correctness of NFSM's responses. An answer can be either yes or no. Based on the answers, the proper DFSM is automatically mined. We assume that the proper oracle is not available to the expert and the expert might have limited time resources for answering the queries. In this context, the expert cannot check the equivalence between a candidate oracle and the unavailable proper oracle; so, polynomial time active learning approaches inspired by L^* [1] are less adequate for devising the proper DFSM. In our approach, distinct responses to the same test data permit to distinguish between candidate oracles. Responses, as well as the corresponding test data, are automatically computed. Our approach is iterative and applies the "divide and conquer" principle over a current set of "good" candidates. At each iteration step, the current candidate set is divided into a subset of "good" candidates exhibiting "expected" responses to test data and the complementary subset of "bad" ones. The approach uses a Boolean encoding of the imprecise oracle; it takes advantage of the efficiency of constraint solvers to facilitate the search of good candidates.

The paper is organized as follows. The next section provides preliminary definitions. In Sect. 3, we describe the oracle mining problem and introduce the steps of our solution to it. In Sect. 4 we propose a Boolean encoding for an imprecise oracle and test-equivalent candidates; then we present the reduction of an imprecise oracle based on the selection of expected responses by experts. In Sect. 5, we propose a procedure for verifying the adequacy of a test data set for mining an oracle and a mining procedure based on automatic generation of test data. Experiments for promoting the applicability of the approach are presented in Sect. 6. In Sect. 7, we present the related work. We conclude our work in Sect. 8.

2   Preliminaries

A *Finite State Machine* (FSM) is a 5-tuple $\mathcal{S} = (S, s^0, X, Y, T)$, where S is a finite set of states with initial state s^0; X and Y are finite non-empty disjoint sets of inputs and outputs, respectively; $T \subseteq S \times X \times Y \times S$ is a transition relation and a tuple $(s, x, y, s') \in T$ is called a transition from s to s' with input x and output y. The set of transitions from state s is denoted by $T(s)$. $T(s, x)$ denotes the set of transitions in $T(s)$ with input x. For a transition $t = (s, x, y, s')$, we define $src(t) = s$, $inp(t) = x$, $out(t) = y$ and $tgt(t) = s'$. The set of uncertain transitions in an object A is denoted by $Unctn(A)$. Transition t is *uncertain* if $|T(src(t), inp(t))| > 1$, i.e., several transitions from the $src(t)$ have the same input as t; otherwise t is *certain*. The number $U_{s,x} = |T(s, x)|$ is called the *uncertainty degree* of state s on input x. $U_S = max_{s \in S, x \in X} U_{s,x}$ defines the uncertainty degree of S. We say that S is *deterministic* (DFSM) if it has no uncertain transition, otherwise it is *non-deterministic* (NFSM). In other words $U_S \leq 1$ if S is deterministic. S is *completely specified* (complete FSM) if for each tuple $(s, x) \in S \times X$ there exists transition $(s, x, y, s') \in T$.

An *execution of S in s*, $e = t_1 t_2 \ldots t_n$ is a finite sequence of transitions forming a path from s in the state transition diagram of S, i.e., $src(t_1) = s$, $src(t_{i+1}) = tgt(t_i)$ for every $i = 1 \ldots n - 1$. Execution e is *deterministic* if every t_i is the only transition in e that belongs to $T(src(t_i), inp(t_i))$, i.e., e does not include several uncertain transitions from the same state with the same input. e is simply called an execution of S if $s = s^0$. S is *initially connected*, if for any state $s' \in S$ there exists an execution of S to s'. A DFSM has only deterministic executions, while an NFSM can have both. A trace $\overline{x}/\overline{y}$ is a pair of an input sequence $\overline{x}$ and an output sequence $\overline{y}$, both of the same length. The trace of e is $inp(t_1)inp(t_2) \ldots inp(t_n)/out(t_1)out(t_2) \ldots out(t_n)$. A trace of S in s is a trace of an execution of S in s. Let $Tr_S(s)$ denote the set of all traces of S in s and Tr_S denote the set of traces of S in the initial state s^0. Given a sequence $\beta \in (XY)^*$, the input (resp. output) projection of β, denoted $\beta_{\downarrow X}$ (resp. $\beta_{\downarrow Y}$), is a sequence obtained from β by erasing symbols in Y (resp. X); if β is the trace of execution e, then $\beta_{\downarrow X} = inp(e)$ (resp. $\beta_{\downarrow Y} = out(e)$) is called the input (resp. output) sequence of e and we say that $out(e)$ is the *response* of S in s to (the application of) input sequence $inp(e)$. $|X|$ denotes the size of set X.

Two complete FSMs are distinguished with an input sequence for which they produce different responses. Given input sequence $\overline{x} \in X^*$, let $out_S(s, \overline{x})$ denote the set of responses which can be produced by S when $\overline{x}$ is applied at state s, that is $out_S(s, \overline{x}) = \{\beta_{\downarrow Y} \mid \beta \in Tr_S(s) \text{ and } \beta_{\downarrow X} = \overline{x}\}$. Given state s_1 and s_2 of an FSM S and an input sequence $\overline{x} \in X^*$, s_1 and s_2 are $\overline{x}$-distinguishable, denoted by $s_1 \not\simeq_{\overline{x}} s_2$ if $out_S(s_1, \overline{x}) \neq out_S(s_2, \overline{x})$; then $\overline{x}$ is called a distinguishing input sequence for s_1 and s_2. s_1 and s_2 are $\overline{x}$-equivalent, denoted by $s_1 \simeq_{\overline{x}} s_2$ if $out_S(s_1, \overline{x}) = out_S(s_2, \overline{x})$. s_1 and s_2 are distinguishable, denoted by $s_1 \not\simeq s_2$, if they are $\overline{x}$-distinguishable for some input sequence $\overline{x} \in X^*$; otherwise they are equivalent. Let $a \in X$. A distinguishing input sequence $\overline{x}a \in X^+$ for s_1 and s_2 is *minimal* if $\overline{x}$ is not distinguishing for s_1 and s_2. Two complete DFSMs $S_1 = (S_1, s_1^0, X, Y, T_1)$ and $S_2 = (S_2, s_2^0, X, Y, T_2)$ over the same input and output alphabets are distinguished with input sequence $\overline{x}$ if $s_1^0 \not\simeq_{\overline{x}} s_2^0$.

Henceforth, FSMs and DFSMs are complete and initially connected.

Given a NFSM $\mathcal{M} = (M, m^0, X, Y, N)$, a FSM $S = (S, s^0, X, Y, T)$ is a *submachine* of $\mathcal{M}$, denoted by $S \in \mathcal{M}$ if $S \subseteq M$, $m^0 = s^0$ and $T \subseteq N$.

We will use a NFSM to represent a set of *candidate* DFSMs. We let $Dom(\mathcal{M})$ denote the set of candidate DFSMs included in NFSM $\mathcal{M}$. Later, we will be interested in executions of $\mathcal{M}$ that are executions of a DFSM in $Dom(\mathcal{M})$. Let e be an execution of a NFSM $\mathcal{M}$ in m^0. We say that e *involves* a submachine $\mathcal{S} = (S, s_0, X, Y, T)$ of $\mathcal{M}$ if $Unctn(e) \subseteq T$, i.e., all the uncertain transitions in e are defined in $\mathcal{S}$. The certain transitions are defined in each DFSM in $Dom(\mathcal{M})$, but distinct DFSMs in $Dom(\mathcal{M})$ define distinct sets of uncertain transitions.

3   The Oracle Mining Problem and Overview of the Proposed Solution

Oracles play an important role in testing and verification activities, especially they define and evaluate the responses of implementations to given tests. The evaluation serves to provide verdicts on the presence of faults in the implementations. Letting experts play the role of an oracle is expensive. The experts will intervene in recurrent test campaigns for judging an important number of responses. For these reasons, automated test oracles are preferred.

Devising precise oracles (shortly oracles) is a challenging task that might require uncertainty resolution, as discussed in Sect. 1. Full automation of this task might result in undesired oracles. Inspired by previous work [5,12], we represent oracles with DFSMs and a *test* with an input sequence.

We propose a semi-automated mining approach for devising oracles. First we suggest modelling uncertainties with non deterministic transitions in a NFSM. This latter NFSM represents an *imprecise oracle* and it defines conflicting outputs for the same input applied in the same state. It also defines a possibly big number of candidate oracles (shortly *candidates*) which are the DFSM included in it. Secondly, experts can take useful decisions for the resolution of uncertainties and the automatic extraction of the proper candidate. The decisions concern the evaluation and the selection of conflicting responses. The fewer are the decisions, the less is the intervention of experts in the mining process and the recurrent testing activities with the selected oracle.

Let a NFSM $\mathcal{M} = (M, m^0, X, Y, N)$ represent an imprecise oracle. We say that $\mathcal{S} \in Dom(\mathcal{M})$ is the *proper* oracle w.r.t. experts if $\mathcal{S}$ always produces the expected responses to every test, according to the point of view of experts; otherwise $\mathcal{S}$ is *inappropriate*. Equivalent DFSMs represent an identical oracle. In practice the uncertainty degree of $\mathcal{M}$ should be much smaller than its maximal value $|M||Y|$; we believe that it could be smaller than the maximum of $|M|$ and $|Y|$. The *oracle mining problem* is to select the proper oracle in $\mathcal{M}$, with the help of an expert. We assume that $Dom(\mathcal{M})$ always contains the proper oracle.

The NFSM in Fig. 1a represents an imprecise oracle. It defines eight candidate oracles with six uncertain transitions, namely $t_5, t_6, t_7, t_8, t_9, t_{10}$. Figure 1c and Fig. 1d present two candidates; one of them is proper.

Mining the proper oracle is challenging even with the help of an expert, especially when the NFSM for an imprecise oracle defines an important number of candidates. The one-by-one enumeration of the candidates might not work because of the sheer number of candidates induced by an imprecise oracle. A naive approach could consist to deactivate in each state of the NFSM,

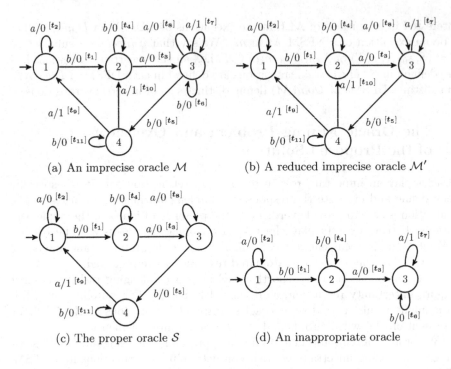

(a) An imprecise oracle $\mathcal{M}$

(b) A reduced imprecise oracle $\mathcal{M}'$

(c) The proper oracle $\mathcal{S}$

(d) An inappropriate oracle

Fig. 1. An imprecise oracle and two plausible oracles

the transitions producing outputs evaluated as unexpected by the expert. This naive approach does not work. For example, the imprecise oracle in Fig. 1 has four executions with input sequence $baba$, namely $t_1t_3t_5t_9$, $t_1t_3t_5t_{10}$, $t_1t_3t_6t_8$ and $t_1t_3t_6t_7$. The two plausible responses for these executions are 0000 and 0001. The latter is expected as it is produced by the proper oracle in Fig. 1c.

All but one executions produce the desired output 1 in state 3 on the last input a. One could deactivate or remove the transition t_8 based on the fact that it produces the last undesired output in the unexpected response. In consequence the reduction of the imprecise oracle will result in an oracle not defining t_8. Any candidate not defining t_8 is not equivalent to the proper oracle. This naive approach of selecting some transitions from transition sequences fails in mining the proper oracle. This is because entire sequences of transitions used to reach states (and so their input-output sequences) define the proper candidate.

Our oracle mining approach relies on the evaluation by experts of responses (instead of isolated outputs) of the candidates to tests. The principle of the approach is iterative and quite simple. At each iteration step, first we use pair of candidates to generate tests. Next, we generate the plausible responses for generated tests. Then we let experts select expected responses. Eventually we remove from the candidate set, the ones producing unexpected responses; this can be done by deactivating transitions in imprecise oracle and removing candidates from the set of solutions of the Boolean formulas. The iteration process continues if two remaining candidates are distinguishable. A lot of memory can be needed to store each and every candidate, especially if a great number of them is available. To reduce the usage of the memory, we encode candidates with Boolean formulas and we use a solver to retrieve candidates from the Boolean encodings. The Boolean encoding is also useful for representing the candidates already used to generate distinguishing tests.

In the next section we propose Boolean encodings for the DFSMs including in a NFSM and the test-equivalent DFSMs. We also present how to deactivate/remove transitions in a NFSM for modelling reduced candidate sets.

4 Boolean Encodings

Let $\mathcal{M} = (M, m_0, X, Y, T)$ be an imprecise oracle. $Dom(\mathcal{M})$ represents a set of candidate oracles, i.e., a set of DFSMs. We encode candidates with Boolean formulas over variables representing the transitions in $\mathcal{M}$. A solution of a formula *determines* the transitions corresponding to the variables it assigns to "true". An FSM is *determined* (encoded) by a formula if exactly all its transitions are determined by a solution of the formula.

4.1 Candidates in an Imprecise Oracle

Let $\tau = \{t_1, t_2, \ldots, t_n\}$ be a set of variables, each variable corresponds to a transition in T. Let us define the Boolean expression ξ_τ as follows:

$$\xi_\tau = \bigwedge_{k=1..n-1} \left(\neg t_k \vee \bigwedge_{j=k+1..n} \neg t_j \right) \wedge \bigvee_{k=1..n} t_k$$

It holds that every solution of ξ_τ determines exactly one variable in τ. Indeed, ξ_τ assigns *True* if both $\bigwedge_{k=1..n-1}(\neg t_k \vee \bigwedge_{j=k+1..n} \neg t_j)$ and $\bigvee_{k=1..n} t_k$ are *True*. $\bigvee_{k=1..n} t_k$ is *True* whenever at least one t_i is *True*. If some t_i is *True*, then every t_j, $i \neq j$ must be *False* in order for $\bigwedge_{k=1..n-1}(\neg t_k \vee \bigwedge_{j=k+1..n} \neg t_j)$ to be *True*. So every solution of ξ_τ determines exactly one transition in T; this transition corresponds to the only variable in τ that the solution assigns to *True*.

We encode the candidates in $Dom(\mathcal{M})$ with the formula

$$\varphi_\mathcal{M} = \bigwedge_{(m,x) \in M \times X} \xi_{T(m,x)}$$

For every state $m \in M$ and every input $x \in X$, every solution of $\varphi_\mathcal{M}$ determines exactly one transition in $\mathcal{M}$, which entails that a solution of $\varphi_\mathcal{M}$ cannot determine two different transitions with the same input from the same state. So $\varphi_\mathcal{M}$ determines exactly the candidates in $Dom(\varphi_\mathcal{M})$.

For the imprecise oracle $\mathcal{M}$ in Fig. 1a, $T(1, b) = \{t_1\}$, $T(3, a) = \{t_7, t_8\}$, $\xi_{T(1,b)} = t_1$ and $\xi_{T(3,a)} = (\neg t_7 \vee \neg t_8) \wedge (t_7 \vee t_8)$. Then, the formula $\varphi_\mathcal{M} :=$ $t_1 \wedge t_2 \wedge t_3 \wedge t_4 \wedge t_{11} \wedge ((\neg t_7 \vee \neg t_8) \wedge (t_7 \vee t_8)) \wedge ((\neg t_5 \vee \neg t_6) \wedge (t_5 \vee t_6)) \wedge ((\neg t_9 \vee \neg t_{10}) \wedge (t_9 \vee t_{10}))$ encodes all the DFSMs included in $\mathcal{M}$. In other words, $\varphi_\mathcal{M}$ determines all the candidates defined by $\mathcal{M}$. The DFSM in Fig. 1c is determined by $\varphi_\mathcal{M}$.

4.2 Candidates Involved in Executions of an Imprecise Oracle

An execution $e = t_1 t_2 \ldots t_n$ of $\mathcal{M}$ *involves* a FSM $\mathcal{S} \in Dom(\mathcal{M})$ if every t_i is defined in $\mathcal{S}$. Recall that all the certain transitions are defined in every candidate. Let us define the formula $\varphi_e = \bigwedge_{i=1..n, t_i \in Unctn(e)} t_i$. Clearly ξ_e determines every uncertain transition in e, so it determines the deterministic and non deterministic FSMs involved in e. However we are interested in DFSMs in $Dom(\mathcal{M})$ only. Remark that if DFSM $\mathcal{S}$ is involved in e, then e is deterministic. Conversely, e is deterministic if $Dom(\mathcal{M})$ includes a DFSM involved in e. An execution of $\mathcal{M}$ must be deterministic for a DFSM to be involved in it. So φ_e determines the DFSMs involved in e if e is deterministic. Let $E = \{e_1, e_2, \ldots, e_m\}$ be a set of deterministic executions of $\mathcal{M}$ and let us define the formula $\varphi_E = \bigvee_{i=1..n} \varphi_{e_i}$. The formula $\varphi_E \wedge \varphi_{\mathcal{M}}$ determines the DFSMs involved in an execution in E.

Consider the NFSM in Fig. 1a and a set $E = \{e_0 = t_1 t_3 t_6 t_8 t_8 t_6, e_1 = t_1 t_3 t_5 t_9 t_2, e_2 = t_1 t_3 t_5 t_{10} t_3 t_5, e_3 = t_1 t_3 t_6 t_7 t_7 t_6\}$ consisting of four executions e_1, e_2 and e_3. Remark that the executions are deterministic and they have the same input sequence *babaab* but distinct responses, namely 000000 for e_0, 000100 for e_1 and e_2 and 000110 for e_3. The formula $\varphi_E = (t_1 \wedge t_3 \wedge t_6 \wedge t_8) \vee (t_1 \wedge t_3 \wedge t_5 \wedge t_9 \wedge t_2) \vee (t_1 \wedge t_3 \wedge t_5 \wedge t_{10}) \vee (t_1 \wedge t_3 \wedge t_6 \wedge t_7) \wedge \varphi_{\mathcal{M}}$ encodes the DFSMs involved in the three executions.

4.3 Test-Equivalent Candidate

Let $\overline{x}$ be a test. To determine the $\overline{x}$-equivalent DFSMs, we can partition $Dom(\mathcal{M})$ into subdomains. The DFSMs in each subdomain produce the same response to test $\overline{x}$. Our encoding of each subdomain with a Boolean formula works as follows.

Let $Y_{\mathcal{M},\overline{x}} = \{\overline{y}_1, \overline{y}_2, \ldots \overline{y}_n\}$ be the set of responses the DFSMs in $Dom(\mathcal{M})$ to test $\overline{x}$. Each response $\overline{y}_i$, with $i = 1 \ldots n$, corresponds a maximal set of deterministic executions of $\mathcal{M}$ with input sequence $\overline{x}$. We denote by $E_{\overline{x}/\overline{y}_i} = \{e_{i_1}, e_{i_2}, \ldots, e_{i_m}\}$ the set of deterministic executions producing $\overline{y}_i$ on input sequence $\overline{x}$. Clearly $E_{\overline{x}/\overline{y}_i}$ characterizes a subdomain of $\overline{x}$-equivalent DFSMs. The maximal size of $Y_{\mathcal{M},\overline{x}}$ equals $|\overline{x}|^{|Y|}$ and it is reached when the imprecise oracle is the universe of all DFSMs, which is not the practical context of our work with imprecise oracles having reasonable uncertainty degrees.

Let $P_{x/\overline{y}_i}$ denote the set of DFSM in $\mathcal{M}$ involved in an execution in $E_{\overline{x}/\overline{y}_i}$. It holds that $P_{\overline{x}/\overline{y}_1}, P_{\overline{x}/\overline{y}_2}, \ldots P_{\overline{x}/\overline{y}_n}$ constitutes a partition of $Dom(\mathcal{M})$, i.e., every deterministic submachine of $\mathcal{M}$ exactly belongs to one $P_{\overline{x}/\overline{y}_i}$, $i = 1..n$ and every DFSM in $P_{\overline{x}/\overline{y}_i}$ is a submachine of $\mathcal{M}$ for every $i = 1..n$.

For each $\overline{y} \in Y_{\mathcal{M},\overline{x}}$, we define the formula $\varphi_{E_{\overline{x}/\overline{y}}}$. It holds that $\varphi_{\mathcal{M}} \wedge \varphi_{E_{\overline{x}/\overline{y}}}$ encodes the maximal set of DFSMs indistinguishable by $\overline{x}$. Indeed, $\varphi_{E_{\overline{x}/\overline{y}}}$ determines exactly the $\overline{x}$-equivalent FSMs involved in deterministic executions in $E_{\overline{x}/\overline{y}}$ and $\varphi_{\mathcal{M}}$ determines the DFSMs in $\mathcal{M}$. We can show that every DFSM included in $\mathcal{M}$ is determined by the formula $\varphi_{\mathcal{M}} \wedge \varphi_{E_{\overline{x}/\overline{y}}}$ for exactly one $\overline{y} \in Y_{\mathcal{M},\overline{x}}$. Furthermore, if $\overline{x}$ is not distinguishing for the DFSMs in $Dom(\mathcal{M})$, then $\varphi_{\mathcal{M}} \wedge \varphi_{E_{\overline{x}/\overline{y}}}$ and $\varphi_{\mathcal{M}}$ are equivalent, i.e., they determine the DFSMs in $Dom(\mathcal{M})$.

Table 1. Partitioning of $\mathcal{M}$ into Subdomains w.r.t input sequence $\bar{x} = babaab$

Response $\bar{y}$	Subdomain for $\varphi_{\mathcal{M}}$	Size	Precise oracles in the subdomain $P_{\bar{x}/\bar{y}_i}$
000100	$\varphi_{\bar{x}/000100} = ((t_5 \wedge t_9) \vee (t_5 \wedge t_{10}))$	4	$\{t_1, t_2, t_3, t_4, t_5, t_7, t_{10}, t_{11}\}$, $\{t_1, t_2, t_3, t_4, t_5, t_7, t_9, t_{11}\}$, $\{t_1, t_2, t_3, t_4, t_5, t_8, t_9, t_{11}\}$, $\{t_1, t_2, t_3, t_4, t_5, t_8, t_{10}, t_{11}\}$
000110	$\varphi_{\bar{x}/000110} = t_6 \wedge t_7$	2	$\{t_1, t_2, t_3, t_4, t_6, t_7, t_{10}, t_{11}\}$, $\{t_1, t_2, t_3, t_4, t_6, t_7, t_9, t_{11}\}$
000000	$\varphi_{\bar{x}/000000} = t_6 \wedge t_8$	2	$\{t_1, t_2, t_3, t_4, t_6, t_8, t_9, t_{11}\}$, $\{t_1, t_2, t_3, t_4, t_6, t_8, t_{10}, t_{11}\}$

where, $\varphi_{\mathcal{M}} = t_1 \wedge t_2 \wedge t_3 \wedge t_4 \wedge t_{11} \wedge ((\neg t_7 \vee \neg t_8) \wedge (t_7 \vee t_8)) \wedge ((\neg t_5 \vee \neg t_6) \wedge (t_5 \vee t_6)) \wedge ((\neg t_9 \vee \neg t_{10}) \wedge (t_9 \vee t_{10}))$

Considering our running example and the test $\bar{x} = babaab$, we have that $Y_{\mathcal{M},babaab} = \{e_0 = t_1 t_3 t_6 t_8 t_8 t_6, e_1 = t_1 t_3 t_5 t_9 t_2, e_2 = t_1 t_3 t_5 t_{10} t_3 t_5, e_3 = t_1 t_3 t_6 t_7 t_7 t_6\}$. Since the four executions have distinct responses (i.e., output sequences), we get $E_{babaab/000000} = \{e_0\}$, $E_{babaab/000100} = \{e_1, e_2\}$ and $E_{babaab/000110} = \{e_3\}$. Table 1 presents the corresponding subdomains and the number of oracles in each subdomain. The two oracles in the subdomain for response 000000 are equivalent. The same for response 000110. The subdomain for response 000100 defines four $babaab$-equivalent candidate oracles. Later, experts are invited to select the expected response that will serve to reduce the imprecise oracle.

4.4 Reducing an Imprecise Oracle

The selection of test-equivalent candidates renders useless transitions of the imprecise oracle unused in the selected candidates. These transitions can be deactivated for obtaining a reduced imprecise oracle.

Let $\mathcal{M} = (M, m^0, X, Y, N)$ be an input complete NFSM and $\bar{x}/\bar{y}$ be a trace. $Dom(\mathcal{M})$ is partitioned into the set $Dom(\mathcal{M})_{\bar{x}/\bar{y}}$ of DFSMs producing $\bar{y}$ on $\bar{x}$ and the set of DFSMs not producing $\bar{y}$ on $\bar{x}$. We say that a transition $t \in N$ is *eligible* for a candidate involved in e if e uses t or $t' \notin N(src(t), inp(t))$ for every t' used in e.

Lemma 1. *There is a submachine $\mathcal{M}_{\bar{x}/\bar{y}}$ of $\mathcal{M}$ such that $Dom(\mathcal{M}_{\bar{x}/\bar{y}}) = Dom(\mathcal{M})_{\bar{x}/\bar{y}}$.*

Proof. Let e be a deterministic execution e in $E_{\bar{x}/\bar{y}}$. Remark that all the transitions in e are eligible for the candidates involved in e. Moreover e is the only execution with input sequence $\bar{x}$ and response $\bar{y}$ in each of these candidates.

We build $\mathcal{M}_{\bar{x}/\bar{y}} = (S, s^0, X, Y, T)$ with $T \subseteq N$ by deactivating (deleting) non eligible transitions for candidates in $Dom(\mathcal{M}_{\bar{x}/\bar{y}})$. Formally $t \in N$ belongs to T if it is eligible for a candidate involved in some deterministic execution $e \in E_{\bar{x}/\bar{y}}$. $m \in M$ belongs to S if m is used in a transition in T. Clearly, $\mathcal{M}_{\bar{x}/\bar{y}}$ is a complete and initially connected submachine of $\mathcal{M}$; $\mathcal{M}_{\overline{x}/\overline{y}}$ is not necessarily deterministic because several executions in $E_{\overline{x}/\overline{y}}$ can use several uncertain transitions defined in the same state and with the same input; these transitions belong to T.

First we show that $Dom(\mathcal{M}_{\overline{x}/\overline{y}}) \subseteq Dom(\mathcal{M})_{\overline{x}/\overline{y}}$ by contradiction. Assume that there is $\mathcal{P}$ in $Dom(\mathcal{M}_{\overline{x}/\overline{y}})$ but not in $Dom(\mathcal{M})_{\overline{x}/\overline{y}}$. $\mathcal{P}$ is deterministic and by construction it defines all the transitions in a deterministic execution $e \in E_{\overline{x}/\overline{y}}$ of $\mathcal{M}$. This implies the response of $\mathcal{P}$ on $\overline{x}$ is $\overline{y}$, which is a contradiction with hypothesis $\mathcal{P} \notin Dom(\mathcal{M})_{\overline{x}/\overline{y}}$. Secondly, we show that $Dom(\mathcal{M})_{\overline{x}/\overline{y}} \subseteq Dom(\mathcal{M}_{\overline{x}/\overline{y}})$. Let $\mathcal{P} \in Dom(\mathcal{M})_{\overline{x}/\overline{y}}$. $\mathcal{P}$ produces $\overline{y}$ on $\overline{x}$ with exactly one of its execution e. The transitions eligible for $\mathcal{P}$ are defined in $\mathcal{M}_{\overline{x}/\overline{y}}$. So $\mathcal{P} \in Dom(\mathcal{M}_{\overline{x}/\overline{y}})$. $\qquad\square$

Consider Table 1 and assume experts choose the expected response 000100. The reduced imprecise oracle for $babaab/000100$, $\mathcal{M}_{babaab/000100}$ is the imprecise oracle in Fig. 1b which was obtained by removing transition t_6 from $\mathcal{M}$ in Fig. 1a. This is because among the two transitions t_5 and t_6 from state 3 with input b, the executions in $E_{babaab/000100}$ only use t_5.

Reducing an imprecise oracle permits to speed up the computation of executions with given tests. Indeed, once it becomes clear that passing some transitions in the imprecise oracle leads to the production of undesired responses, one does not need to consider these transitions in determining new execution sets.

Let $\mathcal{S}$ be a candidate in $Dom(\mathcal{M})$ and $\overline{x}/\overline{y}$ be a test-response pair.

Lemma 2. $\mathcal{S} \in Dom(\mathcal{M}_{\overline{x}/\overline{y}})$ *if and only if* $\mathcal{S}$ *is determined by* $\varphi_{\mathcal{M}} \wedge \varphi_{E_{\overline{x}/\overline{y}}}$.

Remark that in some circumstances $\mathcal{M}_{\overline{x}/\overline{y}}$ is the same as $\mathcal{M}$. This happens when the union of eligible transitions over a set of executions equals the set of transitions of $\mathcal{M}$. Such a case will be presented in Sect. 5.2. Uncertain transitions in $\mathcal{M}$ but not in $\mathcal{M}_{\overline{x}/\overline{y}}$ are not determined by $\varphi_{\mathcal{M}} \wedge \varphi_{E_{\overline{x}/\overline{y}}}$ because other uncertain transitions are determined by $\varphi_{E_{\overline{x}/\overline{y}}}$ and a solution of $\varphi_{\mathcal{M}}$ cannot determine two uncertain transitions from the same state with the same input.

5   Mining an Oracle

To mine an oracle represented with a DFSM, we apply a test set TS on an imprecise oracle $\mathcal{M}$. We say that TS is *adequate* for mining the proper oracle from $\mathcal{M}$ if TS is distinguishing for some $\mathcal{S} \in \mathcal{M}$ and every other candidate in $\mathcal{M}$ that is not equivalent to $\mathcal{S}$; moreover $\mathcal{S}$ is proper. Verifying the mining adequacy of TS is the first step in mining the proper oracle. In case TS is not adequate, new tests can be generated.

5.1   Verifying Adequacy of a Test Set for Mining the Proper Oracle

Our method of verifying the adequacy of a test is iterative. At each iteration step, a test is randomly chosen and the corresponding plausible responses are computed with the imprecise oracle. Then experts select an expected response and send it to an automated procedure. The automated procedure reduces the

---

Algorithm 1: Verifying Test Adequacy For Mining an Oracle.

Input-Output: $\mathcal{M}$ an imprecise oracle

Input: $\varphi_\mathcal{M}$ the boolean encoding of DFSM included in NFSM $\mathcal{M}$

Input: a test set TS

Input: a DFSM S emulating the expert for the response selection

Output: $verdict$, is $true$ or $false$ on whether TS enables mining a DFSM.

Output: φ the Boolean encoding of DFSM consistent with expert knowledge

Output: $\overline{x}_d$ a test that distinguish two DFSM

1 **Procedure** $verify\_test\_adequacy\_for\_mining$ $(\mathcal{M}, \varphi_\mathcal{M}, TS, S)$:

2   Set $\varphi = \varphi_\mathcal{M}$

3   Set $verdict = true$ if φ does not select at least two non equivalent DFSMs; otherwise set $verdict = false$

4   **while** $TS \neq \emptyset$ and $verdict == false$ **do**

5   Let $\overline{x}$ be a test in TS.

6   Remove $\overline{x}$ from TS.

7   Determine $Y_{\mathcal{M},\overline{x}}$ the set of outputs of deterministic executions in $E_{\overline{x}}$ of $\mathcal{M}$ with input $\overline{x}$

8   Show $Y_{\mathcal{M},\overline{x}}$ to experts and let $\overline{y} \in Y_{\mathcal{M},\overline{x}}$ be the output such that $\overline{y} = outs_S(s^0, \overline{x})$, ($\rightarrow$ choice of the expected response by experts)

9   Determine $E_{\overline{x}/\overline{y}} \subseteq E_{\overline{x}}$ the deterministic executions of $\mathcal{M}$ which produce $\overline{y}$ on test $\overline{x}$

10   Determine $\mathcal{M}_{\overline{x}/\overline{y}}$

11   Set $\varphi = \varphi \wedge \varphi_{E_{\overline{x}/\overline{y}}}$ the Boolean encoding of DFSMs in $\mathcal{M}$ which produce $\overline{y}$ on test $\overline{x}$

12   Set $\mathcal{M} = \mathcal{M}_{\overline{x}/\overline{y}}$

13   **if** φ encodes at two non equivalent DFSMs **then**

14   Set $\overline{x}_d$ to a minimal distinguishing test for two non equivalent DFSMs

15   **else**

16   Set $verdict = true$

17   **return** $(verdict, \mathcal{M}, \varphi, \overline{x}_d)$

---

imprecise oracle, i.e., deactivates some transitions from the imprecise oracle. The procedure stops when the responses for every test are examined or no imprecision remains. The procedure *verify_test_adequacy_for_mining* scripted in Algorithm 1 returns a verdict of the verification.

Procedure *verify_test_adequacy_for_mining* takes as inputs an imprecise oracle represented by a NFSM, a test set and the expert knowledge about the expected outputs for the tests. We represent the expert knowledge with a DFSM. It uses Boolean encoding presented in the previous section. The procedure ends the iteration if all the tests were visited or the Boolean encoding defines a single DFSM. If the Boolean encoding of the test-equivalent DFSMs defines two non equivalent DFSMs then the tests do not enable mining an oracle; otherwise one of the remaining equivalent DFSMs is mined. The procedure also returns the

---

Algorithm 2: Mining an Oracle by Test Generation.

Input: $\varphi_{\mathcal{M}}$ the boolean encoding of DFSM included in a NFSM $\mathcal{M}$
Input: a test set $\mathcal{TS}$
Input: a DFSM $\mathcal{S}$ emulating the expert for the response selection
Output: $\mathcal{TS}_m$ a test set that enables mining a DFSM.
Output: $\mathcal{P}$ the proper oracle
1 **Procedure** *precise_oracle_mining* $(\mathcal{M}, \mathcal{TS}, \mathcal{S})$:
2   Set $\varphi = \varphi_{\mathcal{M}}$
3   Set $\mathcal{TS}_m = \mathcal{TS}$
4    $(verdict, \mathcal{M}', \varphi', \overline{x}_d) = verify\_test\_adequacy\_for\_mining(\mathcal{M}, \varphi, \mathcal{TS}, \mathcal{S})$
5   **while** *verdict* == *false* **do**
6   Set $\mathcal{TS}_m = \mathcal{TS}_m \cup \{\overline{x}_d\}$
7      $\varphi = \varphi'$
8      $\mathcal{M} = \mathcal{M}'$
9   Set $\mathcal{TS} = \{\overline{x}_d\}$
10      $(verdict, \mathcal{M}', \varphi', \overline{x}_d) = verify\_test\_adequacy\_for\_mining(\mathcal{M}, \varphi, \mathcal{TS}, \mathcal{S})$
11   Let $\mathcal{P}$ be the DFSM obtained from a solution of φ'
12   **return** $(\mathcal{TS}_m, \mathcal{P})$

Boolean encoding of the selected DFSMs for the tests, i.e., the DFSMs which produce the expected output on every test.

Consider the original imprecise oracle $\mathcal{M}$ in Fig. 1a. For verifying whether the test *babaab* is adequate for mining an oracle, *verify_test_adequacy_for_mining* determines the plausible responses (see Table 1) for the deterministic execution $\mathcal{M}$ on *babaab*. Assume that experts choose expected response 000100. The procedure determines $E_{babaab/000100}$ as we discussed in Sect. 4.3; then it builds $\varphi_{babaab/000100}$ in Table 1 and the reduced imprecise oracle in Fig. 1b as discussed in Sect. 4.4. The formula $\varphi := \varphi_{\mathcal{M}} \wedge \varphi_{babaab/000100}$ determines four *babaab*-equivalent candidates presented in Table 1. Two of these candidates are distinguished with test *babaaa*, namely the oracle in Fig. 1c and the one defining the transition set $\{t_1, t_2, t_3, t_4, t_5, t_7, t_{10}, t_{11}\}$. This latter oracle provides response 000101 whereas the former provides 000100 for test *babaaa*. In conclusion the procedure returns *verdict* = *false* indicating that test *babaab* is not adequate for mining the proper oracle in Fig. 1c; it also returns the reduced imprecise oracle and the encoding with φ of *babaab*-equivalent candidates.

5.2 Test Generation in Mining an Oracle

Procedure *precise_oracle_mining* in Algorithm 2 mines an oracle from an imprecise one by generating tests. The procedure makes a call to semi-automated procedure *verify_test_adequacy_for_mining* in Algorithm 1. If given tests are not adequate for the mining task, procedure *verify_test_adequacy_for_mining* returns a Boolean encoding of a reduced set of test-equivalent candidates. Then, procedure *precise_oracle_mining* generates a distinguishing test for two candidates in the reduced set. Such a test can correspond to a path to a sink state in the distinguishing product [15] of two candidates. The test generation stops if the generated test is adequate for mining the proper oracle in the reduced set of candidates; otherwise another test is generated. Procedure *precise_oracle_mining* always terminates because at each iteration step, the set of candidates is reduced after a call to procedure *verify_test_adequacy_for_mining* and the number of DFSMs included in the original imprecise oracle is finite. On termination of *verify_test_adequacy_for_mining*, the initial tests augmented with the generated ones constitute adequate tests for mining the proper oracle determined by φ'.

Considering the running example, the first call to *verify_test_adequacy_for_mining* in the execution of Procedure *precise_oracle_mining* permits establishing that the test *babaab* is not adequate for mining an oracle. This was discussed at the end of the previous section where the test $\overline{x}_d = babaaa$ was generated as a distinguishing test for two candidates determined by $\varphi' := \varphi_{\mathcal{M}} \wedge \varphi_{babaab/000100}$ and included in the reduced imprecise oracle $\mathcal{M}'$ in Fig. 1b. In the first iteration step of the while loop, Procedure *precise_oracle_mining* makes a second call to *verify_test_adequacy_for_mining* for checking whether the generated test *babaaa* is adequate for mining an oracle from the new context $\mathcal{M} = \mathcal{M}'$ and $\varphi = \varphi'$. Here is what happens within this second call. The plausible responses for *babaaa* belong to $Y_{\mathcal{M}',babaaa} = \{000100, 000101\}$; they are obtained with deterministic executions of $\mathcal{M}'$ in $E_{babaaa} = \{e_0 = t_1 t_3 t_5 t_9 t_2 t_2, e_1 = t_1 t_3 t_5 t_{10} t_3 t_8, e_2 = t_1 t_3 t_5 t_{10} t_3 t_7\}$. Computing executions having input sequence *babaaa* and the plausible responses is more efficient with $\mathcal{M}'$ than with $\mathcal{M}$; this is because $\mathcal{M}'$ does not define t_6. Assume that 000100 is the expected response for *babaaa*. Then $E_{babaaa/000100} = \{e_0 = e_1 = t_1 t_3 t_5 t_9 t_2 t_2, e_2 = t_1 t_3 t_5 t_{10} t_3 t_8\}$ and $\varphi_{babaaa/000100} = t_9 \vee (t_{10} \wedge t_8)$. Using $\mathcal{M}'$ in Fig. 1b, there are two candidates involved in e_0 and the eligible transitions for the two candidates include all the transitions in $\mathcal{M}'$ but t_{10}. Remark that uncertain transitions t_8, t_7 are eligible even if they are not used in e_0. There is one candidate involved in e_1 and the eligible uncertain transitions for this candidate are t_8, t_{10}. So, the set of eligible transitions for the candidates involved in executions in $E_{babaaa/000100}$ are all the transitions in $\mathcal{M}'$. In this particular case, $\mathcal{M}'$ is not reduced with test-response pair *babaaa/000100*. However the $\{babaab, babaaa\}$-equivalent candidates are encoded with $\varphi' \wedge \varphi_{E_{babaaa/000100}} = \varphi_{\mathcal{M}} \wedge \varphi_{E_{babaab/000100}} \wedge \varphi_{E_{babaaa/000100}}$. This latter formula determines two candidates distinguishable with *babaaba* in the reduced imprecise oracle obtained from $\mathcal{M}'$ by deactivating transition t_{10}. Eventually *precise_oracle_mining* generates the test *baa*, terminates and returns adequate test set $\{babaab, babaaa, babaaba, baa\}$ for mining the oracle in Fig. 1c.

6   Experimental Results

We evaluate whether the proposed approach is applicable for mining oracles from imprecise oracles that define a big number of candidate oracles and whether it requires a reasonable number of interventions of experts. For that purpose we implemented a prototype tool, perform multiple atomic experiments, monitor metrics and we compute some statistics. The prototype tool is implemented in

Java; it uses Java libraries of the solver Z3 version 4.8.4 and the compilation tool ANTLR version 4.7.2. The computer has the following settings: WINDOWS 10, 16 Go (RAM), Intel(R) Core i7-3770 @ 3.4 GHz.

An atomic experiment works as follows. We automatically generate a complete DFSM S for given numbers of states, inputs and outputs denoted by $|M|, |X|$ and $|Y|$ respectively. S emulates the experts during the experiments. We set the uncertainty degree U. For a value of U we randomly add transitions to S for generating an imprecise oracle M. Eventually, we extract a DFSM equivalent to S from M by making a call to our implementation of procedure *precise_oracle_mining* in Algorithm 2.

The metrics we monitor in each atomic experiments are: $|Dom(M)|$ the maximum number of candidate oracles in M; $|TS|_{min}$ and $|TS|_{max}$ the minimum and the maximum numbers of generated tests; L_{min} and L_{max} the minimum and the maximum lengths of the generated tests; and T_{min}, T_{max} and T_{med} the minimal, maximal and median processing times (in milliseconds) for the mining procedure. We assumed that it takes almost zero millisecond for emulated experts to select responses, which is insignificant in comparison to the processing time for the plausible responses and solutions of Boolean formulas. We performed 30 atomic experiments to obtain the data in each row of Table 2 and Table 3.

In Table 2, we consider imprecise oracles with 10 states, 3 inputs and 2 outputs. We observe that the values of almost all the metrics augment when the uncertainty degree U increases, especially T_{med}. The generated imprecise oracles in Table 3 have 3 inputs, 2 outputs and uncertainty degree equals to 3. We also observe that almost all the metrics increase when the number of states increases, especially T_{med}. We notice that for $(|M|, |X|, |Y|, U) = (10, 3, 2, 3)$, the gap between the values for T_{med} in Table 2 and Table 3 is minor, which let us believe that T_{med} is significant to evaluate the performance of our approach.

Let us provide a practical perspective on the results in Table 2 and Table 3. Clearly, experts would have took more time than its emulation with a DFSM to select expected responses. Let us assume that it takes on average 1 min to experts for selecting the expected response for a test. Under this assumption and considering the last row of Table 2, the extraction of an oracle over the possible $2.21E23$ candidates could last 106 min since the automated procedure only lasts for 18.26 s. We advocate that if the extracted oracle serve in testing a critical system, taking 106 min to extract the proper oracle is better than using an undesired oracle. If the manual repair of the undesired oracle is not trivial, mutation operations (taking inspiration from [10,19]) can apply to it for generating an imprecise oracle and mining a proper oracle.

The proposed approach could also be lifted for the generation in a distributed way of adequate test sets for mining each and every candidate. This can be done by partitioning the candidate set into subsets, one subset per plausible response. The constraints for each subset can be processed in parallel in other to generate new tests. The generated test sets will be computed without any intervention of experts. After the test set generation and the iterative partitioning of candidate subsets, the experts could passively select expected responses for the generated tests in a passive manner for mining the proper oracle.

Table 2. $(|M|, |X|, |Y|) = (10, 3, 2)$

U	$|Dom(\mathcal{M})|$	$|TS|_{min}$	$|TS|_{max}$	L_{min}	L_{max}	T_{min} (ms)	T_{max} (ms)	T_{med} (ms)
2	1.07E9	21	32	5	8	871	1619	1106.0
3	2.06E14	33	55	5	8	2128	115867	2865.0
4	1.15E18	40	78	5	7	3313	8626	4417.0
5	9.31E20	55	100	5	7	6334	35190	9618.0
6	2.21E23	64	106	5	7	9903	105994	18263.0

Table 3. $(|X|, |Y|, U) = (3, 2, 3)$

$|M|$	$|Dom(\mathcal{M})|$	$|TS|_{min}$	$|TS|_{max}$	L_{min}	L_{max}	T_{min} (ms)	T_{max} (ms)	T_{med} (ms)
7	1.05E10	22	43	4	7	1008	2457	1220.0
8	2.82E11	24	53	4	8	1136	3199	2071.0
9	7.63E12	30	55	5	7	1575	4767	2056.0
10	2.06E14	33	53	5	7	1905	4237	2438.0
11	5.56E15	37	66	5	7	2109	4567	3053.0
12	1.50E17	41	71	5	8	2533	5588	5140.0
13	4.053E18	43	79	5	8	2837	7680	6381.0

7   Related Work

Metamorphic testing [4, 16, 17] applies in devising test oracle when it is difficult to compare an expected response of a system under test with an observed one. It consists in mutating original test input data to build a test set that violates metamorphic relations. These relations can play the role of coarse specifications and can serve to derive test sets. Building the relations requires the expert knowledge and extra-skills. Our approach exonerates testers to building such relations. Candidate oracles allow focusing on revealing deviations in the responses.

In [10, 19] a test-response set is used to repair a system when its formal specification is unavailable. The approach consists in analyzing mutated versions of an implementation (C program) until one is found that retains required functionality and avoids a defect located by the tests. Mutated versions are generated using genetic programming. In our work, the specification and the test-response pairs are unavailable. We generate tests and we rely on experts and the imprecise oracle to obtain the expected responses and to extract the oracle (specification).

In [9], a test set is generated to detect whether a DFSM implementation is a reduction (i.e., is trace included) of a NFSM specification playing the role of an oracle; if so the implementation conforms to the specification. This work presumes that any of the traces of the specification is expected. This differs from our settings where responses from non deterministic executions in the imprecise oracle NFSM cannot be produced by the proper candidate DFSM; so any implementation exhibiting these responses must fail the tests.

The work in [1] addresses the problem of learning a DFSM by using output and equivalence queries to a teacher. The proposed polynomial time active learning algorithm often requires a certain number of queries so that it wont be effective for experts to play the role of the teacher. In practice, the teacher is a black-boxed implementation one wants to infer a DFSM model. In our work, we want to mine a DFSM from a given NFSM by using the expert knowledge. Such a situation happens, e.g., when one needs to choose among multiple implementation models of the same system. In our settings, there is no equivalence query and expert responds few queries on the selection of expected responses.

The work in [13, 15] represents the fault domain for a DFSM specification with a NFSM. Each DFSM in the domain represents a version of the specification seeded with faults. The work addresses the problem of generating a test set [15] or a single test [13] for distinguishing a the specification from the other DFSMs. In this paper we address a different concern, which is selecting a yet unknown oracle (specification) from a set of candidate oracles.

In [14], experts play the role of an ultimate oracle to select one precise oracle from an imprecise oracle. The experts are requested to evaluate pairs of responses produced from too many pairs of candidate oracles. In the current work, candidate oracles having produced unexpected responses are neither analysed, nor compared to the others. The mining approach developed in this paper is clearly more efficient than the one in [14].

8   Concluding Remarks

We have presented an approach to mining a precise oracle from an imprecise one defining a set of candidate oracles. Precise oracles are represented with DFSMs whereas NFSMs represent imprecise oracles. We compactly encoded candidate precise oracles with Boolean formulas. We presented a method of reducing the imprecise oracle for efficient computation of plausible response sets. The proposed approach takes advantage of the efficiency of existing solvers and the reduction of the imprecise oracle for efficient search of distinguishable precise oracles, test generation. It requests experts to select one correct response per test. The experimental results have demonstrated that few tests and few response sets are needed for mining the proper precise oracle from many candidate precise oracles. This indicates that the number of experts' interventions is reasonable and the approach is applicable.

We plan to lift the proposed approach for mining extended finite state machines which are also used to represent test oracles. We also plan investigating automatic construction of imprecise oracles from system requirements, e.g., by modifying machine learning-based translation procedures or investigating mutation operators to be applied on generated "incorrect" oracles.

Acknowledgment. This work was partially supported by MEI (Ministère de l'Économie et Innovation) of Gouvernement du Québec. The author would like to thank Dr. Alexandre Petrenko and anonymous reviewers for their valuable comments.

References

1. Angluin, D.: Learning regular sets from queries and counterexamples. Inf. Comput. **75**(2), 87–106 (1987)
2. Barr, E.T., Harman, M., McMinn, P., Shahbaz, M., Yoo, S.: The oracle problem in software testing: a survey. IEEE Trans. Softw. Eng. **41**(5), 507–525 (2015)
3. Brunello, A., Montanari, A., Reynolds, M.: Synthesis of LTL formulas from natural language texts: state of the art and research directions. In: 26th International Symposium on Temporal Representation and Reasoning (TIME 2019). Schloss Dagstuhl-Leibniz-Zentrum fuer Informatik (2019)
4. Chen, T.Y., Cheung, S.C., Yiu, S.M.: Metamorphic testing: a new approach for generating next test cases. Technical report, HKUST-CS98-01, Department of Computer Science, The Hong Kong University of Science and Technology (1998)
5. Chow, T.S.: Testing software design modeled by finite-state machines. IEEE Trans. Softw. Eng. **4**(3), 178–187 (1978)
6. Fantechi, A., Gnesi, S., Lami, G., Maccari, A.: Applications of linguistic techniques for use case analysis. Require. Eng. **8**(3), 161–170 (2003)
7. Fantechi, A., Gnesi, S., Ristori, G., Carenini, M., Vanocchi, M., Moreschini, P.: Assisting requirement formalization by means of natural language translation. Formal Methods Syst. Des. **4**(3), 243–263 (1994)
8. Fraser, G., Staats, M., McMinn, P., Arcuri, A., Padberg, F.: Does automated white-box test generation really help software testers? In: Proceedings of the 2013 International Symposium on Software Testing and Analysis, pp. 291–301. ISSTA 2013, ACM, New York (2013)
9. Hierons, R.M.: Testing from a nondeterministic finite state machine using adaptive state counting. IEEE Trans. Comput. **53**(10), 1330–1342 (2004)
10. Le Goues, C., Dewey-Vogt, M., Forrest, S., Weimer, W.: A systematic study of automated program repair: fixing 55 out of 105 bugs for $8 each. In: Proceedings of the 34th International Conference on Software Engineering, pp. 3–13. ICSE 2012, IEEE Press, Piscataway (2012)
11. Lee, D., Yannakakis, M.: Principles and methods of testing finite state machines-a survey. Proc. IEEE **84**(8), 1090–1123 (1996)
12. Mavridou, A., Laszka, A.: Designing secure Ethereum smart contracts: a finite state machine based approach. In: Meiklejohn, S., Sako, K. (eds.) FC 2018. LNCS, vol. 10957, pp. 523–540. Springer, Heidelberg (2018). https://doi.org/10.1007/978-3-662-58387-6_28
13. Nguena Timo, O., Petrenko, A., Ramesh, S.: Checking sequence generation for symbolic input/output FSMS by constraint solving. In: Fischer, B., Uustalu, T. (eds.) ICTAC 2018. LNCS, vol. 11187, pp. 354–375. Springer, Cham (2018). https://doi.org/10.1007/978-3-030-02508-3_19
14. Nguena Timo, O., Petrenko, A., Ramesh, S.: Using imprecise test oracles modelled by FSM. In: 2019 IEEE International Conference on Software Testing, Verification and Validation Workshops, ICST Workshops 2019, Xi'an, China, 22–23 April 2019, pp. 32–39. IEEE (2019)
15. Petrenko, A., Nguena Timo, O., Ramesh, S.: Multiple mutation testing from FSM. In: Albert, E., Lanese, I. (eds.) FORTE 2016. LNCS, vol. 9688, pp. 222–238. Springer, Cham (2016). https://doi.org/10.1007/978-3-319-39570-8_15
16. Saha, P., Kanewala, U.: Improving the effectiveness of automatically generated test suites using metamorphic testing. In: ICSE 2020: 42nd International Conference on Software Engineering, Workshops, Seoul, Republic of Korea, 27 June–19 July 2020, pp. 418–419. ACM (2020)

17. Segura, S., Fraser, G., Sanchez, A.B., Ruiz-Cortés, A.: A survey on metamorphic testing. IEEE Trans. Softw. Eng. **42**(9), 805–824 (2016)
18. Stahlberg, F.: Neural machine translation: a review. J. Artif. Intell. Res. **69**, 343–418 (2020)
19. Weimer, W., Nguyen, T., Le Goues, C., Forrest, S.: Automatically finding patches using genetic programming. In: Proceedings of the 31st International Conference on Software Engineering, pp. 364–374. ICSE 2009, IEEE Computer Society, Washington, DC, USA (2009)
20. Weyuker, E.J.: On testing non-testable programs. Comput. J. **25**(4), 465–470 (1982)

Reverse-Engineering EFSMs with Data Dependencies

Michael Foster$^{(\boxtimes)}$ ⓘ, John Derrick ⓘ, and Neil Walkinshaw ⓘ

Department of Computer Science, The University of Sheffield,
Regent Court, Sheffield S1 4DP, UK
{m.foster,j.derrick,n.walkinshaw}@sheffield.ac.uk

Abstract. EFSMs provide a way to model systems with internal data variables. In situations where they do not already exist, we need to infer them from system behaviour. A key challenge here is inferring the functions which relate inputs, outputs, and internal variables. Existing approaches either work with white-box traces, which expose variable values, or rely upon the user to provide heuristics to recognise and generalise particular data-usage patterns. This paper presents a preprocessing technique for the inference process which generalises the concrete values from the traces into symbolic functions which calculate output from input, even when this depends on values not present in the original traces. Our results show that our technique leads to more accurate models than are produced by the current state-of-the-art and that somewhat accurate models can still be inferred even when the output of particular transitions depends on values not present in the original traces.

Keywords: EFSM inference · Model inference · Genetic programming

1 Introduction

Reactive systems – systems that respond to their environment, their users, or other systems – are commonly modelled as Finite State Machines (FSMs). These offer an intuitive basis upon which to model and reason about the sequential behaviours of a wide range of systems from network communication protocols to GUIs, and form the foundation of many verification and testing techniques [24]. Reactive systems that incorporate data (where computation requires a memory, or where data can be supplied and received through inputs and outputs) can be represented as Extended Finite State Machines (EFSMs) [14]. Despite their utility, models can be neglected due to the pressures of system development.

The challenge of reverse-engineering FSMs and EFSMs has been the subject of a considerable amount of research. Where the field of FSM inference is mature and has produced many powerful approaches [11,22,38], current techniques to

Michael Foster and Neil Walkinshaw are funded by the EPSRC CITCoM project.

D. Clark et al. (Eds.): ICTSS 2021, LNCS 13045, pp. 37–54, 2022.
https://doi.org/10.1007/978-3-031-04673-5_3

infer EFSMs tend to suffer from a variety of drawbacks. Some approaches produce results that are only partial, in that they do not infer *how* data variables change throughout execution [26,39], or lack internal data variables entirely [12,34]. Those approaches that do infer fully-fledged EFSMs are limited either in terms of their practical applicability [6,10,13,18,35], or accuracy [37].

Inferring accurate, complete EFSMs is particularly challenging when the update functions have interdependencies; when a function on one transition depends on a value computed by another transition. Empirical work by Androutsopoulos *et al.* [7] suggests that these are widespread, arising in around a third of the transitions in the models that they studied. Current inference approaches, such as MINT [37], cannot handle such interdependencies because they infer transition functions on an individual basis, without considering relationships to other transitions. A further problem in the case of MINT is that it is incapable of inferring variables that are not explicitly part of the execution trace. This means that it is not a truly black-box technique. Finally, its update functions are only inferred *after* the transition structure of the machine has been decided, which is often too late because the underlying structural inference algorithm (which is largely data-insensitive) can end up merging transitions together that should remain separate because they should have different update behaviours [22].

In this work we present a technique that addresses these limitations. The key contributions of this paper are as follows:

- An approach to infer update functions *before* any structural state machine inference has taken place, instead of afterwards, so that transitions with different update functions that should remain separate can be kept apart.
- An approach based on Genetic Programming to infer hidden variables (as part of update inference) using values observed in other transition update functions. This captures interdependencies *between* transitions, enabling the inference of state machines that are more precise than the state-of-the-art.
- An openly available [16] proof-of-concept implementation, along with the full experimental data-set and scripts.
- A small empirical study that assesses the accuracy of our approach in comparison to the state-of-the-art, with respect to two systems.

The rest of this paper is structured as follows. Section 2 introduces a motivating example and gives some necessary background. Section 3 explains the details of our technique, the implementation of which is discussed in Sect. 4. Section 5 evaluates our technique experimentally. Finally, Sect. 6 concludes the paper and discusses possible future work.

2   Background

This section defines EFSMs and traces, and gives an overview of the current state-of-the-art in EFSM inference. We then highlight the limitations of existing techniques. Throughout this work, we draw from a toy example of a simple vending machine. Users first *select* a drink. They then insert *coins*, with the total balance being displayed as output on a small screen. Once sufficient payment has been inserted, the machine *vends* the selected drink.

2.1 Definitions

Traces. As systems execute, we can record the sequence of actions performed, along with any inputs and return values. Figure 1 shows some traces of our simple drinks machine. In our notation, $coin(50)/[100]$ represents the event $coin$ being called with the input 50 and outputting 100. We delimit events with commas and omit the outputs from events like $select(\text{"tea"})$ which do not produce any.

$$\langle select(\text{"tea"}), coin(50)/[50], coin(50)/[100], vend()/[\text{"tea"}]\rangle$$
$$\langle select(\text{"tea"}), coin(100)/[100], vend()/[\text{"tea"}]\rangle$$
$$\langle select(\text{"coffee"}), coin(50)/[50], coin(50)/[100], vend()/[\text{"coffee"}]\rangle$$

Fig. 1. Exemplary traces of the vending machine.

EFSMs. An EFSM is a conventional FSM that has been extended to explicitly model how a system handles data. While there are many different EFSM representations in the literature [14,25], our technique is designed to work with the inference process from [18], so we use that definition [17–20].

Definition 1. *An EFSM is a tuple, (S, s_0, T) where S is a finite non-empty set of states, $s_0 \in S$ is the initial state, and T is the transition matrix $T :$ $(S \times S) \to \mathcal{P}(L \times \mathbb{N} \times G \times F \times U)$ with rows representing origin states and columns representing destination states. In T, L is a set of transition labels. $\mathbb{N}$ gives the transition arity (the number of input parameters), which may be zero. G is a set of Boolean guard functions $G : (I \times R) \to \mathbb{B}$. F is a set of output functions $F : (I \times R) \to O$. U is a set of update functions $U : (I \times R) \to R$.*

In G, F, and U, I is a tuple $[i_1, i_2, \ldots, i_m]$ of values representing the inputs of a transition, which is empty if the arity is zero. Inputs do not persist across states or transitions. R is a mapping from variables $[r_1, r_2, \ldots]$, representing each register of the machine, to their values. Registers are globally accessible and persist throughout the operation of the machine. All registers are initially undefined until explicitly set by an update expression. O is a tuple $[o_1, o_2, \ldots, o_n]$ of values, which may be empty, representing the outputs of a transition.

This differs from the traditional EFSM definition [14] in several ways. In [14], transitions take one literal input, produce one literal output. Our definition assigns each transition an explicit label and allows multiple inputs and outputs (or none at all). Transitions may also produce outputs as a function of input and register values, which allows transition behaviour to be *generalised*.

Definition 1 technically only affords each transition one guard, output, and update, but syntactic sugar allows a transition from state q_m to q_n to take the form $q_m \xrightarrow{label:arity[g_1,\ldots,g_g]/f_1,\ldots,f_f[u_1,\ldots,u_u]} q_n$ in which guards $g_1, \ldots, g_g$ are implicitly conjoined, output functions $f_1, \ldots, f_f$ are evaluated to produce a list of outputs, and update functions $u_1, \ldots, u_u$ are executed simultaneously. We use this notation throughout this work, for example in Fig. 3.

2.2 Genetic Programming

The technique we present in Sect. 3 uses Genetic Programming (GP) [21] to infer expressions which relate sets of input-output pairs from the traces. We therefore provide a brief introduction to the essential notions of GP that we use in this work. For a more comprehensive overview, we refer the reader to [31].

In (tree-based) GP, candidate functions are represented as syntax trees in which branch nodes represent operators ("non-terminals"), and leaf-nodes represent variables and constants ("terminals"). GP is an approach to synthesise these functions by evolution. The basic loop is as follows and iterates for a fixed number of *generations* or until we find a function with optimal *fitness*.

1. Generate an initial population of random functions.
2. Evaluate each expression according to some *fitness function.*
3. Select the best individuals to continue to the next generation.
4. Create a new population by a process of crossover and mutation.
5. Repeat from step 2 until some stopping criterion is met.

The most important aspect of this for our purposes is the *fitness function.* This provides a metric for the suitability of candidate functions. Fitness is evaluated by executing each candidate function on all available inputs and then comparing the resulting set of outputs to the corresponding outputs in the trace data. For numerical values, the fitness function is taken as the average distance between the predicted and the actual values. For nominal outputs, the fitness is calculated as the proportion of instances where the outputs were correct.

Another key step in the algorithm is the creation of a new population by *crossover* and *mutation.* Crossover recombines desirable characteristics from individuals in the population. Mutation simulates the small changes in DNA which occur during natural reproduction, allowing us to introduce new characteristics.

2.3 EFSM Inference

Model inference enables us to make statements about the overall behaviour of a system by generalising from its *traces.* A popular way to do this [18,26,39] is to convert the traces into a tree-shaped model called a prefix tree acceptor (PTA) like in Fig. 2. States in the PTA which are believed to represent the same program state are then merged, resulting in a smaller and more general model.

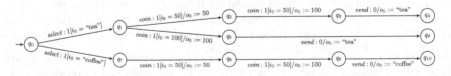

Fig. 2. The PTA of the traces in Fig. 1.

As well as inferring the control flow, we also want to infer the functions that transform inputs into outputs. For example, in Fig. 2, the output of each *vend* event is the input of *select*, and the output of each *coin* event is a running total of the inputs. To express such behaviour, we must use the internal data state of the model. The EFSM in Fig. 3 uses a register, r_1, to keep track of the inputs to *coin*, and uses a second register, r_2, to store the input of *select* for later use as the output of *vend*. These registers affect the behaviour of the model, but do not appear in its traces—they are *latent*.

2.4   Limitations of Existing Approaches

Figure 3 shows the ideal EFSM model of the drinks machine, but there are currently no techniques in the literature which can infer this effectively from the traces in Fig. 1. A major obstacle to overcome is that registers r_1 and r_2 are latent variables, so their existence and usage must be inferred. One technique [18] allows users to provide *data abstraction heuristics* to facilitate this. To provide these heuristics, the user requires a prior understanding of the system, which means that this technique cannot be applied to any realistic inference scenario.

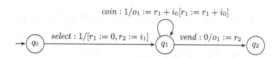

Fig. 3. The EFSM representing the traces in Fig. 1.

MINT [37] is an alternative approach which uses GP to infer update functions for variables. This is done as a postprocessing step for existing models. Having inferred a model from a set of traces, the first stage of postprocessing is to execute the model on these traces. For each transition, the anterior and posterior variable values are recorded. These are then used as the inputs and outputs for GP to evolve individual update functions for each variable of each transition.

Figure 4 shows a model MINT might infer of the traces in Fig. 1. Crucially, the *longitudinal dependency* between *vend* and *select* is missed. There are two reasons for this. Firstly, MINT infers data updates per-transition, so cannot discover relationships between different transitions. Secondly, a variable is required to store the input to *select* for later reuse. Figure 3 uses r_2 for this, but MINT only considers variables that appear in the traces, so has no way to facilitate the relationship. The technique we present in Sect. 3 overcomes these limitations to enable Fig. 3 to be effectively inferred from the traces in Fig. 1.

This work tackles the problem of *passive* inference—inferring a model using only the traces provided—but there is also much literature on *active* inference [8]. Here, the learner asks questions about the system under inference of the form "Is this trace acceptable behaviour?". These are often answered by running the proffered traces directly on the system under inference. There are many active

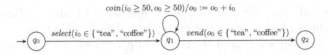

Fig. 4. An EFSM of the traces in Fig. 1 as might be inferred by MINT. MINT has no notion of outputs, so o_0 here represents an internal register.

EFSM inference techniques [5, 6, 10, 13, 35], but these do not support arithmetic operations in data updates, only simple assignments. Functions that update registers in terms of their anterior values, such as the *coin* transition in Fig. 3, are beyond them. Another limitation of all active learners is the requirement to run arbitrary traces to answer queries, which may not always be viable.

Another group of approaches [12, 33] rephrase the EFSM inference problem as an instance of SAT. The solution is then a set of boolean variables which together represent the automaton. Unfortunately, these approaches only consider boolean data values and do not support internal variables, so have limited applicability.

3   Inferring Output and Update Functions

This paper addresses the challenge of inferring EFSMs from truly black-box systems where we cannot inspect the internal state or ask arbitrary queries. Instead, we must reason about the system purely in terms of the observable behaviour recorded in a fixed set of its traces. The key challenge here is to infer the necessary internal variables that enable us to capture functionality where there is a dependence on some input data that might have been provided several steps previously, without relying on the visibility of the internal data state.

Our approach works by inferring the key internal variables and the functions that update them during an execution. This allows for "longitudinal" dependencies, where an input is provided at one point (e.g. the user selects a drink), and referenced several steps later in the machine (e.g. the machine dispenses the drink, but only after the user has paid for it). As established by Androutsopoulos *et al.* [7], such dependencies are common in EFSM specifications.

To infer these functions accurately, we cannot adopt the approach of existing techniques such as MINT, which infer the transition functions as a postprocessing step *after* the transition structure has been inferred. The process of state merging leads to a loss of information which is vital to track these longitudinal dependencies. Hence, the situation in Fig. 4, where the inferred model allows for the undesirable situation where a user selects tea but receives coffee.

To avoid this information loss, our approach operates as a *pre*processing technique. We take advantage of the detailed trace-by-trace information in the PTA before it is merged, inferring internal variables and associated update functions directly from the prefix tree. We therefore retain flexibility as our approach does not impose any restrictions on the state merging algorithm that is subsequently used to infer the model structure. Our approach tackles three interdependent inference challenges: (1) the functions to compute output from transition inputs, (2) the registers needed to support this, and (3) the functions required to update register values to ensure they hold the correct values when evaluated.

Algorithm 1: Outline of our GP preprocessing technique.

Input: A set of traces T
Output: A prefix tree pta
// Generate a PTA from the traces using the conventional approach.
1   $pta \leftarrow$ BUILDPTA(T);
   /* Group transitions by their structure (label and arity) and history (to restrict the inference challenge for each group to the same context).   */
2   $groups \leftarrow$ GROUPTRANSITIONS(pta);
3   **for** $g_1 \in groups$ **do**
     /* Use GP to infer functions that accurately predict outputs for group, including the ability to infer the presence of memory registers that can be presumed to contain any missing values if required.   */
4      $fun \leftarrow$ INFEROUTPUTFUN(g_1);
     // Replace literal outputs with inferred functions.
5      $newPTA \leftarrow$ REPLACELITWITHFUN(pta, g_1, fun);
     // Infer updates to the inferred memory registers.
6   **for** $r_n \in fun.latentVars$ **do**
7   **for** $g_2 \in groups$ **do**
8          $newPTA \leftarrow$ INFERUPDATEFUNS(g_2, TARGETVALUES(pta, r_n));

     // Check that inferred functions are compatible with traces.
9   **if** ACCEPTS($newPTA, T$) **then**
10        $pta \leftarrow newPTA$;
     /* Combine functions for transitions that were put into separate groups because they had different histories (line 2).   */
11      $pta \leftarrow$ STANDARDISE(pta);

12   $pta \leftarrow$ DROPGUARDS(pta);
13   **return** RESOLVENONDETERMINISM(pta);

Algorithm 1 outlines our technique. We first group related transitions in the PTA together (line 2). We then infer output and update functions for each group using GP. This works in two steps. In the first step (line 4), the GP infers functions to compute output from input and identifies the use of registers if required (addressing challenges 1 and 2 above). In the second step (lines 6–8) it ensures that these registers are correctly updated by other transitions in the PTA before they are evaluated. The rest of this section elucidates the process.

GroupTransitions (line 2) forms groups of transitions that represent the same behaviour. Transitions are grouped together if they have the same *structure*, i.e. the same label, arity, and produce the same number and types of outputs. The PTA in Fig. 2 has three structural transition groups: *select*, *coin*, and *vend*.

Latent variables can lead to side effects [7] such that transitions with the same structure may be subject to different data states depending on where in a trace they occur. To provide a degree of uniformity for the GP, we only place transitions into the same group if they share the same *history*.

To account for contiguous blocks of the same event, we cannot simply look at the previous transition. Instead, we look backwards in time until we find one which is *structurally different*. For example, the most recent structurally different transition of all the *coin* transitions in Fig. 2 is *select*. Consecutive structurally identical transitions (like $q_1 \xrightarrow{coin} q_2 \xrightarrow{coin} q_3$ in Fig. 2) represent the same behaviour so have consistent side effects. By contrast, if our simple drinks machine had a *refund* event to reset the balance to zero, *coins* inserted after this event would be grouped separately to those that follow *select*.

InferOutputFun (line 4) takes a set of input/output pairs and uses GP to infer a function to relate them. The key challenge here is getting the GP to work with *latent variables*; registers like r_1 and r_2 which are absent from the traces. As mentioned in Sect. 2, this is not something which MINT can do. To infer Fig. 3 from the PTA in Fig. 2, we need to be able to do this.

To introduce new registers, we simply add them to the set of variables used by the GP, but this causes a problem. As discussed in Sect. 2, the fitness of candidate functions is assessed by executing them on the inputs from the traces. Unfortunately, register values do not appear in the traces, so we cannot evaluate functions involving them. Our solution is to look to the inputs and outputs in the traces, and assign each register the value that yields the closest output to the target. The justification for this is that register values are usually either set to a particular input or observed as an output. Full details can be found in [17].

Latent variables give the GP a lot of freedom when evolving expressions, so we want to minimise their use. We expect transitions like *coin* to use their non-latent inputs as part of the output, so want to find an expression involving them if we can. Thus, we penalise the fitness of expressions which use latent variables without using all the non-latent ones. In situations where ignoring inputs is the correct solution, expressions cannot achieve optimal fitness but, since our GP has a set maximum number of generations, this will not stop it from terminating.

To further limit the use of latent variables, we first call the GP without them. If this fails, we add one latent register to the set of variables and run GP again. If either attempt is successful, REPLACELITWITHFUN (line 5) replaces the literal outputs of the transition group with the inferred function. For example in Fig. 2, the output behaviour of the *coin* transitions generalises to $i_0 + r_1$. Replacing the concrete outputs with this function gives Fig. 5a. If the GP fails both attempts, we keep the literal outputs from the PTA. We could continue adding registers until the GP succeeds, but we here choose to stop after one.

Update Function Inference (lines 7–9). To ensure that registers introduced by INFEROUTPUTFUN hold the correct values when evaluated, we walk each trace in the PTA annotating each state with target register values, as illustrated in Fig. 5a. These are propagated backwards so every state in the prefix path has a target value. This is what allows r_2 in Fig. 3 to be initialised by *select*. Without it, registers could only be initialised immediately prior to use, which would not allow us to discover longitudinal relationships between transitions.

Starting at the root of the PTA, we call GP again (without latent variables) for each group. The "inputs" are the transition input values and the anterior register value, if defined. The "output" is the target register value. For example, in q_2 and q_8 of Fig. 5a, we need r_1 to hold the value 50. The input to the respective incident *coin* transitions is 50, and the anterior value of r_1 must have been zero. Thus, $r_1 := r_1 + i_0$ works as possible update, as shown in Fig. 5b.

Accepts (lines 9–10). After inferring output and update functions for a transition group, we check to ensure that the new PTA still accepts the original traces and produces the correct outputs. If not, we must reject our inferred functions and default back to the literal outputs from the PTA for that particular group.

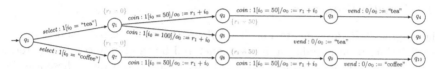

(a) The PTA after inferring output functions for the *coin* transitions.

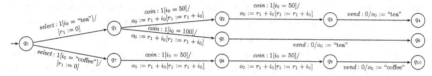

(b) The PTA after inferring update functions for the *coin* transitions.

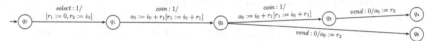

(c) The PTA after inferring output and update functions for all transitions, dropping guards, and resolving nondeterminism.

Fig. 5. Preprocessing the PTA in Fig. 2.

Standardise (line 11) takes a PTA and attempts to "standardise" output and update functions between transitions with the same structure that were grouped separately due to their histories. For example, in our *refund*ing vending machine from earlier, we want our two groups of *coin* transitions to have the same output and update functions. The full details of this process can be found in [17].

Generalisation (lines 12–13). Currently, the model has symbolic output and update functions, but each transition still has its literal input guards. We want our final model to be more responsive, so we drop these guards at this stage. This can introduce nondeterminism, which is undesirable in a PTA as trace prefixes no longer necessarily share a common path. In fact, this nondeterminism is simply an indication that the model contains duplicated behaviour and is easily resolved by merging states and transitions [18]. This results in Fig. 5c. This is smaller than Fig. 2 as the top and bottom branches are "zipped" together.

Having processed the PTA, we then perform the conventional state merging process [18] to produce Fig. 3. This perfectly models the drinks machine, capturing data dependencies using internal registers. To the best of our knowledge, this is the first technique to infer such relationships using only system traces.

4 Implementation

We built our implementation on two frameworks. For the GP component, we significantly enhanced the GP implementation used for MINT [37]. For the underlying PTA, we built upon our Isabelle/HOL state-merging framework [16,18]. This section provides details of these enhancements and adaptations.

4.1 Genetic Programming

The original GP implementation [37] follows the basic steps outlined in Subsect. 2.2. An initial population is first generated by randomly combining terminals and non-terminals[1] to form syntactically valid expressions. These are then evolved through crossover and mutation, with only the best surviving to the next generation. Our main addition was a fitness function to enable latent registers to be introduced, as discussed in Sect. 3. In addition, several other changes were necessary to improve the performance of the GP in this new context.

The mutation operator used in [37] simply replaces a random node with a new random subtree, but we found that this failed to produce satisfactory outcomes. We created a richer set of mutation operators inspired by a different open-source GP implementation [1] which offers more scope for useful mutations during evolution (details in [17]). To further enhance the impact of mutation operators, we also took inspiration from Doerr *et al.* [15] and apply up to three mutations in sequence as making occasional large changes to individuals has been shown to help escape local optima and avoid premature convergence.

Another implementational issue we faced was *bloat* [23]. While [37] applies some basic simplification to expressions, it still yielded more complex expressions than were desirable, often including redundant operations like +0. To mitigate this, we used Z3 [30] to simplify our expressions. This can reveal semantic duplicates in the population, which become identical when simplified. We replace these duplicates with new random individuals to keep the population distinct and diverse. To further manage bloat, we also use *lexicographic parsimony pressure* [27] to break ties in fitness, favouring smaller expressions over larger ones.

4.2 PTA Preprocessing

Our technique is designed to work with the inference tool from [18], which is implemented in Isabelle/HOL with executable Scala code exported using Isabelle's code generator. To incorporate Algorithm 1, we defined the functions in Isabelle and then automatically generated the Scala code using the code generator. While [18] uses Isabelle to verify certain aspects of transition merging, we here use Isabelle purely for compatibility reasons. Rather than formalising our GP in Isabelle, we specified INFEROUTPUTFUN and INFERUPDATEFUN

---

[1] The inference tool we use here [18] currently supports only $+$, $-$, and $\times$ for integers, and literal assignment for strings, although our GP has broader support [16,37].

abstractly and hooked their Scala counterparts into our Java implementation from Subsect. 4.1 using a thin wrapper function.

The implementation for this work comes to around 1000 lines of Java on top of [37] to implement our GP (INFEROUTPUTFUN and INFERUPDATEFUN) and an additional 551 lines of Isabelle code (translating to 2010 lines of automatically generated Scala code) and 496 lines of manually written Scala code on top of [18] to implement the rest of Algorithm 1. All of this code is available at [16].

5 Evaluation

This section describes a small experiment where we compare our approach against MINT [37] (the current state-of-the-art of passive EFSM inference). For our technique to be successful, we want to infer models which can correctly predict system outputs for unseen traces. We also want our technique to be robust to data values being absent from the traces. Our research questions are as follows.

RQ1 Does the processing of the PTA by our technique prior to state merging lead to more accurate models than the current state-of-the-art?
RQ2 How robust is our technique to latent variables?

5.1 Methodology

Metrics. Both our RQs are concerned with model accuracy. To evaluate this, we use one set of traces (the *training set*) to infer a model and then use another set of traces (the *test set*) to compute various accuracy metrics. In this evaluation, we use the following two metrics, in which the *accepted prefix* is the first part of the trace, where the outputs produced by the model match those of the system.

$$\text{Sensitivity} = \frac{\text{number of accepted positive traces}}{\text{total number of positive traces}} \quad \text{Accepted prefix length} = \frac{\text{length of accepted prefix}}{\text{length of trace}}$$

Sensitivity is the proportion of positive traces in the test set accepted by a model. This is often paired with *specificity*, which is the proportion of negative traces rejected by the model. Here though, we are more concerned with whether our models correctly calculate the output values in response to the given inputs than whether it can correctly classify traces as positive or negative. Our models produce outputs in response to inputs, so traces are only accepted if the correct outputs are produced. Thus, there is much less risk of overgeneralisation here, making specificity an inappropriate metric for this evaluation.

Subject Systems. To illustrate the performance of our technique, we evaluate it on the two published models summarised below. The first is a lift door controller published in [32] and used in [17,37] to evaluate inference tools. The second system [2] is a Java accompaniment to [28] based on the game Space Invaders.

System	States	Variables	Transitions	Traces/Events
LIFTDOORS [17,32,37]	6	*timer*	10	348/9333
SPACEINVADERS [17]	4	*x, aliens, shields*	7	100/2580

Our work is motivated by the fact that existing EFSM inference approaches do not consider the possibility of internal variables which do not appear explicitly as transition inputs. Thus, we chose our subject systems for their use of these variables, and the *relationships* between data values used by different transitions, rather than for the complexity of any individual function. We also chose systems which differ in terms of the number of state variables as this is identified in [37] as being a factor which has a significant effect on the accuracy of MINT.

To an extent, the values above mask the complexity of the two systems. LIFT-DOORS has only one system variable, but this is shared between and modified by every transition. Despite the heavy data dependencies of LIFTDOORS, it is SPACEINVADERS which is the more complex case study. There are three state variables here, and the system is much more reactive. All but one of the transitions in this model emanate from the same state, giving a much greater variation in the traces produced by this system. By contrast, LIFTDOORS has only one or two transitions from each state, so the traces are more constrained.

RQ1 (Assessing Accuracy). This RQ asks whether our *pre*processing approach infers more accurate models than the *post*processing used by MINT. This work focuses on *latent variables* which do not appear in traces, allowing us to infer models from traces that only contain information observable from outside the system without probing the internal program state. MINT, however, is not applicable to this scenario. To compare it to our technique, we must work with traces where the output of each transition depends only on its input.

To evaluate the accuracy of our models, we followed the standard procedure of creating a training set and a test set, where the former is used to infer a model and the latter is used to compare the predictions made by the model to the ground truth. For LIFTDOORS, we used the same traces [3] as [37]. For SPACEINVADERS, we modified the code to log certain actions [17] and obtained traces by manually playing the game. For each system, we then took random samples of 60 traces and divided them in half to form the training and test sets, each of 30 traces. These are available online alongside our implementation [16].

The accuracy of our inferred models depends on the selection of training traces and the random seed passed to the GP. To control for these we ran the inference tools with 30 seeds each for 30 sets of traces. Thus, we inferred a total of 900 models for each technique. As well as the random seed, our GP technique has a number of configurable parameters. These are the population size, μ, the number of new individuals per generation, λ, and the number of generations. Here, we use $\mu = 100$, $\lambda = 10$, and 100 generations. MINT has a similar set of configurable parameters, all of which we left at their default values.

We anticipate that both techniques will perform well here but that our technique will outperform MINT. Because we infer output and update functions prior to merging, they play an active role in the inference process and help to shape the structure of the final model. By contrast MINT infers functions after state merging, when this structure has already been determined. MINT also requires every event to report the value of every variable, so can be led astray by superfluous information. Our technique does not require this, so is more targetted.

RQ2 (Assessing Robustness to Missing Variables). This RQ investigates how robust our technique is to variables being absent from the traces. Such variables indicate potential dependencies between the data values of different transitions. To investigate this, we took the training and test sets we used for RQ1 and elided one input at a time. For SPACEINVADERS, we also elided combinations of two variables. Thus, we are no longer in the purely functional domain: the output of certain events depends on values which are missing from the traces. The main challenge here is inferring the correct use of internal registers as part of the output functions, and then inferring suitable updates to facilitate this.

MINT has no notion of hidden variables, so is simply not applicable to systems where we cannot inspect the internal data state during execution. Thus, we must evaluate our technique in isolation. We anticipate that obfuscating variables will lead to a drop in the accuracy of the models produced by our technique since the GP has less information to guide it and must use latent variables in expressions, which gives it much more freedom to produce esoteric functions which do not properly generalise. It must also infer update functions in addition to output functions, which gives it extra opportunities to make mistakes.

5.2   Results and Discussion

The raw data from all of our experiments is available online [4]. The distributions of accuracy values, in terms of sensitivity and accepted prefix-lengths, are shown in Fig. 6. We will proceed to answer both RQs in terms of these box-plots.

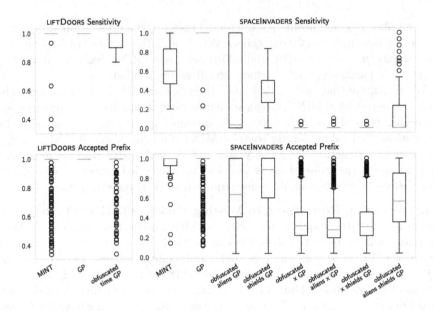

Fig. 6. Accuracy metrics for the two systems.

RQ1 (Assessing Accuracy). This RQ concerns the GP and MINT plots. Figure 6 shows that our technique (GP) achieves a perfectly accurate model in all but a few outlying cases of SPACEINVADERS. MINT performs comparably for LIFTDOORS but only achieves a median sensitivity of 0.6 for SPACEINVADERS.

These results are not surprising. When we preprocess with GP, we generalise concrete data values from the traces to symbolic functions. This is not a particularly difficult task in the purely functional scenario, and our GP is correct in all but a few outlying cases of SPACEINVADERS. This then enables many states to be merged, leading to a very accurate model. While MINT also uses GP to infer functions, it does so *after* the structure of the model has been inferred. It also tries to infer transition guards during inference to aggregate the observed data values (where our technique simply discards them). This is a particular problem for systems like SPACEINVADERS with multiple variables as these often cause MINT to infer spurious guards, leading to an inaccurate model structure.

RQ2 (Assessing Robustness to Missing Variables). This RQ concerns all plots except MINT. Since MINT has no notion of latent variables, it is simply not applicable here. Figure 6 shows that obfuscating the system timer for LIFTDOORS has a relatively small effect on the accuracy of the models inferred by our system, but that the effect of obfuscation is much greater for SPACEINVADERS.

Again, this is not surprising. The two contributing factors here are the two calls to GP detailed in Sect. 3. Here, we must use latent variables in the output functions as the result depends on variables absent from the traces. This gives the GP much more freedom when inferring functions, so it is more likely to be incorrect. We also need to infer update functions for each latent variable. This was not necessary in RQ1, so there is an extra opportunity to make mistakes.

For both subject systems, the main cause of inaccuracy is a failure to *recognise* events rather than a failure to adequately calculate output from input. This is because, if our GP makes a mistake or fails to come up with a function, the dropping of transition guards in the generalisation step is detrimental to state merging. More states must remain separate and share the underlying functionality between them. This leads to models that are both larger and less reactive.

For SPACEINVADERS, the variable we obfuscate has a huge effect on the accuracy of the model. The *aliens* and *shields* variables do relatively well when obfuscated, but the *x* variable leads to very poor models. There are two reasons for this. Firstly, most events in the traces are movement events, which depend on *x*, so any mistake with these is given much more opportunity to reveal itself. Secondly, because our technique introduces one register per transition group and there are two movement events (left and right) which both mutate *x*, our technique struggles to work out what is going on here.

Discussion. While Fig. 6 shows that our technique infers more *accurate* models than MINT, it does not show what these models actually look like. Figure 7 shows a model of SPACEINVADERS inferred by our technique in the purely functional setting of RQ5. This model concisely shows the behaviour of the system. By contrast, most of the models inferred by MINT are too large to effectively display here. The same is true for LIFTDOORS. Where our technique drops the guards on transitions before state merging, MINT tries to infer guards to aggregate the observed data values. These are often overly specific, which leads to cluttered and chaotic models, even if they are accurate in terms of traces.

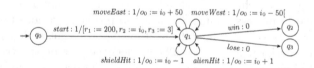

Fig. 7. A model of SPACEINVADERS inferred by our technique.

5.3 Threats to Validity

This evaluation cannot be used to (and does not aim to) draw general conclusions about the accuracy or scalability of either our technique or MINT. Our main aim here is illustrate each technique performs "out of the box", its applicability, and factors which affect model accuracy. There are, however, certain aspects of the study that must be taken into account when reviewing the results.

Choice of Systems. For this study we used two fully specified EFSMs. Although these present us with valuable insights here, it will require a larger, more diverse selection of systems to produce more generalisable results.

Selection of Parameters. We did not spend time optimising the configuration parameters used by either our technique or MINT. This avoids the threat of overfitting values to these subject systems, biasing the results in favour of either technique, but opens up the threat that there may be more suitable configurations. A more specific selection of parameters may lead to more accurate results, but parameter optimisation falls outside the intended scope of this investigation.

6   Conclusion

This paper presented a GP-based technique to infer functions that relate inputs, outputs, and internal variables of EFSM models. We use this as part of preprocessing step for the inference process to generalise the initial PTA before merging states. To the best of our knowledge, this is the first technique to do this in a truly black-box setting. Our results indicate that our technique leads to more accurate models than those inferred by MINT [37], the current state-of-the-art.

A key aspect of our technique is the ability to infer output functions involving variables which do not appear in the traces, and update functions to ensure these variables hold the correct values when evaluated. While eliding variables from the traces reduces the accuracy of the models we can infer, our technique still improves upon MINT, which cannot be applied at all in this scenario.

There are many applications of GP [21], but [37] is the only work which applies it to EFSM inference. Work in [9] applies similar techniques to learn *feature models,* but these do not model control flow. Work in [10,18] considers latent variables but relies on simple heuristics, which limits applicability. Active techniques such as [6,13,35] build on the L^* algorithm [8] to infer EFSMs with data updates, but these techniques rely on submitting queries about the system under inference. Our technique is entirely passive, using only on the traces provided. The field of process mining [36] has also produced various techniques to infer models from traces. The main focus, though, is on control flow rather than data usage. Research carried out in [29] considers the data perspective, but does not attempt to infer models which can predict system behaviour for new traces.

One possible line of future work is to increase the set of operations for the GP, including the ability to handle floating-point numbers. This would make our technique applicable to a broader range of systems. Another line of work would be a more comprehensive evaluation involving more systems, which would enable us to draw more general conclusions about accuracy and scalability.

References

1. https://github.com/lagodiuk/genetic-programming. Accessed 03 Feb 2020
2. http://www.doc.ic.ac.uk/~jnm/book/book_applets/concurrency/invaders. Accessed 15 May 2020
3. http://www.cs.le.ac.uk/people/nw91/Files/ICSMEData.zip. Accessed 15 April 2020
4. https://doi.org/10.15131/shef.data.15172969

5. Aarts, F.: Tomte : Bridging the gap between active learning and real-world systems. Ph.D. thesis, Radboud University Nijmegen (2014)
6. Aarts, F., Heidarian, F., Kuppens, H., Olsen, P., Vaandrager, F.: Automata Learning through Counterexample Guided Abstraction Refinement. In: Giannakopoulou, D., Méry, D. (eds.) FM 2012. LNCS, vol. 7436, pp. 10–27. Springer, Heidelberg (2012). https://doi.org/10.1007/978-3-642-32759-9_4
7. Androutsopoulos, K., Gold, N., Harman, M., Li, Z., Tratt, L.: A theoretical and empirical study of EFSM dependence. In: 2009 IEEE International Conference on Software Maintenance, pp. 287–296 (2009)
8. Angluin, D.: Learning regular sets from queries and counterexamples. Inf. Comput. **75**(2), 87–106 (1987)
9. Arcaini, P., Gargantini, A., Radavelli, M.: Achieving change requirements of feature models by an evolutionary approach. J. Syst. Softw. **150**, 64–76 (2019)
10. Berg, T., Jonsson, B., Raffelt, H.: Regular inference for state machines using domains with equality tests. In: Fiadeiro, J.L., Inverardi, P. (eds.) Fundamental Approaches to Software Engineering. vol. 4961 LNCS, pp. 317–331. Springer, Berlin (2008). https://doi.org/10.1007/978-3-540-78743-3_24
11. Biermann, A.W., Feldman, J.A.: On the synthesis of finite-state machines from samples of their behavior. IEEE Trans. Comput. **C-21**(6), 592–597 (1972)
12. Buzhinsky, I., Vyatkin, V.: Automatic inference of finite-state plant models from traces and temporal properties. IEEE Trans. Indust. Inf. **13**(4), 1521–1530 (2017)
13. Cassel, S., Howar, F., Jonsson, B., Steffen, B.: Learning extended finite state machines. In: Giannakopoulou, D., Salaun, G. (eds.) Software Engineering and Formal Methods, pp. 250–264. Springer, Cham (2014). https://doi.org/10.1007/978-3-319-10431-7_18
14. Cheng, K.T., Krishnakumar, A.S.: Automatic functional test generation using the extended finite state machine model. In: Proceedings of the 30th International Design Automation Conference, pp. 86–91. ACM Press (1993)
15. Doerr, B., Le, H.P., Makhmara, R., Nguyen, T.D.: Fast genetic algorithms. In: Proceedings of the Genetic and Evolutionary Computation Conference, pp. 777–784. Association for Computing Machinery (2017)
16. Foster, M.: EFSM inference (2020). https://github.com/jmafoster1/efsm-inference
17. Foster, M.: Reverse Engineering Systems to Identify Flaws and Understand Behaviour. Ph.D. thesis, The University Of Sheffield (2020)
18. Foster, M., Brucker, A.D., Taylor, R., North, S., Derrick, J.: Incorporating data into EFSM inference. In: Olveczky, P., SalaUn, G. (eds.) Software Engineering and Formal Methods. SEFM 2019. LNCS, vol. 11724, pp. 257–272. Springer, Cham (2019). https://doi.org/10.1007/978-3-030-30446-1_14
19. Foster, M., Brucker, A.D., Taylor, R.G., Derrick, J.: A formal model of extended finite state machines. Archive of Formal Proofs (2020). https://isa-afp.org/entries/Extended_Finite_State_Machines.html, Formal proof development
20. Foster, M., Taylor, R., Brucker, A.D., Derrick, J.: Formalising extended finite state machine transition merging. In: Sun, J., Sun, M. (eds.) Formal Methods and Software Engineering. ICFEM 2018. LNCS, vol. 11232, pp. 373–387. Springer, Cham (2018). https://doi.org/10.1007/978-3-030-02450-5_22
21. Koza, J.R.: Genetic Programming: On the Programming of Computers by Means of Natural Selection. MIT Press (1992)
22. Lang, K.J., Pearlmutter, B.A., Price, R.A.: Results of the Abbadingo One DFA learning competition and a new evidence-driven state merging algorithm. In: Grammatical Inference, pp. 1–12. Springer, Berlin (1998). https://doi.org/10.1007/BFb0054059

23. Langdon, W.B.: Quadratic bloat in genetic programming. In: Proceedings of the 2nd Annual Conference on Genetic and Evolutionary Computation, pp. 451–458. GECCO'00, Morgan Kaufmann Publishers Inc., San Francisco, CA, USA (2000)

24. Lee, D., Yannakakis, M.: Principles and methods of testing finite state machines-a survey. Proc. IEEE **84**(8), 1090–1123 (1996)

25. Lorenzoli, D., Mariani, L., Pezzè, M.: Inferring state-based behavior models. In: Proceedings of the 2006 International Workshop on Dynamic Systems Analysis, p. 25. ACM Press (2006)

26. Lorenzoli, D., Mariani, L., Pezzè, M.: Automatic generation of software behavioral models. In: Proceedings of the 13th International Conference on Software Engineering, p. 501. ACM Press (2008)

27. Luke, S., Panait, L.: Lexicographic parsimony pressure. In: Proceedings of the 4th Annual Conference on Genetic and Evolutionary Computation, pp. 829–836. Morgan Kaufmann Publishers Inc. (2002)

28. Magee, J., Kramer, J.: State Models and Java Programs, 2nd edn. Wiley Hoboken (2006)

29. Mannhardt, F.: Multi-perspective process mining. Ph.D. thesis, TU Eindhoven (2018)

30. de Moura, L., Bjørner, N.: Z3: An efficient SMT solver. In: Ramakrishnan, C.R., Rehof, J. (eds.) Tools and Algorithms for the Construction and Analysis of Systems, pp. 337–340. Springer, Heidelberg (2008). https://doi.org/10.1007/978-3-540-78800-3_24

31. Poli, R., Langdon, W.B., McPhee, N.F.: A field guide to genetic programming (2008). http://www.gp-field-guide.org.uk

32. Strobl, F., Wisspeintner, A.: Specifcation of an elevator control system. Technical report, TUM (1999). https://wwwbroy.in.tum.de/publ/papers/elevator.pdf

33. Ulyantsev, V., Tsarev, F.: Extended finite-state machine induction using sat-solver. In: 2011 10th International Conference on Machine Learning and Applications and Workshops, vol. 2, pp. 346–349 (2011)

34. Ulyantsev, V., Buzhinsky, I., Shalyto, A.: Exact finite-state machine identification from scenarios and temporal properties. Int. J. Softw. Tools Technol. Transfer **20**(1), 35–55 (2016)

35. Vaandrager, F., Midya, A.: A Myhill-Nerode theorem for register automata and symbolic trace languages. In: Holm, C., Kremer, K. (eds.) Theoretical Aspects of Computing, vol. 221, pp. 43–63. Springer, Cham (2020). https://doi.org/10.1016/j.tcs.2022.01.015

36. Van Der Aalst, W.: Process mining. Commun. ACM **55**(8), 76–83 (2012)

37. Walkinshaw, N., Hall, M.: Inferring computational state machine models from program executions. In: 2016 IEEE International Conference on Software Maintenance and Evolution, pp. 122–132. IEEE (2016)

38. Walkinshaw, N., Lambeau, B., Damas, C., Bogdanov, K., Dupont, P.: STAMINA: a competition to encourage the development and assessment of software model inference techniques. Emp. Softw. Eng. **18**(4), 791–824 (2013)

39. Walkinshaw, N., Taylor, R., Derrick, J.: Inferring extended finite state machine models from software executions. Emp. Softw. Eng. **21**(3), 811–853 (2016)

Testing Against Non-deterministic FSMs: A Probabilistic Approach for Test Suite Minimization

Natalia Kushik[1](✉), Nina Yevtushenko[2,3], and Jorge López[4]

[1] Télécom SudParis, Institut Polytechnique de Paris, Palaiseau, France
natalia.kushik@telecom-sudparis.eu
[2] Ivannikov Institute for System Programming of the Russian Academy of Sciences, Moscow, Russia
evtushenko@ispras.ru
[3] Higher School of Economics, Moscow, Russia
[4] Airbus Defence and Space, Issy-Les-Moulineaux, France
jorge.lopez-c@airbus.com

Abstract. The paper is devoted to model based testing against non-deterministic specifications. Such test derivation strategies are well developed, for example against non-deterministic Finite State Machines, however the length of the corresponding test suite can be exponential w.r.t. the number of specification states. We therefore discuss how a test suite can be minimized or reduced when certain level of guarantee concerning its fault coverage is still preserved. The main idea behind the approach is to augment the specification by assigning probabilities for the non-deterministic transitions and later on evaluate the probability of each test sequence to detect the relevant faulty implementation. Given a probability P which is user-defined, we propose an approach for minimizing a given exhaustive test suite TS such that, it stays exhaustive with the probability no less than P.

Keywords: Model based testing · Non-deterministic finite state machines · Guaranteed fault coverage · Probabilistic approach

1 Introduction

Model based testing has been actively developing in the past decades; the interested reader can find various recent works, in particular, when checking the proceedings of related conferences such as the International Conference on Testing Software and Systems (ICTSS), the International Symposium on Software Testing and Analysis (ISSTA), the Workshop on Model-Based Testing (MBT), the International Conference on Software Testing, Verification and Validation (ICST), etc. Finite State Machine (FSM) based testing assumes that the specification of the System Under Test (SUT) and its implementations are given

The work was partially supported by Erasmus program.

as FSMs and usually the possible implementations share the same input/output alphabets with this specification FSM. In this paper, we study non-deterministic FSMs as related specifications. We note that various (preset and adaptive) testing strategies have been previously proposed for such machines, considering not only the test suite derivation but also learning the specification, test suite minimization and complexity estimation for the aforementioned tasks (see for example, [2,4,5,10]).

In this paper, we consider a white box testing approach, where all the possible faulty implementations are explicitly enumerated [4,7]. A complete test suite is built in such a way that each faulty implementation is *killed* (detected) by some test case of the test suite (test suite exhaustiveness). Such a test suite can be derived, for example, via adding to the test suite each sequence that distinguishes a potential faulty implementation from the specification machine. However, when the conformance relation is represented by non-separability[1], the length of a separating sequence can be exponential (w.r.t. the number of the specification states) [8], and this makes the approach unpractical, even if the fault coverage can be guaranteed. We propose to preserve the fault coverage up to a given level of certainty through augmenting the specification FSM with probabilities. Indeed, whenever for a given input at a given state two or more outputs are possible, these outputs can appear with certain probability. Note that in this paper, we do not discuss how such probabilities are assigned or obtained; they can be provided due to some additional knowledge of an SUT, or its stochastic behavior which can be revealed, for example, during the system monitoring. We only assume that the augmentation of the specification with probabilities is possible.

Once the specification FSM is augmented with probabilities for each non-deterministic transition, a given complete test suite can be *filtered*, i.e., the sequences that are derived for detecting some faulty implementations can be deleted depending on the likelihood of being detected by other test sequences. The level of such likelihood is determined by a user defined probability P. We propose a method for calculating the related likelihood and also discuss how a given exhaustive test suite can be minimized in such a way that it stays exhaustive at least with probability P. Note that we are not aware of any works for test suite minimization with guaranteed fault coverage against probabilistic non-deterministic FSMs and this is thus, the first attempt.

2   Preliminaries

When testing against FSMs, guaranteed fault coverage can be achieved when a corresponding fault model is properly defined. A *fault model* [6] is a triple $\langle \mathcal{S}, @, FD \rangle$ where $\mathcal{S}$ is the specification of the system behavior, $@$ represents the conformance relation between an implementation $\mathcal{I}_j$ under test and the specification $\mathcal{S}$, while FD is a fault domain which limits the set of possible implementations, i.e., $\mathcal{I}_j \in FD$. We are interested in an *exhaustive* test suite, i.e., a test suite

---

[1] There exists an input sequence such that output responses of the specification and an implementation to this sequence do not intersect.

that detects each implementation $\mathcal{I}_j \in FD$ that is not conforming to $\mathcal{S}$ ($\mathcal{I}_j \not\cong \mathcal{S}$). Moreover, we work under the white box testing methodology, which means that the implementations from FD are explicitly enumerated, $FD = \{\mathcal{I}_1, \mathcal{I}_2, \ldots, \mathcal{I}_k\}$. Usually, each $\mathcal{I}_j \in FD$ corresponds to a potential faulty implementation and thus, represents a *mutant* (transfer and/or output) of the specification $\mathcal{S}$. In this work, @ is the non-separability relation ($\cong$) which we further adjust to *probabilistic* non-separability while the specification is represented by an initialized complete non-deterministic observable FSM $\mathcal{S}$.

An *FSM* is a 5-tuple $\mathcal{S} = \langle S, I, O, h_S, s_0 \rangle$ where S is a finite nonempty set of states with the designated initial state $s_0 \in S$, I and O are finite input and output alphabets, and $h_S \subseteq S \times I \times O \times S$ is a *transition relation*. The FSM $\mathcal{S}$ is *non-deterministic* if for some pair $(s, i) \in S \times I$, there exist several pairs $(o, s') \in O \times S$ such that $(s, i, o, s') \in h_S$; otherwise, the FSM is *deterministic*. The FSM $\mathcal{S}$ is *observable* if for every two transitions (s, i, o, s_1), $(s, i, o, s_2) \in h_S$ it holds that $s_1 = s_2$; otherwise, the FSM is *non-observable*. The FSM $\mathcal{S}$ is *complete* if for every pair $(s, i) \in S \times I$, there exists a transition $(s, i, o, s') \in h_S$; otherwise, the FSM is *partial* (partially specified).

Let each $\mathcal{I}_j \in FD$ and $\mathcal{S}$ share the same input alphabet I. We say that $\mathcal{I}_j \not\cong \mathcal{S}$ if there exists a *separating* sequence $\alpha \in I^*$ for $\mathcal{I}_j$ and $\mathcal{S}$, i.e., the set of output reactions of $\mathcal{I}_j$ and $\mathcal{S}$ to α do not intersect, i.e., $out(\mathcal{I}_j, \alpha) \cap out(\mathcal{S}, \alpha) = \emptyset$, where $out(\mathcal{I}_j, \alpha)$ (resp. $out(\mathcal{S}, \alpha)$) is the set of output responses on α at the initial state of the FSM $\mathcal{I}_j$ (resp. FSM $\mathcal{S}$). Otherwise, $\mathcal{I}_j$ is non-separable from the specification machine $\mathcal{S}$. Note that TS is an exhaustive test suite w.r.t. the fault model $\langle \mathcal{S}, \cong, FD = \{\mathcal{I}_1, \mathcal{I}_2, \ldots, \mathcal{I}_k\} \rangle$, if for each $\mathcal{I}_j \in FD$, there always exists such $\alpha_j \in TS$ that separates $\mathcal{I}_j$ from $\mathcal{S}$.

Deriving such complete test suite TS is possible and this problem has been well studied previously (see, for example [4,10]). However, the length of the corresponding separating sequence (even for a given mutant) can be exponential w.r.t. the number of states of the specification FSM $\mathcal{S}$. Therefore, an iterative test suite derivation even for the white box testing approach can return a test suite of exponential length. Correspondingly, in this paper, we discuss how such test suite (length) can be reduced via introducing probabilities to the specification FSM and a given level of certainty about the TS exhaustiveness.

3 Introducing the Probabilities in the Specification

Given the specification machine $\mathcal{S} = \langle S, I, O, h_S, s_0 \rangle$, we augment each non-deterministic transition $(s, i, o, s') \in h_S$ with the probability p. The probabilistic specification is thus the FSM $\mathcal{S} = \langle S, I, O, h_S, s_0, pr \rangle$, where pr is the function that defines the probability for the output o to be produced at state s under input i, $pr : S \times I \times O \longrightarrow [0, 1]$. Note that, we restrict the assignation of pr in such a way that $\forall s \in S \; \forall i \in I \sum_{o \in O} pr(s, i, o) = 1$. The function pr can be extended over input/output sequences from $(IO)^*$; given an input/output sequence $\alpha/\beta = (\alpha'/\beta').(i/o)$, $pr(s_0, \alpha, \beta) = pr(s_0, \alpha', \beta') * pr(s, i, o)$, where s is the α'/β'-successor of the state s_0 of the specification FSM $\mathcal{S}$; if the trace α'/β'

is not defined at state s_0 then this probability equals 0. Note also, that for the defined sequence γ such a successor is unique due to the observability of the specification FSM S. Note as well, that as usual $pr(s, \varepsilon, \varepsilon) = 1$.

As an example, consider the FSM in Fig. 1 where transitions at states 1 and 2 are non-deterministic and augmented with probabilities.

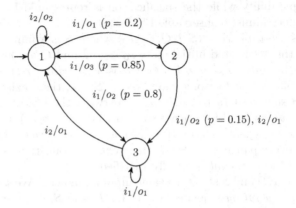

Fig. 1. An example probabilistic FSM S

The notion of a probabilistic FSM has been introduced before, as well as the notion of distinguishability (as non-equivalence) for such machines (see for example, [1,3,9]). However, in this work, we consider the non-separability conformance relation that we adjust, having such an augmented probabilistic specification FSM S.

For a fault model $\langle S, \cong, \{\mathcal{I}_1, \mathcal{I}_2, \ldots, \mathcal{I}_k\}\rangle$ we thus define a *probabilistic separability* for a given implementation $\mathcal{I}_j$ from the specification S. Given P as a user defined probability[2], a sequence $\alpha \in I^*$ is a *P-probably separating* sequence for $\mathcal{I}_j$ and S, if $\sum_{\beta \in out(\mathcal{I}_j, \alpha) \cap out(S, \alpha)} pr(s_0, \alpha, \beta) \leq 1 - P$. Note that $\mathcal{I}_j$ is not probabilistic, and $pr(s_0, \alpha, \beta)$ is the probability to observe β when α is applied at the initial state s_0 of S. For the considered example FSM S (shown in Fig. 1), and a potential implementation $\mathcal{I}_1$ shown in Fig. 2, by direct inspection one can observe that $\alpha = i_1 i_2$ is a 0.8-probably separating sequence.

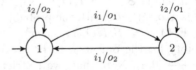

Fig. 2. An implementation FSM $\mathcal{I}_1 \in FD$

---

[2] A level of certainty that a sequence separates the specification and an implementation.

For a fault model $\langle \mathcal{S}, \cong, FD = \{\mathcal{I}_1, \mathcal{I}_2, \ldots, \mathcal{I}_k\}\rangle$, we say that the test suite $P\text{-}TS$ is P-*probably exhaustive* if $\forall \mathcal{I}_j \in FD \; \exists \alpha \in P\text{-}TS$ such that α is a P-probably separating sequence for $\mathcal{I}_j$ and $\mathcal{S}$. We aim at deriving such test suites for user defined probabilities via *filtering* a given exhaustive test suite TS for the fault model $\langle \mathcal{S}, \cong, FD = \{\mathcal{I}_1, \mathcal{I}_2, \ldots, \mathcal{I}_k\}\rangle$.

4 Minimizing an Exhaustive Test Suite Against $\langle \mathcal{S}, \cong, \{\mathcal{I}_1, \mathcal{I}_2, \ldots, \mathcal{I}_k\}\rangle$

Given an exhaustive test suite $TS = \{\alpha_1, \ldots, \alpha_l\}$ derived for the fault model $\langle \mathcal{S}, \cong, FD = \{\mathcal{I}_1, \mathcal{I}_2, \ldots, \mathcal{I}_k\}\rangle$, given also a user defined probability P, we propose to derive a test suite $P\text{-}TS \subseteq TS$, aiming at reducing $|P\text{-}TS|$ (in size), and which is P-probably exhaustive for $\langle \mathcal{S}, \cong, FD = \{\mathcal{I}_1, \mathcal{I}_2, \ldots, \mathcal{I}_k\}\rangle$. In order to do so, we propose to build a matrix M whose rows correspond to the test sequences of TS while columns correspond to all the implementations from FD. $m_{i,j}$ contains the maximal guaranteed probability $p_{i,j}$ for the sequence α_i (in lexicographical order) to separate the implementation I_j (also in lexicographical order) from the specification FSM $\mathcal{S}$. This probability is calculated as $p_{i,j} = 1 - \sum_{\beta \in out(\mathcal{I}_j, \alpha_i) \cap out(\mathcal{S}, \alpha_i)} pr(s_0, \alpha_i, \beta)$.

Note that, by construction, each column of the matrix M contains at least one 1, as the test suite TS is exhaustive. After M is derived what is left to do is to build a minimal cover of it, such that a subset $P\text{-}TS$ corresponding to the rows covers all columns $\{\mathcal{I}_1, \mathcal{I}_2, \ldots, \mathcal{I}_k\}$, where each probability $p_{i,j} \geq P$. The latter means that for each potential faulty implementation from FD there exists at least one test sequence from $P\text{-}TS$ that P-probably separates it from the specification $\mathcal{S}$.

We omit the discussion about how such a row cover can be constructed - it can be done through an explicit combinatorial enumeration or various (combinatorial) optimization strategies can be applied. The solution to the problem always exists and in the worst case scenario, when nothing could be minimized, $P\text{-}TS = TS$.

Consider again the example FSM $\mathcal{S}$, and the $FD = \{\mathcal{I}_1, \mathcal{I}_2, \mathcal{I}_3\}$, where $\mathcal{I}_1$ is the mutant from Fig. 2; it is separated from $\mathcal{S}$ via $\alpha = i_1 i_2 i_1 \in TS$. $\mathcal{I}_2$ shown in Fig. 3 is separated from $\mathcal{S}$ via the application of $\alpha = i_1 i_1$, and 0.2-probably separated via $\alpha = i_1 i_2$. Finally, the mutant $\mathcal{I}_3$ is shown in Fig. 4. The corresponding separating sequence is $\alpha = i_1 i_2$.

Assume that the $TS = \{i_1 i_1, i_1 i_2, i_1 i_2 i_1\}$; the matrix M for the example FSM, mutants $\mathcal{I}_1, \mathcal{I}_2$ and $\mathcal{I}_3$ and this test suite is the following:
$$\begin{pmatrix} 0.97 & 1 & 0.2 \\ 0.8 & 0.2 & 1 \\ 1 & 0.36 & 1 \end{pmatrix}.$$

As an example, note that the M cover that only consists of first two rows provides 0.97-probably exhaustive[3] $P\text{-}TS = \{i_1 i_1, i_1 i_2\}$. The last test sequence thus can be omitted, preserving the exhaustiveness with the probability 0.97.

---

[3] This is just an illustrative example; some other pair of rows can even return an exhaustive test suite, nonetheless longer.

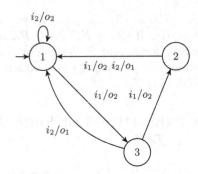

Fig. 3. An implementation FSM $\mathcal{I}_2 \in FD$

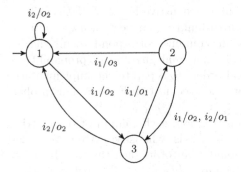

Fig. 4. An implementation FSM $\mathcal{I}_3 \in FD$

5   Conclusion

In this paper, we discussed a possibility of reducing an exhaustive test suite built for a non-deterministic specification, via augmenting this specification with probabilities. The proposed technique relies on a user defined probability P that each potential faulty implementation will be detected (with this probability). The same approach can be applied for a test suite with adaptive separating sequences. In this case, the probability of a test case is the minimum probability of all test case traces. Note also that the proposed approach can also be applied for filtering a non-exhaustive test suite, as long as the sequences left, respect the P-separability relation with the specification.

As a future work, we plan to extend this short paper by considering other fault models, as the proposed technique only considers the non-separability conformance relation and only relies on the white box testing assumption. At the same time, we plan to investigate the model learning strategies for obtaining the probabilities of interest. Finally, as for test derivation, it is interesting to consider how an augmented specification can be used for choosing input sequences, which are more efficient for distinguishing faulty implementations from the specification.

References

1. Alur, R., Courcoubetis, C., Yannakakis, M.: Distinguishing tests for nondeterministic and probabilistic machines. In: Leighton, F.T., Borodin, A. (eds.) Proceedings of the Twenty-Seventh Annual ACM Symposium on Theory of Computing, 29 May–1 June 1995, Las Vegas, Nevada, USA, pp. 363–372. ACM (1995). https://doi.org/10.1145/225058.225161
2. El-Fakih, K., Hierons, R.M., Türker, U.C.: K-branching UIO sequences for partially specified observable non-deterministic FSMS. IEEE Trans. Softw. Eng. **47**(5), 1029–1040 (2021). https://doi.org/10.1109/TSE.2019.2911076
3. Hierons, R.M., Merayo, M.G.: Mutation testing from probabilistic and stochastic finite state machines. J. Syst. Softw. **82**(11), 1804–1818 (2009). https://doi.org/10.1016/j.jss.2009.06.030
4. Kushik, N., Yevtushenko, N., Cavalli, A.R.: On testing against partial non-observable specifications. In: 9th International Conference on the Quality of Information and Communications Technology, QUATIC 2014, Guimaraes, Portugal, 23–26 September 2014, pp. 230–233. IEEE Computer Society (2014). https://doi.org/10.1109/QUATIC.2014.38
5. Petrenko, A., Avellaneda, F.: Learning and adaptive testing of nondeterministic state machines. In: 19th IEEE International Conference on Software Quality, Reliability and Security, QRS 2019, Sofia, Bulgaria, 22–26 July 2019, pp. 362–373. IEEE (2019). https://doi.org/10.1109/QRS.2019.00053
6. Petrenko, A., Yevtushenko, N., von Bochmann, G.: Fault models for testing in context. In: Gotzhein, R., Bredereke, J. (eds.) Formal Description Techniques IX: Theory, application and tools, IFIP TC6 WG6.1 International Conference on Formal Description Techniques IX/Protocol Specification, Testing and Verification XVI, Kaiserslautern, Germany, 8–11 October 1996. IFIP Conference Proceedings, vol. 69, pp. 163–178. Chapman & Hall (1996)
7. Poage, J.F., McCluskey, E.J.: Derivation of optimum test sequences for sequential machines. In: 1964 Proceedings of the Fifth Annual Symposium on Switching Circuit Theory and Logical Design, pp. 121–132 (1964). https://doi.org/10.1109/SWCT.1964.7
8. Spitsyna, N., El-Fakih, K., Yevtushenko, N.: Studying the separability relation between finite state machines. Softw. Test. Verif. Reliab. **17**(4), 227–241 (2007). https://doi.org/10.1002/stvr.374
9. Vidal, E., Thollard, F., de la Higuera, C., Casacuberta, F., Carrasco, R.C.: Probabilistic finite-state machines-part I. IEEE Trans. Pattern Anal. Mach. Intell. **27**(7), 1013–1025 (2005). https://doi.org/10.1109/TPAMI.2005.147
10. Yenigün, H., Kushik, N., López, J., Yevtushenko, N., Cavalli, A.R.: Decreasing the complexity of deriving test suites against nondeterministic finite state machines. In: 2017 IEEE East-West Design and Test Symposium, EWDTS 2017, Novi Sad, Serbia, September 29–October 2, 2017, pp. 1–4. IEEE Computer Society (2017). https://doi.org/10.1109/EWDTS.2017.8110091

Test Generation and Selection

Test Quotation and Selection

Automatic Test Generation with ASMETA for the Mechanical Ventilator Milano Controller

Andrea Bombarda⬤, Silvia Bonfanti⁽⊠⁾⬤, and Angelo Gargantini⬤

Dipartimento di Ingegneria Gestionale, dell'Informazione e della Produzione,
Università degli Studi di Bergamo, Bergamo, Italy
{andrea.bombarda,silvia.bonfanti,angelo.gargantini}@unibg.it

Abstract. This paper presents an automatic test cases generation method from Abstract State Machine specifications. Starting from the ASMETA specification, the proposed approach applies the following steps: 1. Generation of abstract tests from a ASMETA model; 2. Optimization of the abstract tests; 3. Concretization of the abstract tests in GoogleTest; 4. Execution of the concrete tests on C++ code. We have applied this approach to the Mechanical Ventilator Milano (MVM) project, which our research group has contributed to develop, test, and certify during the Covid-19 pandemic.

1 Introduction

In response to the lack of ventilators due to Covid-19, a group of physicists, engineers, physicians, computer scientists, and others from 12 countries around the world has developed a simplified mechanical lung ventilator, called MVM (Mechanical Ventilator Milano)[1]. The project started from an idea of the physicist Cristiano Galbiati, who was also the leader, and our research group has been involved in the development and testing of the device, in order to get the certifications from local authorities and distribute the MVM in the hospitals of different countries. In only 42 d from the initial prototype production to the demonstration of performances, the FDA (Food and Drug Administration) declared that the MVM falls within the scope of the Emergency Use Authorization (EUA) for ventilators and, during the following months, it has obtained the Health Canada and the CE marking as well. Thanks to these achievements, the MVM can be sold and used in the USA, but also in Canada and Europe.

During the development, as required by the standards, we (together with other colleagues) started to design the MVM controller (more details can be found in [1]) and we have used the Yakindu Statechart Tool. Regarding unit testing, since Yakindu does not provide an automatic test generator, tests were manually written and we were able to test the entire machine in a satisfactory way, enough to obtain the required certifications. As well known, writing tests manually should be discouraged, especially if a model is present, since it requires a significant amount of time and can be an error-prone activity. Therefore, after the completion of the development and certification process, we have wondered if test generation starting from formal specifications would have

---

[1] https://mvm.care/.

© IFIP International Federation for Information Processing 2022
Published by Springer Nature Switzerland AG 2022
D. Clark et al. (Eds.): ICTSS 2021, LNCS 13045, pp. 65–72, 2022.
https://doi.org/10.1007/978-3-031-04673-5_5

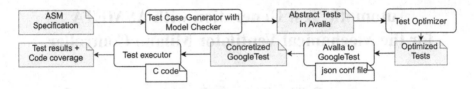

Fig. 1. Test generation and execution process

been applicable in this case and since we still have access to the source code of the MVM, we decided to apply a Model-based-testing (MBT) method to this project. We have decided to use the ASMETA [2] framework which we are familiar with and which offers all the necessary techniques (including those for V&V, missing in Yakindu).

We have started from the ASM specifications of the MVM controller and we have validated and verified our formal specification. Using a model checker we have generated abstract test sequences, that have been optimized and, then, concretized in order to be executable on the C++ implementation of the MVM controller. By evaluating the coverage reached with this testing process, we have obtained better results than the one got with manual tests. The entire process is presented in the following sections.

2   Test Generation

The testing process applied to the case study is depicted in Fig. 1. It starts from the ASM specifications, which have been validated, and verified - but the modeling activity is not reported here for brevity. Starting from the ASM model, abstract tests are generated by the ATGT tool, exploiting the counterexample generation of the model checker. Tests are saved in Avalla, the language used to write scenarios in ASMETA [2]. In this paper, we extend the approach presented in [11] by generating test sequences using the bounded model checker (BMC) and Linear Temporal Logic (LTL) properties. ATGT generates the test predicates which are then translated to suitable LTL temporal properties, called *trap properties* whose counterexamples generated by the BMC are the tests we are looking for. Test predicates are generated by applying the following coverage criteria: 1. *Basic rule* (every rule r_i is executed at least once), 2. *Complete rule* (every rule is executed and performs a non trivial update), 3. *Rule update* (every update is performed once and it is not trivial), 4. *Rule guard* (every guard is evaluated true at least once, and false at least once), 5. *MCDC* (Modified Condition Decision coverage of the guards), 6. *2-wise* (pairwise testing of all the inputs - with a limited domain).

In this case study, tests are generated using the *monitoring* optimization: when a test sequence *ts* is generated for a test predicate yet to cover, the algorithms checks if *ts* covers accidentally other test predicates and it skips the test predicates already covered.

Moreover, we have introduced a *timeout*: for every test predicate *tp* to be covered, the model checker is interrupted if it reaches the timeout before producing a test, either because the test that covers *tp* exists but the model checker is unable to find it or because *tp* is unfeasible, i.e. there is no test that covers it and the trap property is actually true. However, because ATGT uses the classical bounded model checking, it is unable to distinguish the two cases by proving test predicates unfeasibility.

Table 1. Comparison between different criteria for automatic test cases generation

Criteria	#Tps	Timeout 10 min					Timeout 40 min				
		#Tests	#Time-outs	Generation time [min]	#Tps covered	%Tps covered	#Tests	#Time-outs	Generation time [min]	#Tps covered	%Tps covered
Basic rule	72	13	29	345	43	60%	24	11	773	61	85%
Complete rule	2	0	0	0	2	100%	0	0	0	2	100%
Rule guard	124	1	60	601	64	52%	1	27	1080	97	78%
Rule update	89	0	52	520	37	42%	0	25	1000	64	72%
MCDC	148	10	55	581	93	63%	9	24	997	124	84%
2-wise	420	77	0	1	420	100%	73	0	1	420	100%
All criteria	853	101	196	2048	659	77%	107	87	3852	768	90%

Code 1. Original scenario

```
scenario
check apneaAlarm = false;
check iValve = CLOSED; ...
set respirationMode := PCV; ...
step
check apneaAlarm = false;
check iValve = CLOSED; ...
set respirationMode := PCV; ...
step
check iValve = OPEN; ...
```

Code 2. Check Opt.

```
scenario
check apneaAlarm = false;
check iValve = CLOSED; ...
set respirationMode := PCV; ...
step ...
set respirationMode := PCV; ...
step
check iValve = OPEN; ...
```

Code 3. Set Opt.

```
scenario
check apneaAlarm = false;
check iValve = CLOSED; ...
set respirationMode := PCV; ...
step ...
step
check iValve = OPEN;
```

Table 1 reports the comparison in terms of test predicates, number of generated tests, number of timeouts, generation time, and number of test predicates covered for each coverage criteria by setting two different timeouts of 10 and 40 min.

We can observe that by increasing the timeout, the total number of covered test predicates increases (from 77% with timeout 10 min to 90% with timeout 40 min) as well as the number of generated tests and the generation time. For each coverage criterion, the number of *tps* covered increases from 10 min timeout to 40 min timeout, except for *complete rule* and *2-wise* criteria. Considering *complete rule*, no test is generated because, due to the *monitoring* optimization, all *tps* are already covered by tests generated with *basic rule* criteria. For the *2-wise* criterion, in both cases all the *tps* are covered. There is a difference in the number of generated tests that is greater with 10 min timeout. This is because of the lower timeout, fewer tests are generated before trying to cover *2-wise*, so more *tps* will result uncovered and they will need more tests.

Remark: We suspect that many of the uncovered test predicates are unfeasible. Being able to prove unfeasible test requirements is necessary to give complete information about the real coverage of the specification. We plan to extend ATGT in order to support proof by induction using the IC3 algorithm (as we did for property verification).

Test Optimization. Once the abstract tests are generated, we perform the following (optional) test optimizations, which do not change the semantic of the tests but improve the readability and the translatability of the abstract tests to concrete ones.

1. Check optimization: This operation removes unchanged controlled locations. If a controlled location in state s_i has not changed w.r.t. state s_{i-1}, the corresponding **check**

```
[{"asmName": "startVentilation",          "cName": "defaultMock->getInValveStatus",
  "cName": "startVentilation",            "commandType": "OPERATION"
  "commandType": "IN_EVENT"             },{"asmName": "state", "cName": "state",
},{"asmName": "time", "cName": "time",     "commandType": "STATE"
  "commandType": "TBD"                 },{"asmName": "mode", "cName": "mode",
},{"asmName": "iValve",                    "commandType": "VAR"}]
```

Code 4. JSON file for function mapping

is removed, if present. For instance, in Code 1 **check** command on the location *iValve* is repeated, so it is possible to remove the second one (see Code 2).

2. Set optimization: It aims to remove **set** commands of monitored variables in state s_{i-1} if they are not actually asked to compute the update set for state s_i. In Code 2, the second instance of **set** respirationMode = PCV is removed in Code 3 since it is useless.

The average number of **check** and **set** per state in the generated scenarios without optimization is respectively 37 and 15. By applying the check optimization technique the optimized scenarios have an average of 11.22 **check** per state, while by applying the set optimization the average of **set** per state became 3.31.

3   Test Concretization

We have concretized Avalla tests as unit tests in the GoogleTest framework, in order to be executed on the C++ code of the MVM controller generated by Yakindu. The concretization process consists of the following three consecutive steps explained below.

1. Mapping of ASMETA functions to state machine variables. To map each ASM function with the corresponding function in C++ code, we introduce a configuration file in the JSON format. It is automatically generated and filled with all the functions set or checked in the Avalla scenarios which can be adjusted manually.

For each function, the JSON file contains: • asmName, i.e., the name of the function in the ASMETA model; • cName, representing the name of the corresponding function in C++ code; • commandType indicating the type of the function chosen between IN_EVENT, VAR, OPERATION, STATE, and TBD (TBD is the default type and TBD functions are ignored during test concretization).

An example of the JSON file is reported in Code 4. The functions startVentilation is IN_EVENT since it is raised by the user. mode is VAR because it represents an internal field of the state machine, and iValve is OPERATION function type because it interacts with hardware components, i.e. the input valve. Functions used only in the ASMETA model but not in the C++ code (e.g. time) are set to be ignored (TBD type).

2. Hardware mocking: Since the MVM state machine interacts with hardware, during test concretization we needed to append in the generated C++ test file some hardware mock. It has been written using the same interface as the real classes of the hardware components and it is included automatically by the scenario concretization process.

3. GoogleTest code generation: Starting from the Avalla scenarios and using the JSON configuration and the mocking files, we have concretized the tests in GoogleTest. MVM has been developed as a cycle-based state machine. For this reason, we have defined the

set mode := PSV;
set startVentilation := true;
step
check time = 3;
check oValve = CLOSED;
check iValve = OPEN;
check state =
    MAIN_REGION_PSV_R1_INSPIRATION;
	sm−>setMode(PSV);
	sm−>raiseStartVentilation();
	runner−>proceed_time(100);
	
	EXPECT_EQ(valveMock−>getOutValveStatus() , CLOSED);
	EXPECT_EQ(valveMock−>getInValveStatus() , OPEN);
	EXPECT_TRUE(sm−>isStateActive(
	    MAIN_REGION_PSV_R1_INSPIRATION));

Code 5. Test concretization from an Avalla scenario fragment to a GoogleTest test case

main cycle duration of 100 ms as in the C++ implementation, which is used to convert the step command in proceed_time(100) command in GoogleTest. The other Avalla commands are concretized as explained in Table 2. Code 5 shows a test concretization example of an Avalla scenario. IN_EVENT functions (such as startVentilation) are raised only when they are set to true in the Avalla scenario. VAR functions, like mode, are set in the GoogleTest test case when there is a corresponding set in the Avalla scenario, while OPERATION functions, such as iValve, are translated in method calls. VAR and OPERATION functions are controlled when they are checked in the Avalla scenario. Finally, the STATE function represents the active state of the machine.

4 Test Execution

Having concretized the optimized tests, we have tested the C++ code of the MVM controller with them. Table 3 reports the incremental coverage reached with the tests. These results confirm those reported in Table 1: increasing the timeout leads to an increment of the covered test predicates and the code. The table shows that every criterion, except *complete rule* and *rule update* for which no test is generated, improves the code coverage, so we cannot claim that any criterion could have been skipped.

We believe that higher values of coverage are difficult to be obtained since we started from the code generated by Yakindu SCT and many parts of the code are only used by Yakindu itself and can not be mapped in external calls.

Remark: Generating code automatically may hinder testers in reaching a complete code coverage because some code could never be covered or because it would require adding ad hoc tests that can not be easily derived from the behavior specifications.

With automatic test case generation, we are able to improve the coverage of the controller compared to the coverage obtained with handwritten test cases. Nevertheless unit testing the MVM controller was not mandatory in order to obtain the safety

Table 2. Translation rules between Avalla and GoogleTest instructions (sm is the generic name used to indicate the state machine object in Yakindu)

Function type	Set	Check
STATE	//	EXPECT_TRUE(sm->isStateActive([stateName]))
IN_EVENT	sm->raise[cName]()	//
VAR	sm->set[cName]([value])	EXPECT_EQ(sm->get[cName](),[value])
OPERATION	[cName]([value])	EXPECT_EQ([cName](),[value])

Table 3. Coverage reached using different timeouts and coverage criteria

Criteria	Timeout 10 min			Timeout 40 min		
	Statement cov.	Branch cov.	Function cov.	Statement cov.	Branch cov.	Function cov.
Basic rule	65.69%	63.48%	59.46%	80.97%	81.32%	79.05%
Complete rule	65.69%	63.48%	59.46%	80.97%	81.32%	79.05%
Rule guard	66.19%	63.91%	60.47%	81.48%	81.74%	80.07%
Rule update	66.19%	63.91%	60.47%	81.48%	81.74%	80.07%
MCDC	70.24%	69.85%	65.54%	81.48%	81.74%	80.07%
2-wise	70.24%	69.85%	65.54%	81.98%	82.17%	81.08%
All criteria	70.24%	69.85%	65.54%	81.98%	82.17%	81.08%

certification, it is important, since its behavior affects the valves position. However, these tests can be used for integration testing, which is mandatory for the certification.

5   Related Works

In this paper, we generate concrete tests starting from the formal specification of the MVM controller. In [5,6], from an ASMETA specification, C++ unit tests are automatically generated (using the Boost Test library) and they are executed against the C++ code automatically generated from the ASMETA specification. The main difference with the approach presented in this paper is that the code is already available and a map between ASMETA functions and C++ functions is required. This is a widely used methodology, especially when the formal model of the SUT is available [10,12]. In this work and in [4], we start from the ASM specification of the SUT, but many other techniques have been used in the literature. For example, in [3] tests are generated off-line, starting from a Timed Output Input Symbolic Transition System. This process is known as *conformance testing* since the testers want to check the conformance between formal specifications and the actual system [8]. FSMs, or their extensions, are often used for this purpose [9,13,14]. However, the concretization of the generated tests has to be performed in different ways in order to be executed against the actual implementation. In this paper, we propose a test concretization methodology starting from Avalla scenarios and resulting in a collection of GoogleTest test cases. Other approaches exploit different tools, such as the ACT one [7] that can be used for concretizing abstract tests from formal specifications of web applications. Though Yakindu does not have an integrated model checker, other tools like Gamma [15] provide an environment to verify properties but they do not generate automatically an entire test suite.

6   Conclusion

In this paper, we have presented an approach to automatically generate test cases from ASMETA specification. The ATGT tool generates abstract tests by means of the model checker and then they are concretized into GogoleTest cases. The unit tests are then executed on C++ code and test results and code coverage are collected. This approach has been successfully applied to the MVM case study, the code coverage is increased compared to the one obtained with handwritten tests. As future work, we plan to compare probabilistic random test generation instead of using the model checker, since the counterexample generation is very time-consuming.

References

1. Abba, A., et al.: The novel mechanical ventilator milano for the COVID-19 pandemic. Phys. Fluids **33**(3), 037122 (2021). https://doi.org/10.1063/5.0044445
2. Arcaini, P., Bombarda, A., Bonfanti, S., Gargantini, A., Riccobene, E., Scandurra, P.: The ASMETA approach to safety assurance of software systems. In: Raschke, A., Riccobene, E., Schewe, KD. (eds.) Logic, Computation and Rigorous Methods. Lecture Notes in Computer Science(), vol. 12750, pp. 215–238. Springer, Heidelberg (2021). https://doi.org/10.1007/978-3-030-76020-5_13
3. Bannour, B., Escobedo, J.P., Gaston, C., Le Gall, P.: Off-line test case generation for timed symbolic model-based conformance testing. In: Nielsen, B., Weise, C. (eds.) Testing Software and Systems. ICTSS 2012. Lecture Notes in Computer Science, vol. 7641. Springer, Heidelberg (2012). https://doi.org/10.1007/978-3-642-34691-0_10
4. Bombarda, A., Bonfanti, S., Gargantini, A., Radavelli, M., Duan, F., Lei, Y.: Combining model refinement and test generation for conformance testing of the IEEE PHD protocol using abstract state machines. In: Medina-Bulo I., MerayoRobert, M.G., Hierons, R. (eds.) Testing Software and Systems, Lecture Notes in Computer Science book series (LNCS), vol. 11146, pp. 67–85. Springer, Heidelberg (2019). https://doi.org/10.1007/978-3-030-31280-0_5
5. Bonfanti, S., Gargantini, A., Mashkoor, A.: Generation of C++ unit tests from abstract state machines specifications. In: 2018 IEEE International Conference on Software Testing, Verification and Validation Workshops (ICSTW). IEEE (2018). https://doi.org/10.1109/icstw.2018.00049
6. Bonfanti, S., Gargantini, A., Mashkoor, A.: Design and validation of a C++ code generator from Abstract State Machines specifications. J. Softw. Evol. Process **32**(2) (2019)
7. Bubna, K., Chakrabarti, S.: Act (abstract to concrete tests) - a tool for generating concrete test cases from formal specification of web applications. In: ModSym+SAAAS@ISEC (2016)
8. Cavalli, A.R., Maigron, P., Kim, S.U.: Automated protocol conformance test generation based on formal methods for LOTOS specifications. In: Proceedings of the IFIP TC6/WG6.1 Fifth International Workshop on Protocol Test Systems V, pp. 237–248. North-Holland Publishing Co., NLD (1992)
9. Dorofeeva, R., El-Fakih, K., Maag, S., Cavalli, A.R., Yevtushenko, N.: FSM-based conformance testing methods: a survey annotated with experimental evaluation. Inf. Softw. Technol. **52**(12), 1286–1297 (2010). https://doi.org/10.1016/j.infsof.2010.07.001
10. Fraser, G., Wotawa, F., Ammann, P.E.: Testing with model checkers: a survey. Softw. Test. Verific. Reliabil. **19**(3), 215–261 (2009). https://doi.org/10.1002/stvr.402
11. Gargantini, A., Riccobene, E.: ASM-based testing: coverage criteria and automatic test sequence generation. JUCS - J. Univ. Comput. Sci. **7**(11), 1050–1067 (2001). https://doi.org/10.3217/jucs-007-11-1050
12. Hong, H., Lee, I., Sokolsky, O.: Automatic test generation from statecharts using model checking. Technical Reports (CIS) (2001)
13. Kalaji, A., Hierons, R.M., Swift, S.: A search-based approach for automatic test generation from extended finite state machine (EFSM). In: 2009 Testing: Academic and Industrial Conference - Practice and Research Techniques, pp. 131–132 (2009). https://doi.org/10.1109/TAICPART.2009.19

14. Merayo, M.G., Núñez, M., Rodríguez, I.: Formal testing from timed finite state machines. Comput. Netw. **52**(2), 432–460 (2008). https://doi.org/10.1016/j.comnet.2007.10.002
15. Molnár, V., Graics, B., Vörös, A., Majzik, I., Varró, D.: The Gamma statechart composition framework: design, verification and code generation for component-based reactive systems. In: Proceedings of the 40th International Conference on Software Engineering: Companion Proceeedings, pp. 113–116. ACM (2018). https://doi.org/10.1145/3183440.3183489

Locality-Based Test Selection
for Autonomous Agents

Sina Entekhabi[1]([⊠]), Wojciech Mostowski[1], Mohammad Reza Mousavi[2],
and Thomas Arts[3]

[1] Halmstad University, Halmstad, Sweden
{sina.entekhabi,wojciech.mostowski}@hh.se
[2] King's College London, London, UK
mohammad.mousavi@kcl.ac.uk
[3] Quviq AB, Gothenburg, Sweden
thomas.arts@quviq.com

Abstract. Automated random testing is useful in finding faulty corner
cases that are difficult to find by using manually-defined fixed test suites.
However, random test inputs can be inefficient in finding faults, particularly in systems where test execution is time- and resource-consuming.
Hence, filtering out less-effective test cases by applying domain knowledge constraints can contribute to test effectiveness and efficiency. In
this paper, we provide a domain specific language (DSL) for formalising
locality-based test selection constraints for autonomous agents. We use
this DSL for filtering randomly generated test inputs. To evaluate our
approach, we use a simple case study of autonomous agents and evaluate
our approach using the QuickCheck tool. The results of our experiments
show that using domain knowledge and applying test selection filters
significantly reduce the required number of potentially expensive test
executions to discover still existing faults. We have also identified the
need for applying filters earlier during the test data generation. This
observation shows the need to make a more formal connection between
the data generation and the DSL-based filtering, which will be addressed
in future work.

Keywords: Test input generation · Domain specific languages · Test
selection · Autonomous agents · Scenario-based testing · Model-based
testing

1 Introduction

It is well-known [22] that testing and debugging account for more than half
of the development costs. Test automation, e.g., using Model-Based Testing
(MBT) [16], mitigates this problem by generating tests at low additional cost
once a model is in place. However, in some application areas, test execution is
very time- and resource-intensive. In particular, this applies to our research

© IFIP International Federation for Information Processing 2022
Published by Springer Nature Switzerland AG 2022
D. Clark et al. (Eds.): ICTSS 2021, LNCS 13045, pp. 73–89, 2022.
https://doi.org/10.1007/978-3-031-04673-5_6

project SafeSmart[1], where we consider cooperative (semi-)autonomous vehicles supported by V2X communication [29]. In our project, testing cooperative behaviour in complex urban traffic scenarios requires full simulation cycle for each test and is hence, extremely resource consuming. Our main objective is thus to identify *interesting* tests, i.e., ones that can effectively provide challenging scenarios that may stress the system under test and reveal severe faults by triggering failures.

To address this objective, we introduce a Domain Specific Language (DSL) for defining locality-based constraints for our autonomous agents moving on a grid. We implement this DSL for filtering the test cases randomly generated by the QuickCheck tool that we use in our project. To evaluate our approach, we implement and use a downsized form of the project case study, namely a set of autonomous agents moving in a grid, which we call *SafeTurtles* [8]. We use SafeTurtles for conducting an experiment with a few filtering constraints, defined by our DSL, and analyse and compare the results of testing with and without filters. This analysis is mainly in terms of the most expensive task in our testing approach, i.e., the number of test executions until a failure is found. Using this experiment, we answer the following two research questions:

Q1 Can filtering test inputs make fault detection more efficient?
Q2 Can filtering test inputs lead to a more efficient process for finding the most concise failing test input?

The answers to these research questions have a significant impact on reducing the test execution time: Q1 implies that we can find challenging test cases more efficiently and Q2 implies that we can close up on the "causes" for such failures more efficiently.

Finally, we also discuss the need of having a tailored data generator in the first place for the approach to be meaningful, while the natural step of deriving test cases directly from the DSL is a topic for future work.

In the remainder of this paper, we present a brief overview of our context in Sect. 2. Our testing methodology and our proposed DSL for formalising test selection constraints are explained in Sect. 3 and Sect. 4, respectively. To evaluate our approach, an experiment is designed, carried out, and its results are analysed in Sect. 5. Finally, related work is discussed in Sect. 6, and the paper is concluded in Sect. 7.

2   Context

2.1   SafeSmart Project

The wider context of our work is the SafeSmart project [29] that investigates *Safety of Connected Intelligent Vehicles in Smart Cities* from different angles, including vehicle-to-X (V2X) communication, localisation of objects on the road,

---

[1] https://hh.se/safesmart.

and control of vehicles. These topics are investigated in the context of dense urban traffic, and the primary technique to validate the developments is simulation. Our particular objective is the application of model-based techniques [16] for testing systems in this domain. We start off by using Property-Based Testing (PBT) with random test data generation.

2.2 QuickCheck

In the context of the SafeSmart project, we use an advanced PBT tool QuickCheck[2] [1]. Random input data generation in QuickCheck is supported by dedicated data generators for different data types (numbers, lists, vectors) with capping and distribution parameters, and the ability to combine the generators to build more complex data structures.

In QuickCheck, when a generated test fails, to ease debugging, the tool looks for and reports the most concise test failing input to report by modifying a failing test input into a "smaller" input and retrying the test. The way the data is modified is inherent in each particular data generator following a data type specific heuristic. This process is called *shrinking*. If a smaller test still fails, QuickCheck has gotten one step closer to the most concise failing input; this is called a *successful shrinking step*. Otherwise, if a smaller input data does not lead to a failed test, the process may back-track and try other ways of reducing the test input. This is called a *failed shrinking step*. This process continues up to the point, where no more successful shrinking is possible, and the last modified input is reported as the most concise input.

3   Methodology

While automated random testing can be useful in generating unforeseen scenarios, the test execution cost can become prohibitive in using it for embedded autonomous systems. Hence, we propose to exploit domain knowledge in selecting tests along with having the randomness factor. In our methodology, we first define a random data generator and use a DSL to formalise the domain knowledge for filtering the uninteresting cases from test execution. Filtering, hence, aims to increase the fault detection capability of the generated test cases.

Our target domain for SUTs is the domain of autonomous agents moving on a grid. Each of these agents has a goal coordinate on the grid and plans a path to reach the goal, including some forced waiting steps. However, the agents do not have to follow the planned path, if they need to avoid a collision. The input of the test process is the grid size (X, Y), the number of agents within the grid, and the number of the their waiting and displacement (action) steps. The output is the sequence of actual movement steps of the agents in response to the planned paths. The testing property of concern is the existence of a collision event in the system execution output, see Fig. 1.

---

[2] http://www.quviq.com/products.

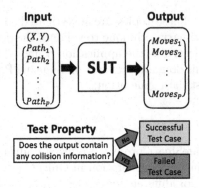

Fig. 1. The SUT of autonomous agents and the testing property

3.1 Testing Module

In our methodology, the testing module generates random inputs, filters them based on the given constraints, and executes the selected tests (after filtering) on the SUT. After executing each selected test input, the existence of collisions is checked. If no collision is detected another set of inputs is generated in the next attempt.

The module presented in Mod. 1.1 is the specification for testing our SUT using QuickCheck. The parameters of this module are respectively the grid dimensions, the number of agents in the gird, the number of displacement and waiting steps of each agent, and the filtering function (predicate) that is used for selecting the generated set of test inputs. In this module, first, a set of random paths is generated for the agents by a function which we named **pathGenerator** (line 3). Then, the SUT is executed to move all the agents based on the suggested generated paths in the given grid (line 6), and the existence of collisions is checked in the output trace afterwards (line 7).

Module 1.1. QuickCheck module for testing the SUT of autonomous agents

```
1   testCollision(X,Y,AgentsNum, ActionSteps, WaitSteps, FilterFunc)->
2     ?FORALL(AgentsPaths,
3             pathGenerator(X, Y, AgentsNum, ActionSteps, WaitSteps),
4             ?IMPLIES(FilterFunc(AgentsPaths),
5                 begin
6                     Trace = sut:run(AgentsPaths, X, Y),
7                     not lists:keymember({event, collision}, 1, Trace)
8                 end)).
```

3.2 Random Data Generation

Although randomness enables contrived corner case discovery, the whole process is still likely to statistically produce much more passing test scenarios rather than failing ones. Therefore, the way random inputs are generated can have a significant effect on fault detection capability and efficiency. In this work, a random data generator is specified for paths of a given length (line 3 in Mod. 1.1). In the remainder of this section, we discuss two approaches to generating random paths.

Uniform Random Data Generator. A random path with displacement length n can be generated by picking a random initial position in the grid, such as (x, y), and picking n sequential random actions (by uniformly random generators) from the *Action* list $\{$ *Up, Down, Left, Right* $\}$. Although at first this may be a natural way of generating paths, in practice this method generates *clustered* paths making them unsuitable for triggering collisions.

By definition, having a set of elements and a uniform random generator, in random selection of n elements from this set when n is very large, the number of each element of the set in the selected sequence is statistically the same. Therefore, when n is very large, the number of *Up*-s and *Down*-s and the number of *Left*-s and *Right*-s would be equal in a randomly selected sequence, the agents would end up close to their initial position at the end of their travel. Therefore, by testing the SUT with these generated paths, the collision avoidance feature of the SUT is rarely tested, as illustrated in Fig. 2a.

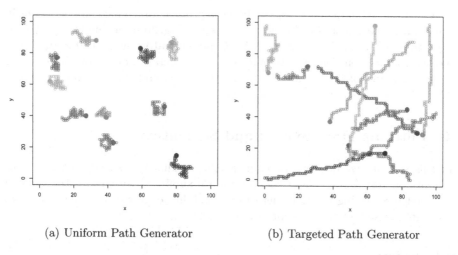

(a) Uniform Path Generator   (b) Targeted Path Generator

Fig. 2. Examples of generating random paths of length 100 in 100 × 100 grid for 10 agents with the uniform- and targeted generators

Targeted Data Generation. To address the problem of generating more diverse paths, we guide the path generation by defining and targeting random endpoint N for paths. Namely, we first select a random endpoint that is reachable in n moves from the initial state of the agent (i.e., a point in the circle centered at M and with radius n). Then, we generate a random simple path that reaches from M to N; if the path involves less moves than n moves then random pairs of {*Left*, *Right*} and/or {*Up*, *Down*} are added to the path. Finally, the moves of the planned path are shuffled to add more randomness to the moves. An outcome of this strategy for data generation is illustrated in Fig. 3.

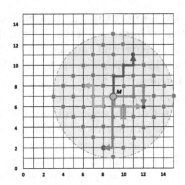

Fig. 3. The possible end points and some random paths with length 6 starting from point M

Our targeted data generator resolves the problem of having compact paths in the uniform data generator, as it can be seen in Fig. 2b. In a simple experiment, we generated paths for 100 agents by these generators in a 1000×1000 grid having displacement length 100. With the first generator, on average, the agents move in squares of 11×10 area. However, this is extended to an average area of 42×43 by using the targeted generator.

4   Filtering DSL: Syntax and Semantics

In this section, we define a domain-specific language to specify filtering constraints on test cases. These constraints are supposed to capture the domain knowledge regarding the fault-detection capability of test cases. This is akin to the criteria used for test-case prioritisation [26].

4.1   Syntax

The syntax of our DSL is presented in Mod. 1.2. According to this syntax, a filtering constraints can be specified as a simple area condition (in line 1 of Mod. 1.2) or a logical combination of constraints NOT, and combination of Constraint-s with AND and OR operators (in lines 2–4 of Mod. 1.2). An area constraint first specifies an area, which can be defined as a circle with a specified radius or a square with a specified side as an integer (in lines 6 and 7 of Mod. 1.2). The second and final part involves locality conditions that specify a minimum number of agents at some arbitrary time in a given area (in line 9) and a minimum number "n" of path intersections of degree "d" (in line 10). The intersection degree for a point is the number of agents that visit that point sometime in their route in a given area. Similar to `Constraint`, locality conditions can also be combined using logical connectives. This syntax can be extended with other domain-specific objects of our target domain to cater for other notions of fault detection capability.

Module 1.2. The DSL for locality-based test selection constraint definition for autonomous agents

```
1   Constraint  ->     IN Area Condition |
2                      AND Constraint Constraint |
3                      NOT Constraint |
4                      OR Constraint Constraint
5
6   Area        ->     Circle Integer |
7                      Square Integer
8
9   Condition   ->     Count Integer |
10                     Intersection Integer Integer |
11                     And Condition Condition |
12                     Not Condition |
13                     Or Condition Condition |
```

To illustrate the syntax, a few test selection constraints are defined next for the test input represented in Fig. 4, which includes the suggested movement paths of four agents in a 7×7 grid. All the agents plan to start their moves at the same time $t = 0$, and stop movement after 6 moves at time $t = 6$. The actual running actions in different times will be obviously affected by the decisions of the agents adapting to the traffic.

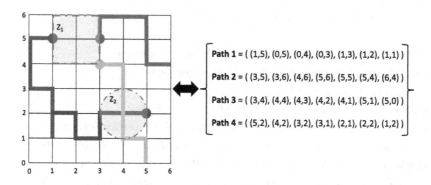

Path 1 = ((1,5), (0,5), (0,4), (0,3), (1,3), (1,2), (1,1))

Path 2 = ((3,5), (3,6), (4,6), (5,6), (5,5), (5,4), (6,4))

Path 3 = ((3,4), (4,4), (4,3), (4,2), (4,1), (5,1), (5,0))

Path 4 = ((5,2), (4,2), (3,2), (3,1), (2,1), (2,2), (1,2))

Fig. 4. Test input example including the suggested paths of four autonomous agents

- `IN Square 2 Count 3`: This constraint is satisfied for the test input since there are three agents (i.e., agents $1, 2, 3$) that in a particular time ($t = 0$) could stand in positions that are included in a square with side length 2 (the Z_1 area).
- `IN Circle 1 Intersection 1 2`: This constraint is satisfied for the test input since there is an occurrence of two agents (3 and 4) crossing a particular point (($4, 2$)) and that the point is included in a circle with radius 1 (the Z_2 area).
- `IN Square 2 (Intersection 1 2 And Count 3)`: This constraint is not satisfied for the test input since there is no square area with side length 2 that both of the conditions "`Intersection 1 2`" and "`Count 3`" are satisfied in that area.

4.2   Semantics

The formal semantics of our DSL is defined in Mod. 1.2 in terms of an *eval* function that maps every constraint and a list of paths to a Boolean. Our semantics assumes a $g \times g$ grid containing m agents with l number of actions (including waiting steps) in total. The only non-trivial case in the definition of *eval*, which uses the auxiliary function *evalCon*; the application of the latter function checks whether there exists an area that satisfies a constraint. The geometric definition of the area is ascertained by function *areaContains*, while the condition to be satisfied in the specified area is checked by function *getCases*; the latter function makes a case distinction based on the type of condition to be satisfied and generates the associated constraint on the involved paths.

$eval :: Constraint \rightarrow [Path] \rightarrow Boolean$

$eval\ (IN\ a\ c\ )\ P = \exists\ x, y \in \{0, \ldots, (g - 1)\}\ evalCon(AreaInstance\ a\ (x, y)\ ))\ c\ P$

$eval\ (NOT\ f)\ P = \neg\ eval(f\ P)$

$eval\ (f_1\ AND\ f_2)\ P = (eval\ f_1\ P) \wedge (eval\ f_1\ P)$

$eval\ (f_1\ OR\ f_2)\ P = (eval\ f_1\ P) \vee (eval\ f_1\ P)$

$evalCon :: AreaInstance \rightarrow Condition \rightarrow [Path] \rightarrow Boolean$

$evalCon\ (AreaInstance\ a\ (x, y))\ c\ P = \exists\ z \in (getCases\ c\ P)$

$\qquad areaContains\ (a\ (x, y))\ z$

$evalCon\ (Not\ (i\ c\ P)) = \neg\ evalCon(i\ c\ P)$

$evalCon\ (AreaInstance\ a\ (x, y))\ (c_1\ And\ c_2)\ P = \exists\ z \in getCases\ (c_1\ P)$

$\qquad (areaContains\ (a\ (x, y))\ z) \wedge (evalCon\ (AreaInstance\ a\ (x, y))\ c_2\ P)$

$evalCon\ (AreaInstance\ a\ (x, y))\ (c_1\ Or\ c_2)\ P = \exists\ z \in getCases\ (c_1\ P)$

$\qquad (areaContains\ (a\ (x, y))\ z) \vee (evalCon\ (AreaInstance\ a\ (x, y))\ c_2\ P)$

$getCases :: Condition \rightarrow [Path] \rightarrow [checkCase]$

$getCases\ (Count\ n)\ P\ =\ (S, n)\ where$

$\quad S = \{\ s\ |\ t \in \{1, \ldots, l\} \wedge Q = \{P[1][t], \ldots, P[m][t]\} \wedge s \subseteq 2^Q \wedge |s| = n\ \}$

$getCases\ (Intersection\ d\ n)\ P\ =\ (S, n)\ where$

$\quad S = \{s\}, s = \{(x, y)\ |\ \exists Q \subseteq P\ |Q| = d\ \forall q \in Q\ \exists t\ (x, y) = w_i[t]\ \}$

$areaContains :: AreaInstance \rightarrow CheckCase \rightarrow Boolean$

$areaContains\ (AreaInstance\ (Circle\ r)\ c)\ (S,\ n) = \exists Q \in S$

$\quad \forall q \in Q\ (q_x - c_x)^2 + (q_y - c_y)^2 \leq r^2$

$areaContains\ (AreaInstance\ (Square\ d)\ c)\ (S,\ n) = \exists Q \subseteq S[1]\ |Q| = n$

$\quad \forall q \in Q\ |q_x - c_x| \leq \dfrac{d}{2} \wedge |q_y - c_y| \leq \dfrac{d}{2}$

Here are the used types:

$\quad type\ Point\ =\ (Integer, Integer)$

$\quad type\ Path\ =\ [Point]$

$\quad type\ CheckCase\ =\ ([Path], Integer)$

$\quad newtype\ AreaInstance\ =\ AreaInstance\ Area\ Point$

5 Experiments

In this section, we design and conduct an experiment to answer the research questions set forth in the introduction, which we recall below:

Q1 Can filtering test inputs make fault detection more efficient?

Q2 Can filtering test inputs lead to a more efficient process for finding the most concise failing test input?

QuickCheck is used for tool support in this experiment where the test inputs are generated randomly with and without filters defined with our DSL, and the results are compared with each other at the end. The chosen experiment size is a 100×100 grid including 5 agents where each agent has 5 displacement steps and 5 waiting steps in total.

The SUT instance of this experiment is a set of autonomous agents called SafeTurtles [8], which are implemented in Erlang. The choice of language is mainly dictated by the ease of interfacing to QuickCheck, but otherwise any other programming language could be used for the SUT, as QuickCheck is very flexible to make any kind of a connection to the SUT. In SafeTurtles, there are a few agents, called turtles, that can move on the grid. Each turtle has a goal and a planned path for reaching its goal. The control algorithm of each turtle is supposed to observe the environment and autonomously avoid collisions with other turtles. However, due to the intentional weakness of the collision avoidance mechanism, the turtles do not take move prediction into account. Therefore, if more than one turtle try to step onto the same position at the very same time, they will collide.

In this experiment, the following filtering constraints F1, F2 and F3 are used along with the targeted data generator (explained in Sect. 3.2), and for a better evaluation of the results, the tests are repeated 100 times in each case to get good statistics.

- **F1**: In Circle 5 Count 2
- **F2**: In Circle 3 Count 2
- **F3**: In Circle 1 Intersection 1 2

Among these filters, F2 is defined to be stricter than F1, i.e., for all sets of test cases, F2 accepts a subset of those test cases accepted by F1. However, rejecting many test inputs does not necessarily mean that the filter makes fault detection more efficient. Among the mentioned filters, the concern captured by F3 is different from both F1 and F2. Choosing these different types of filters is expected to give us more insight on the effect of filtering the test cases.

5.1   Fault Detection Time

The total testing time comprises two major parts: test input generation time and test execution time. Test execution requires execution or simulation of the SUT and hence, the test execution time is expected to be significantly larger than test input generation time. While, for the sake of completeness, we also consider test input generation time, we expect test execution time to be much more significant and hence, will be the focus of our experiment results.

Test Execution Time. Figure 5a represents the number of (passed) test cases up to detecting the first fault by using different filters. To make a rigorous analysis of the obtained results, statistical hypothesis testing is used. Here, the considered statistical question concerns if the mean of one population is significantly smaller than the other one. To start with, we applied the *Kruskal-Wallis* test [19], to check if there is any significant difference in the mean of these four populations; we got the p-value less than $2.2e^{-16}$; meaning with confidence level 99% the test detects that there is some significant difference among the groups. To zoom into the differences, we next performed pairwise tests between all pairs of populations (due to space restrictions, we report only some of them below and in Table 1).

We first checked the normality of the data distributions. For this purpose, *Shapiro-Wilk* test [27] is applied on the data, and since the calculated p-values are below 0.05 (and even below 0.01) for the number of executed tests for each of the filtering cases, the data are supposed not normal[3]. As a result, based on

---

[3] The experimental data and the code of statistical tests are available in "**exp**" sub-directory of [8].

the required statistical question, one tailed *Mann-Whitney-Wilcoxon u-test* [30] is selected for doing statistical analysis on the number of executed tests.

As shown in Table 1, having the alternative hypothesis "the number of required test executions till reaching the failed test by having the filter F1 is significantly smaller than the case of having no filter", the p-value of the t-test is less than 0.01 for our data. It means with confidence level 99% the supposed alternative hypothesis is valid. Applying other u-tests for similar hypotheses also show that with confidence level 99% the number of tests by having F2 is significantly smaller that F1, and the number of tests by having F3 is significantly smaller than F2. These results indicate that having each of these filters lead to detecting the intended fault with smaller number of test cases than having no filter. However, for the particular fault of the system, the filter F3 has better results than F2 and F1.

Figures 5b and 5c show the number of discarded test cases and the relative portions of accepted and discarded cases for each case, respectively. In Fig. 5c, it can be seen that from a total of over 400 generated test inputs, more than 300 were discarded by any filtering strategy.

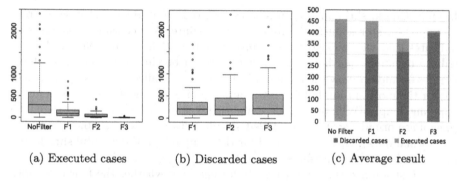

(a) Executed cases   (b) Discarded cases   (c) Average result

Fig. 5. The number of executed (accepted) and discarded test cases up to detecting the failure

Valid Test Input Generation Time. Test input generation time depends on the complexity of the data generator. When applying filtering, the complexity filtering can increase the test input generation time. However, there is a delicate interaction between data generation and filtering: "smarter" data generation schemes may take more time, but at the same time may lead to fewer ineffective test cases; the latter will lead to fewer discarded test cases and hence, save some time in the filtering phase. For instance, for the proposed generators of Sect. 3.2 and the SUT parameters of Fig. 2, to generate a single valid test input having filter F3 with uniform data generator, about 87 test inputs are discarded on average (calculated from 100 attempts). However, the targeted data generator reduces this number to only 7 discarded cases for a single valid test input. This shows that, as expected, the test data generator is much less costly than the uniform data generator in generating valid test inputs when the test selection constraint is a filter like F3.

Table 1. The p-values of applying statistical tests on our experiment results with the alternative hypothesis that "applying no test input filter results in a higher number of executed test-cases before reaching the first failure (resp. successful and failed shrinking steps) than applying filters F1, F2, or F3".

	P-value		
	Executed test cases (u-test)	Successful shrink steps (t-test)	Failed shrink steps (u-test)
F1	$2.149e^{-08}$	0.3443	0.001143
F2	$<2.2e^{-16}$	0.06088	$4.426e^{-06}$
F3	$<2.2e^{-16}$	0.0329	$3.214e^{-09}$

5.2 Shrinking Time

In QuickCheck, shrinking is a mechanism to reduce a failing test case in order to help the tester identify the root cause of failure. A successful shrinking step indicates that the failed test cases involved steps that did not effectively contribute to failure and hence, the test case could be shrunk by removing them. Figures 6a and 6b show the number of successful and failed shrink steps in reaching for the most shrunk failing test inputs in our experiment. As the p-values of applying Shapiro-Wilk test on successful shrink step results are greater than 0.05 (meaning normal data) and on failed shrink steps are less than 0.05 (meaning not normal data), *t-test* [28] is used for the comparison of successful shrink step results and u-test for the failed ones.

We first applied the *Anova* test [9] for checking whether the four categories show a significant difference in the means of *successful* shrinking steps. (In this case, *Bartlett* test with p-value 0.43 indicated that the variances of the groups are not significantly different and we can apply Anova test on them). It turns out that the successful shrinking steps are not significantly different according to the Anova test. Namely, the Anova test shows p-value 0.169 (greater than 0.01), meaning that at least with confidence level 95% the groups are not significantly different than each other. As shown in Table 1, we also considered pairwise differences, defining the alternative hypothesis to "having no filters leads to a smaller number of *successful* shrink steps"; in this case, the p-values amount to about 0.3, 0.06, and 0.03 for filters F1, F2 and F3, respectively. It means at least with confidence level 95%, only the filter F3 significantly reduce the number of successful shrink steps in this experiment.

On the other hand, the data indicates that the case for *failed* shrinking steps is clearer: the Kruskal-Wallis test on the number of failed shrinking tests leads to the p-value $1.345e-08$ (less than 0.01); hence, with confidence level 99%, at least one of the groups is significantly different than one other. Our pair-wise u-tests in the paper goes deeper into that and confirms this result as follows. As shown in Table 1, for the target alternative hypothesis of "having significantly smaller number of *failed* shrink steps by having filters", it results in p-values less than 0.01 for each the filters F1, F2 and F3. It means that with confidence level 99% there is a significant improvement in decreasing the number of failed shrink steps by having these filters. This happens because the filtering constraints directly eliminate the (modified) inputs from test execution that cannot result in failure. In addition, doing u-test for a similar hypothesis shows that with confidence level 95% the number of failed shrink steps by F3 is significantly less than F1 and F2 as well. Figure 6c shows the average number of successful and failed shrink steps in this experiment. The average number of successful shrinking steps is very close in all of the cases. Nevertheless, due to discarding some of the idle test inputs by filtering in the shrinking process, smaller number of test execution is required by having the filters on average in the shrinking process.

In order to analyse further the mutual effect of filtering and shrinking it is useful to apply different strategies and constraints in initial data generation and shrinking. However, QuickCheck does not support this feature yet.

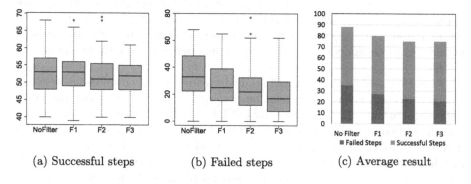

| (a) Successful steps | (b) Failed steps | (c) Average result |

Fig. 6. The number of shrinking steps

Threats to Validity. The subject system used in our experiments is an abstraction of real-world autonomous systems. To address this threat, we plan to extend our SUT to accommodate more domain concepts in our project and in tandem extend our DSL to reflect the extended domain knowledge. Although our experiments show promising results with our specific targeted data generator and filtering constraints, the results cannot be generalised to other data generators or filtering constraints. We would like to consider a wider variety of data generators and incorporate filtering constraints in them, and also study the relative effect of different data generators, filtering constraints and their complexity, and test execution platforms in our future work.

6 Related Work

Random testing has been used as a lightweight method for testing systems, particularly at their early stages of development and deployment [5,14,21]. To mitigate the prohibitive cost of test execution, one could augment random testing with either more intelligent test generation algorithms or filtering and test selection criteria. From the former category, using constraint solvers and search-based algorithms are prominent examples. The latter approach, i.e., filtering, has the advantage of being compositional, i.e., different filters can be composed to cover different aspects of test design. Furthermore, constraint solving would typically lead to the same test values for a particular constraint, while random data generation with filtering provides certain degree of test data variability each time.

Considering code level constraints, TestEra [17] and Korat [3] are examples of having pure filtering style; ASTGen [6] has a pure generating style, and UDITA [13] can be used for both filtering and generating of test cases. For defining test harnesses, TSTL [15] also provides a DSL for test data generation. Our approach puts much more emphasis on embedding domain knowledge in filtering rather than test generation. However, the principles of our approach can also be applied to design intelligent generators and a thorough empirical comparison of the two alternative approaches remains as future work, especially that we witnessed a clear dependency of results on the link between the data generator and the filter.

Scenario-based testing is a well-studied area in testing autonomous systems. Concrete scenarios for testing can be designed by either analysing the crash data [4,23] or naturalistic driving data (NDD) [18,25]. For analysis and simulation of particular scenarios in cyber-physical systems (CPS), several DSLs are designed [2,10,11,24]. Fremount et al. [12] used SCENIC [11] for defining parametric scenarios for testing autonomous vehicles and used VERIFAI toolkit [7] for the analysis of the scenarios and generating concrete test case and used SVL [20] simulator for executing test cases. Our main departure point from much of the informal scenario-definition languages [2,10,24] is the rigorous geometric and logical basis for our DSL. Compared to other languages that do have a formal basis [7,12], our focus on locality of grid-based agents is a distinctive feature of our DSL. We do expect that our DSL can be extended with other features in the aforementioned languages and our concrete filters can be composed with theirs to cover different aspects of the domain.

7 Conclusions and Future Work

In this paper, we proposed a methodology for filtering randomly generated test cases in order to make fault detection more efficient. We have implemented our methodology in QuickCheck and used a case study of autonomous agents to empirically evaluate the proposed methodology. Our empirical results indicate that filters reflecting domain knowledge can significantly reduce the time to reach failures. Also our results indicate that in the process of shrinking a failing test case into a minimal one, using filters can lead to fewer failed shrinking attempts.

As a natural next step, we would like to incorporate the definition of filters into the data generators. In other words, instead of generating and then filtering, we would like to generate test data (also with possible randomness) from the DSL specification. This would involve extending QuickCheck with new DSL-based data generators that would also allow for better results in the test shrinking process.

Finally, we would like to scale up our case study towards our demonstrator within the SafeSmart project. The next step is using the existing Robot Operating System (ROS) version of our case study, which features more elaborate decision making by the agents as well as continuous dynamics of agents. Further, we shall apply our method in the context of SUMO/Veins simulations of communicating vehicles (V2X). Our objectives will go beyond collision-freedom and consider other dangerous or undesired configurations of the system, e.g., excessive braking of the vehicles [29]. The semantics of our DSL should also be extended to not only consider possible failures, but also consider severity and likelihood of undesired situations. This will lead to a model-based framework for evaluating both safety and comfort of the autonomous system under test.

Acknowledgements. We thank Jan Tretmans, Verónica Gaspes, and the anonymous reviewers of ICTSS for their valuable comments on this work. Our research has been partially funded by the Knowledge Foundation (KKS) in the framework of "Safety of Connected Intelligent Vehicles in Smart Cities – SafeSmart" project (2019–2023). Mohammad Reza Mousavi has been partially supported by the UKRI Trustworthy Autonomous Systems Node in Verifiability, Grant Award Reference EP/V026801/1.

References

1. Arts, T., Hughes, J., Johansson, J., Wiger, U.: Testing telecoms software with QUVIQ quickcheck. In: Proceedings of the 2006 ACM SIGPLAN Workshop on Erlang, pp. 2–10 (2006)
2. ASAM: ASAM openSCENARIO (2021). https://www.asam.net/standards/detail/openscenario/
3. Boyapati, C., Khurshid, S., Marinov, D.: Korat: Automated testing based on java predicates. ACM SIGSOFT Softw. Eng. Notes **27**(4), 123–133 (2002)
4. Carsten, O., Merat, N., Janssen, W., Johansson, E., Fowkes, M., Brookhuis, K.: Human machine interaction and safety of traffic in europe. HASTE final Report 3 (2005)
5. Chen, T.Y., Kuo, F.C., Merkel, R.G., Tse, T.: Adaptive random testing: the art of test case diversity. J. Syst. Softw. **83**(1), 60–66 (2010)
6. Daniel, B., Dig, D., Garcia, K., Marinov, D.: Automated testing of refactoring engines. In: Proceedings of the the 6th Joint Meeting of the European Software Engineering Conference and the ACM Sigsoft Symposium on the Foundations of Software Engineering, pp. 185–194 (2007)

7. Dreossi, T., et al.: Verifai: a toolkit for the formal design and analysis of artificial intelligence-based systems. In: Dillig, I., Tasiran, S. (eds.) Computer Aided Verification. CAV 2019. LNCS, vol. 11561, pp. 432–442. Springer, Cham (2019). https://doi.org/10.1007/978-3-030-25540-4_25

8. Entekhabi, S., Arts, T.: Safesmartturtle (2021). https://github.com/ThomasArts/SafeSmartTurtle

9. Fisher, R.A.: Xv.-the correlation between relatives on the supposition of mendelian inheritance. Trans. Roy. Soc. Edinburgh **52**(2), 399–433 (1919). https://doi.org/10.1017/S0080456800012163

10. Foretellix Inc.: M-SDL (2021). https://www.foretellix.com/open-language/

11. Fremont, D.J., Dreossi, T., Ghosh, S., Yue, X., Sangiovanni-Vincentelli, A.L., Seshia, S.A.: Scenic: a language for scenario specification and scene generation. In: Proceedings of the 40th ACM SIGPLAN Conference on Programming Language Design and Implementation, pp. 63–78 (2019)

12. Fremont, D.J., et al.: Formal scenario-based testing of autonomous vehicles: from simulation to the real world. In: 2020 IEEE 23rd International Conference on Intelligent Transportation Systems (ITSC), pp. 1–8. IEEE (2020)

13. Gligoric, M., Gvero, T., Jagannath, V., Khurshid, S., Kuncak, V., Marinov, D.: Test generation through programming in Udita. In: Proceedings of the 32nd ACM/IEEE International Conference on Software Engineering-Volume 1, pp. 225–234 (2010)

14. Hamlet, D.: When only random testing will do. In: Proceedings of the 1st International Workshop on Random Testing, pp. 1–9 (2006)

15. Holmes, J., et al.: TSTL: the template scripting testing language. Int. J. Softw. Tools Technol. Transfer **20**(1), 57–78 (2018)

16. Broy, M., Jonsson, B., Katoen, J.-P., Leucker, M., Pretschner, A. (eds.): Model-Based Testing of Reactive Systems. LNCS, vol. 3472. Springer, Heidelberg (2005). https://doi.org/10.1007/b137241

17. Khurshid, S., Marinov, D.: Testera: specification-based testing of java programs using sat. Autom. Softw. Eng. **11**(4), 403–434 (2004)

18. Kruber, F., Wurst, J., Botsch, M.: An unsupervised random forest clustering technique for automatic traffic scenario categorization. In: 2018 21st International Conference on Intelligent Transportation Systems (ITSC), pp. 2811–2818. IEEE (2018)

19. Kruskal, W.H., Wallis, W.A.: Use of ranks in one-criterion variance analysis. J. Am. Stat. Assoc. **47**(260), 583–621 (1952)

20. LG Electronics Inc.: SVL Simulator (2021). https://www.svlsimulator.com/

21. Liu, H., Xie, X., Yang, J., Lu, Y., Chen, T.Y.: Adaptive random testing through test profiles. Softw.: Pract. Exper. **41**(10), 1131–1154 (2011)

22. Myers, G.J., Sandler, C., Badgett, T.: The Art of Software Testing, 3rd edn. Wiley Publishing (2011)

23. Najm, W.G., Toma, S., Brewer, J., et al.: Depiction of priority light-vehicle pre-crash scenarios for safety applications based on vehicle-to-vehicle communications. Technical report, United States. National Highway Traffic Safety Administration (2013)

24. Queiroz, R., Berger, T., Czarnecki, K.: Geoscenario: an open DSL for autonomous driving scenario representation. In: 2019 IEEE Intelligent Vehicles Symposium (IV), pp. 287–294. IEEE (2019)

25. Roesener, C., Fahrenkrog, F., Uhlig, A., Eckstein, L.: A scenario-based assessment approach for automated driving by using time series classification of human-driving behaviour. In: 2016 IEEE 19th International Conference on Intelligent Transportation Systems (ITSC), pp. 1360–1365. IEEE (2016)

26. Rothermel, G., Untch, R.H., Chu, C., Harrold, M.J.: Test case prioritization: An empirical study. In: Proceedings IEEE International Conference on Software Maintenance-1999 (ICSM 1999). 'Software Maintenance for Business Change'(Cat. No. 99CB36360), pp. 179–188. IEEE (1999)

27. SHAPIRO, S.S., WILK, M.B.: An analysis of variance test for normality (complete samples). Biometrika **52**(3–4), 591–611 (1965). https://doi.org/10.1093/biomet/52.3-4.591

28. Student: The probable error of a mean. Biometrika, pp. 1–25 (1908)

29. Thunberg, J., Sidorenko, G., Sjöberg, K., Vinel, A.: Efficiently bounding the probabilities of vehicle collision at intelligent intersections. IEEE Open J. Intell. Transp. Syst. **2**, 47–59 (2021). https://doi.org/10.1109/OJITS.2021.3058449

30. Wilcoxon, F.: Individual comparisons by ranking methods. Biom. Bull. **1**, 80–83 (1945)

Improving Model Inference via W-Set Reduction

Moritz Halm[1], Rafael S. Braz[2], Roland Groz[1], Catherine Oriat[1(✉)], and Adenilso Simao[2]

[1] Univ. Grenoble Alpes, CNRS, LIG, 38000 Grenoble, France
moritz.halm@student.kit.edu,
{Moritz.Halm,Roland.Groz,Catherine.Oriat}@grenoble-inp.fr
[2] Universidade de São Paulo, São Paulo, Brazil
rafaelbraz@usp.br, adenilso@icmc.usp.br

Abstract. Model inference is a form of systematic testing of black-box systems while learning at the same time a model of their behaviour. In this paper, we study the impact of W-set reduction in hW-inference, an inference algorithm for learning models from scratch. hW-inference relies on progressively extending a sequence h into a homing sequence for the system, and a set W of separating sequences into a fully characterizing set. Like most other inference algorithms, it elaborates intermediate conjectures which can be refined through counterexamples provided by an oracle. We observed that the size of the W-set could vary by an order of magnitude when using random counterexamples. Consequently, the length of the test suite is hugely impacted by the size variation of the W-set. Whereas the original hW-inference algorithm keeps increasing the W-set until it is characterizing, we propose reassessing the set and pruning it based on intermediate conjectures. This can lead to a shorter test suite to thoroughly learn a model. We assess the impact of reduction methods on a self-scanning system as used in supermarkets, where the model we get is a finite state machine with 121 states and over 1800 transitions, leading to an order of magnitude of around a million events for the trace length of the inference.

1 Introduction

Model inference derives state machine models of software systems, for various tasks, such as verification [13], documentation, test generation or all sorts of model-driven engineering tasks [2,17]. Active inference techniques for reactive systems learn a model by interacting with the System Under Learning (SUL), sending inputs and observing outputs. Thus, they can be seen as a form of systematic testing of a system, as well as a machine learning activity.

Active inference algorithms rely on input sequences that can separate (i.e., distinguish) different states of the SUL. In algorithms based on observation tables, such as L^* [1] and L_m [15], such sequences appear in the columns. The sequence or adaptive sequences as trees appear in algorithms based on tree structures, such as TTT [9] and ZQuotient [14]. Sequences separating states have been

© IFIP International Federation for Information Processing 2022
Published by Springer Nature Switzerland AG 2022
D. Clark et al. (Eds.): ICTSS 2021, LNCS 13045, pp. 90–105, 2022.
https://doi.org/10.1007/978-3-031-04673-5_7

at the core of conformance testing methods [10]. Following the seminal paper by Vasilievskii [18], a set of sequences that characterize all states of a finite state machine (FSM) has been called a W-set.

hW-inference [6,7] is a recent algorithm that, contrary to other inference algorithms, makes it possible to infer a SUL without resetting it. As its name indicates, it is fundamentally based on the use of homing and characterizing sequences. It learns a model by repeatedly homing into some state, transferring to an unknown transition to be learnt, applying the input corresponding to that transition, and applying one of the characterizing sequences to check the transition's tail (final) state. As in testing algorithms based on a W-set, the number of sequences in the W-set acts as a multiplier on the length of the global test, as the same preamble (homing and transfer) followed by the transition itself has to be repeated as many times as there are sequences in W to be concatenated at the end. A full discussion of hW-inference related to other inference methods is outside the scope of this paper but can be found in [7].

In conformance testing, it is easy to optimize the use of sequences from W, such as in the Wp method [4], based on the knowledge of the reference state machine (the specification). In the case of hW-inference, the W-set is learnt incrementally, and it grows along the inference process. More precisely, W is extended when processing counterexamples provided by an oracle, or when an inconsistency called W-ND is detected. A counterexample is an input sequence for which the model and SUL yield different outputs; when no such input sequences, the oracle is expected either to confirm equivalence of the model and the SUL.

In this paper, we propose to reassess and reduce the W-set learnt in the course of inference, to limit its growth, while still trying to keep the level of characterization reached, which we can assess thanks to intermediate conjectures. Finding optimal preset W-sets for a given FSM is known to be a PSPACE-complete problem [10]. Thus, we do not look for a minimal W-set that could be computed from a conjectured machine, but we use sub-optimal W-sets that can be efficiently computed with greedy heuristics. We assess the impact of several reduction methods on the inference of a medium-sized model (121 states and 15 inputs), corresponding to a case study that has been used to compare various machine learning techniques [16].

The remainder of this paper is organised as follows. We first give an overview of hW-inference and the elements of the algorithm that are affected by modifications of W. Then, we present in Sect. 4 the reduction approaches we propose. The results on our case study are in Sect. 5. Finally, perspectives are presented in the conclusion.

2   Definitions

In this paper, an FSM is assumed to be a *strongly connected* complete deterministic Mealy machine $M = (Q, I, O, \delta, \lambda)$, with finite state, input and output sets Q, I, O, $\delta : (Q \times I) \to Q$ and $\lambda : (Q \times I) \to O$ as transition and output mappings. We do not define an initial state in the absence of a reset operation. We lift δ and λ to input sequences in the usual way.

Two states $q, q' \in Q$ are separable by a set $H \subset I^*$ if there exists a *separating sequence* $\gamma \in H$ such that $\lambda(q, \gamma) \neq \lambda(q', \gamma)$. An FSM is *minimal* if all states are pairwise separable. A set W of sequences of inputs (therefore conventionally called a W-set) is a *characterization set* for an FSM M if each pair of states is separable by W. An input sequence h is said to be homing for a Mealy machine if the corresponding output sequence observed when applying it to the machine uniquely determines the state reached at the end of the sequence, i.e., $\lambda(q, h) = \lambda(q', h)$ implies that $\delta(q, h) = \delta(q', h)$.

3 Overview of hW-Inference

hW-inference is an active inference algorithm. Given a black-box system (SUL) whose behaviour can be modelled by an FSM, it will produce an FSM that is minimal and equivalent to the SUL. As other inference algorithms, it only assumes that we know the full input set of the SUL, and that we can send to it inputs and observe the outputs. Contrary to most inference algorithms, it does not require the ability to reset the SUL.

Presenting the full hW-inference method has been done in [6]. Here, we just provide a brief overview of it (as in [3]) focusing on the elements that are impacted by the reassessment of W-sets.

Actually, hW-inference exists in two forms.

- Preset: using preset sequences [10]. This was presented and assessed in detail in [7].
- Adaptive: using adaptive homing and characterization [6], so that trees are used instead of sequences. This means that the next input to be applied while homing or characterizing can depend on the outputs observed in response to the prefix of the homing or characterizing sequence of inputs.

In this paper, we only consider the preset version, because W-sets are actually sets of sequences.

hW-inference assumes that the SUL behaves as an unknown FSM, for which I is known, and it will progressively build Q, δ and λ while observing outputs in O.

3.1 Main Algorithm of hW-Inference

The core idea of the algorithm is to apply h to place the SUL in a recognizable state. If the state reached is not fully characterized, we apply one sequence of W to improve the characterization of the state. Otherwise, we learn transitions by applying an input symbol and then applying a sequence of W to improve the characterization of the tail state of the transition. A characterization of a state is a mapping from W to output sequences. Thus, in our approach, states are indeed just mappings from W to O^*, and Q is a set of such mappings.

The inner **repeat** loop of the algorithm iteratively starts by applying the current homing sequence h. If the tail state of this homing sequence is not yet known, we improve our knowledge of it with a further element w from the W-set, until we can associate a full characterization of it by associating a state $H(r)$ to the response r of the SUL to the homing sequence. If the tail state is known (as $H(r)$), then we can proceed with learning the next unknown transition from that tail state. It is possible that the transition starts directly from the tail state of h, but it may also be possible that all transitions from the tail state are known, in which case we find a shortest α sequence leading to an unknown transition.

Algorithm 1. Simplified hW-inference (preset) algorithm [7]

1: **procedure** INFER
2:     initialize : $h \leftarrow \epsilon$; $W \leftarrow \{\epsilon\}$ ▷ (equivalent to $W \leftarrow \emptyset$ here)
3:     **repeat**
4:         $Q, \lambda, \delta \leftarrow \emptyset$
5:         **repeat**
6:             apply h and observe $r \in O^*$
7:             **if** $H(r)$ is undefined **then**
8:                 $H(r) \leftarrow \emptyset$
9:             **end if**
10:            **if** $H(r)$ is undefined for some $w \in W$ **then**
11:                apply w, observe y, $H(r) \leftarrow H(r) \cup \{w \mapsto y\}$
12:            **else**
13:                let $q = H(r)$ be the state reached at end of h;
14:                find shortest input sequence $\alpha \in I^*$ leading from q to a state $q' \in Q$
    with incompletely known transition (q', x);
15:                apply $\alpha.x.w$ observe $\beta.o.y$;
16:                $\lambda(q', x) \leftarrow o$ and $\delta(q', x)(w) \leftarrow y$
17:            **end if**
18:        **until** $M = (Q, I, O, \delta, \lambda)$ contains a strongly connected complete component
19:        ask for a counterexample.
20:        process counterexample as a W-ND inconsistency
21:    **until** no counterexample can be found
22: **end procedure**

3.2 Refining h and W

hW-inference algorithm can start with any hint for a homing sequence and a W-set, but is usually started with an empty homing sequence and an empty characterization set. The algorithm will automatically refine them when there is an indication that h is not homing or W is not characterizing the SUL, which shows up as observable non-determinism. [6] categorizes several types of situations where h or W must be refined.

- h-ND inconsistency: this occurs when after applying h and getting the same response r in two different occasions, we have applied after h a same sequence β of inputs, and we get different responses for β. This implies that h/r was in fact ending in two different states that can be separated by β; thus, we extend h to $h\beta$.
- W-ND inconsistency is similar, except in the case we have come into a state (defined by its characterization as a mapping from W to O^*) and we observe different outputs on the same sequence from that state. The difference is that we may have come to the state from two different homing responses. Formally, W-ND inconsistency occurs when the global trace contains a sequence $h/r.\alpha/u.\beta/v$ and another sequence $h/r'.\alpha'/u'.\beta/v'$ such that $r \neq r'$ or $\alpha \neq \alpha'$, $\delta(H(r),\alpha) = \delta(H(r'),\alpha')$ and $v \neq v'$. This implies that $\delta(H(r),\alpha)$ and $\delta(H(r'),\alpha')$ can be separated by β. So W can be enhanced with β or a subsequence of β.
- Other types of inconsistencies are discussed in [6], which we do not detail here, as they are not relevant for this paper.

3.3 Oracles and Counterexamples

Like most active learning algorithms, following L^*, hW-inference performs a number of tests before being able to build a complete model, called a conjecture, that could still be only an approximation of the real behavioural model of the SUL: at this point, it will require a counterexample to refine that model by a new round of tests to come up with a more precise conjecture.

This is why the outer **repeat** loop will use the inner loop to get a model (called a conjecture) that is complete (all transitions known) and consistent (resolving h-ND and W-ND and other inconsistencies), at which point it will ask for a counterexample to refine the model if needed, until the model is found equivalent to the SUL. Each round of the outer **repeat** loop is called a subinference.

To decide whether the model is indeed equivalent to the SUL requires calling an oracle. Such an oracle is expected either to confirm equivalence or to provide a counterexample, i.e. an input sequence for which the model and the SUL do not yield the same response. In the reset case, the counterexample is an input sequence applied from the initial state. In our case, it has to be applied from the current state reached at the end of the inner learning loop.

In our experiments for this paper, we used the simplest type of oracle: a bounded random walk over the graph of the conjecture until an observed output differs from the prediction of the conjecture (thus yielding a counterexample), or the bound is reached; in the latter case, the conjecture is the final model learnt. Randomness in the oracle implies that the trace to fully learn a model of a system can be different depending on the seed provided to the random generator. As shown in Fig. 1, the trace length can vary a lot between runs for the same system.

3.4   Dictionary

hW-inference also incorporates a number of heuristics to improve the efficiency of learning. They are detailed and evaluated in [7]. The most significant one, the use of a dictionary, is heavily impacted by approaches that revise h or W in the course of inference. A dictionary stores the output result of an input sequence that has been applied in a subinference, so that later subinferences will not query again the SUL for the same combination of homing, transfer, transition and characterization. Dictionaries have proven quite efficient since they were advocated by O. Niese for L^* [12].

4   Approach

4.1   Motivation

In hW-inference, every refinement of W either through W-ND or counterexample processing either adds a new sequence into W or extends an existing one. However, we never remove sequences in W that are separated by sequences that were added later. The size of W thus increases monotonically. *The idea explored in this paper is to reassess W during inference and replace it by a smaller set W' that separates the same states as W does.* To this end, we require that W' is a characterization set for the conjecture inferred by hW-inference.

There are two measures implied by the term "size of W": the number of sequences in it and their average length. To learn a transition, we apply an input sequence $h.\alpha.x.w$ for every sequence $w \in W$; thus, the number of input-output queries depends linearly on both measures.

Experiments confirm that the size of W varies a lot depending on the provided counterexamples, as well as the order in which inputs or transfers are used. This translates to a large variation regarding the length of the total trace. In Table 1, we can observe that in a lucky case, the final W-set was made up of 6 sequences totalling 28 inputs[1]. However, on average (over 40 inferences with different random seeds for the oracle), there were 26 elements in W (with average total length of 236 inputs), with up to 62 sequences totalling 860 inputs. The trace length varies from 3.33E5 inputs to 1.22E7, with an average of 3.09E6. Figure 1 visualizes the correlation between the size of W and the trace length.

This shows that the size of the final W-set can be vastly greater than needed, leading to a dramatic increase in the trace length.

4.2   Methods for W-Set Reduction

There are two possible approaches to compute a reduced W-set, based on the current conjecture: either we just use the conjecture or we start from the existing W. In both cases, we can recompute it every time a new conjecture is found (see Sect. 4.7), or only from time to time.

---

[1] Actually, the 121 states of the FSM can be characterized by a W-set with as few as 4 sequences totalling 11 inputs or 3 sequences totalling 23 inputs (and it might even not be minimal).

Algorithm 2. Generate W using partitions

1: **procedure** GENWPART(conjecture $M = (Q, I, O, \delta, \lambda)$)
2:     $W \leftarrow \emptyset$
3:     $D \leftarrow \{(q, q') \mapsto \bot \mid (q, q') \in Q \times Q \wedge q \neq q'\}$ ▷ P_1 are implicitly defined as the partition induced by the equivalent relation $q \equiv q' \iff D(q, q') = \bot$. Similarly for the other tables.
4:     **for all** $(q, q') \in Q \times Q$ **do**
5:         **if** $\exists y \in W : \lambda(q, y) \neq \lambda(q', y)$ **then** $D(q, q') \leftarrow y$ **end if**
6:     **end for**
7:     **while** $\exists (q, q')$ with $D(q, q') = \bot$ **do**
8:         **if** $\exists x \in I : D(\delta(q, x), \delta(q', x)) = w \neq \bot$ **then**
9:             $W \leftarrow W \cup \{x.w\}$
10:            $D(q, q') \leftarrow x.w$
11:        **end if**
12:    **end while**
13: **end procedure**

Compute from Scratch. We could compute a characterization set for the current conjecture from scratch. Although the problem of finding a minimal characterization set for an FSM is PSPACE-complete [10], there are many heuristic algorithms to compute small W-sets for a given FSM, e.g. P_k approach in [5], or via product machines [10]. The main drawback of these approaches is that the computed W-set can be very different from the previous one. Since in hW-inference there is an extensive caching of responses to sequences in W through the dictionary, *the positive impact of a smaller W-set on the trace length can be effectively outweighed by the effect of cache misses.*

Prune Existing W. To keep the benefits of caching in the dictionary, we propose to take the current W as a starting point and greedily shrink it to find a smaller characterization set (see Algorithm 4).

4.3   Partitions

The P_k approach (Algorithm 2) constructs a series of tables $P_1, P_2, ..., P_k$, where the states are partitioned into classes so that two states are in the same class in P_i if they cannot be separated by sequences of length i. Notice that in the algorithm, the partitions are implicitly defined by the pairs of separated states. They can be computed in the following way. In P_1, the pairs of states which can be separated by a single input, by looking in the output function λ, are put in separate classes. For $i > 1$, in P_i, the pairs of states which lead to states in different classes in P_{i-1}, by looking in the next state function δ, are put in separate classes. The iterative process terminates when either all classes are singletons or, in case the machine is not minimal, $P_k = P_{k-1}$. The characterization set is obtained by collecting the sequences which determined that each pair of states are separated.

Algorithm 3. Generate W with a product machine

1: **procedure** GENWPROD(conjecture $M = (Q, I, O, \delta, \lambda)$)
2:      $Q_P \leftarrow Q \times Q, \lambda_P \leftarrow \emptyset, \delta_P \leftarrow \emptyset$
3:      **for all** $q, q' \in Q_p, x \in I$ **do**
4:          **if** $\lambda(q, x) = \lambda(q', x) =: o$ **then**
5:              $\lambda_P((q, q'), x) \leftarrow o$
6:          **else**
7:              $\lambda_P((q, q'), x) \leftarrow fail$
8:          **end if**
9:          $\delta_P((q, q'), x) \leftarrow (\delta(q, x), \delta(q', x))$
10:     **end for**
11:     $W \leftarrow \emptyset$
12:     **for all** $q, q' \in Q_p$ **do**
13:         **if** $\nexists w \in W \; \lambda(q, w) \neq \lambda(q', w)$ **then**
14:            $t \leftarrow$ shortest $t \in I^*$ s.t. $\lambda_P((q, q'), t) = \ldots fail$
15:            $W = W \cup \{t\}$
16:         **end if**
17:     **end for**
18:     **return** W
19: **end procedure**

4.4 Computing from Product

The product machine approach (Algorithm 3) starts by computing a product machine $M \times M = (Q \times Q, I, O \cup \{fail\}, \delta_P, \lambda_P)$, where for every $q, q' \in Q, x \in I$, $\delta_P((q, q'), x) = (\delta(q, x), \delta(q', x))$, and $\lambda_P((q, q'), x) = o$, with $o = \lambda(q, x)$, if $\lambda(q, x) = \lambda(q', x)$, and $o = fail$, otherwise. The characterization set is obtained by collecting, for each pair of states, the shortest path to a transition with output *fail*.

4.5 Pruning

As W grows monotonically by adding new sequences to an existing set, it is often the case that sequences that are included earlier during the learning process become obsolete later. The pruning (Algorithm 4) is a simple approach to tackle this problem. There are two cases. First, we test if there exists a sequence $w \in W$, such that $W \backslash \{w\}$ is characterizing. If so, then we remove w from W. Second, we test if there exists a sequence w and an input x, such that $w.x \in W$ and $W \backslash \{w.x\} \cup \{w\}$ is characterizing. If so, then we replace $w.x$ by w, which means that we have shortened one of the sequences in W. The pruning can continue as long as one of the two cases applies. However, as a heuristic, we try the second case when we have exhausted the possibility of applying the first case.

4.6 Combining Methods to Get a W-Set Reduction

Neither GENWPART nor GENWPROD produces optimal W-sets, as they are just greedy algorithms to address a PSPACE-complete problem. They can indeed

---

Algorithm 4. W-set pruning

1: **procedure** PRUNEW(conjecture $\mathcal{M}'$, current W-set W)
2:    **while** $\exists w \in W : W \leftarrow W \backslash \{w\}$ is characterizing for $\mathcal{M}'$ **do**
3:        $W \leftarrow W \backslash \{w\}$
4:    **end while**
5:    **while** $\exists w.x \in W : (W \backslash \{w.x\}) \cup \{w\}$ is characterizing for $\mathcal{M}'$ **do**
6:        $W \leftarrow (W \backslash \{w.x\}) \cup \{w\}$
7:    **end while**
8: **return** W
9: **end procedure**

---

produce sets with redundant sequences. So we can get smaller sets by systematically pruning the computed W-sets.

In our experiments, we assess the performance of 3 types of W-set reductions.

Pruning. This uses PRUNEW as the sole method for W-set reduction. In that way, after reduction, all the sequences that are kept in the W-set had already been applied at the tail of $h.\alpha.x.w$ sequences that have been cached in the dictionary, thus saving on the next subinference.

PartR. Discards the previous W-set, computes a W' with GENWPART followed by PRUNEW applied to W' to get the new W.

ProdR. Discards the previous W-set, computes a W' with GENWPROD followed by PRUNEW applied to W' to get the new W.

4.7 When to Apply W-Set Reduction?

We can reduce W every time the inner **repeat**-loop of the algorithm terminates and before processing the counterexample (i.e. in line 19 of Algorithm 1). This order is essential because the counterexample contradicts by definition the conjecture. The characterization sequence found by the counterexample thus would be removed during the pruning, which uses the conjecture as a reference.

Moreover, the conjecture does not necessarily change after a refinement of W. This can happen in particular for Moore locks [11]. In a Moore lock there is a pair of states that can only be separated by one specific sequence. Because in hW-inference W is extended by suffixes of counterexamples (the so-called Suffix1by1 method for counterexample processing [8]), the separating sequence may not be included in the first subinferences, until we include the separating suffix in W. In this case, multiple counterexamples are needed until W separates a new state and the conjecture changes. We address this issue by only deploying W-set reduction when the conjecture has increased in size.

5   Experiments

In this section, we experiment with the proposed improvements and show how the various approaches for W-set reduction impact the overall performance of

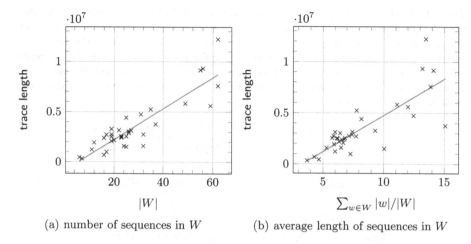

(a) number of sequences in W (b) average length of sequences in W

Fig. 1. Relation between the size of W and the trace length for 40 inferences of Scanette.

hW-inference. All experiments were repeated 40 times with different random seeds (used by hW-inference for the random walk oracle), and Table 1, 2, 3, 4 and 5 analyze the results on the average values. For the record, we provide in Table 6 results for the 40 seed values.

5.1   Case Study and Basic hW-Inference Without Reduction

We applied hW-inference on "Scanette", a supermarket self-service scanning system that has been used as a case study for other learning techniques. For a precise description of it, we refer the reader to [16], a paper that presents both the case study and results of statistical machine learning techniques on the reduction of regression tests from analysis of logs (thus, this is a different goal that cannot be compared to the active model inference we are doing in the present paper). The full system includes counters (to count the number of each type of item in the cart), as well as non-deterministic (random) checks on customers. We reduced the counters and number of items to small values, and made checks in a deterministic way (every other time a customer checks out). With those necessary adaptations to make Scanette equivalent to an FSM, it has 121 states and 15 inputs (totalling over 1800 transitions). Probably due to the presence of counters, some states are hard to reach by random walk, so we had to give a high bound (at least 3.0E5) for the maximal length of a walk before concluding the conjecture was final and giving up searching for a counterexample.

The key measure for performance of an active inference algorithm is the trace length, viz. the number of input symbols applied on the SUL. On average over 40 seeds, hW-inference had a trace length of 3.09E6 inputs, ranging from 3.33E5 to 1.22E7 with a standard deviation of 2.66E6. Thus, the trace length varies by an order of magnitude depending on the counterexamples provided by the oracle.

Table 1. Key figures of basic hW-inference on Scanette. From left to right: the effective trace length, the number of subinferences, the number of sequences in the final W-set and their total size, and the percentage of queries that found an answer in the dictionary (so they did not add any length to the trace). We present figures for three sample inferences (a), (b) and (c) and the mean and standard deviation over 40 inferences. Tables 2, 3 and 4 have the same structure and (a), (b) and (c) correspond to the same seeds for the random oracle.

	Trace length	#subinf.	$|W|$ ($\sum_W |w|$)	Dict hits
(a)	4.45E+05	18	6 (28)	21.0%
		...		
(b)	2.51E+06	35	23 (143)	65.7%
		...		
(c)	5.83E+06	61	49 (544)	82.7%
Mean	3.09E+06	38.2	25.7 (236.0)	62.4%
Stddev.	2.66E+06	17.1	15.6 (240.3)	19.1%

Table 1 contains key figures for a representative sample of inferences and the average over all 40 inferences. We see that longer inferences involve more subinferences and also use a larger final W-set. Figure 1 plots the trace length of all inferences over the number of sequences in W and their average length. There is a linear correlation for the number of sequences (Pearson correlation coefficient 0.90) and the trace length, similar for the average length of the sequences in W (PCC 0.83).

These correlations are expected, as for every sequence in W and every transition there is one iteration of the inner loop in hW-inference and a sequence $h.\alpha.x.w$ is applied to the SUL. Moreover, the size of W also depends on the number of subinferences. If a characterizing W-set is not found until a late subinference, the tentative W is increased with every subinference.

5.2 Impact of W-Set Pruning

The impact of the W-set on the trace length motivates reducing the size of W. To this end, we augmented the implementation of hW-inference in the SIMPA framework[2] with W-set reduction methods as described in Sect. 4.6.

W-set reduction was triggered sparsely (on average 6 times) during hW-inference (see Table 2). Using W-set pruning as the sole reduction method reduced the average trace length by 22.5% as compared to basic hW-inference. This decrease is consistent, i.e., in almost all samples W-set pruning led to a shorter trace length, although with a varying gain.

---

[2] The SIMPA software can be downloaded from:
http://vasco.imag.fr/tools/SIMPA or directly from
https://gricad-gitlab.univ-grenoble-alpes.fr/SIMPA/SIMPA.

Table 2. Key figures for W-set pruning. The trace length difference is in comparison with basic hW-inference. #reduce indicates the number of times W-set pruning was applied during inference.

	Trace length (*rel. diff.*)	#subinf.	$\lvert W \rvert$ ($\sum_W \lvert w \rvert$)	Dict hits	#reduce
(a)	3.71E+05 (-16.7%)	18	3 (23)	17.2%	3
		...			
(b)	2.18E+06 (-13.3%)	39	11 (64)	56.4%	8
		...			
(c)	2.73E+06 (-53.1%)	51	25 (302)	74.0%	4
Mean	2.40E+06 (-22.5%)	39.7	12.1 (100.4)	54.5%	6.0
Stddev.	1.92E+06	15.8	6.6 (89.7)	17.7%	2.2

Note that the number of sequences in the final W-set (and their total length) is on average reduced by half from 26 to 12 (and 236 to 100 for the length). The smaller W-set does not translate, however, proportionally to a shorter trace length (as it does without pruning, cf. Fig. 1). This is expected, since intermediate W-sets before pruning can be larger than the final W-set.

Despite the general decrease in the size of W and the trace length due to W-set pruning, both measures still vary significantly. The effect of pruning W is limited to reducing the trace length per subinference, but not the number of subinferences (although there are exceptions, such as seed (c), where hW-inference with W-set pruning lowers the number of subinferences from 61 to 51). On the contrary, pruning W decreases the number of states of the SUL that are separated by W, which could slow down the convergence of W to characterization set for the SUL. We observed only a small increase in the average number of subinferences from 38.2 to 39.7 though.

This shows that the deployment of W-set pruning considerably decreases the trace length of a single subinference but does not impact the total number of subinferences.

5.3 Impact of W-Set Reduction Through Recomputation from Scratch

As for PartR and ProdR (Tables 3 and 4) the average trace length is slightly increased (by 4% and 9% respectively). In particular, on short inferences, i.e. with less than a million input symbols, generating a new W-set leads to vast increase of the trace length (e.g. by factor 5.5 for seed (a)). On the contrary, on seeds with a trace length (significantly) above average for basic hW-inference (such as (c)), GENWPART and GENWPROD outperform basic hW-inference and even pruning. However, the applicability and positive impact of the methods cannot be predicted in advance, and their average impact remains negative.

These large differences in trace lengths indicate that generating W from scratch discards advantages of the W-set found through random counterexample.

Table 3. Key figures for PartR

	Trace length (*rel. diff.*)	#subinf.	$|W|$ ($\sum_W |w|$)	Dict hits	#reduce
(a)	2.88E+06 (*547.9%*)	39	24 (221)	67.8%	6
		...			
(b)	1.74E+06 (*−30.6%*)	30	8 (20)	30.7%	7
		...			
(c)	1.19E+06 (*−79.6%*)	23	8 (19)	31.1%	8
Mean	3.22E+06 (*4.2%*)	40.5	14.2 (94.1)	50.2%	6.5
Stddev.	2.23E+06	16.9	7.1 (87.6)	16.1%	1.9

Table 4. Key figures for ProdR

	Trace length (*rel. diff.*)	#subinf.	$|W|$ ($\sum_W |w|$)	Dict hits	#reduce
(a)	2.88E+06 (*547.4%*)	39	24 (221)	67.9%	6
		...			
(b)	2.47E+06 (*−1.8%*)	38	9 (25)	43.4%	6
		...			
(c)	1.20E+06 (*−79.4%*)	22	10 (27)	29.6%	7
Mean	3.36E+06 (*8.8%*)	41.6	14.1 (93.9)	51.8%	6.4
Stddev.	2.21E+06	16.9	7.2 (86.6)	14.6%	1.9

Table 5. Trace lengths of hW-inference with different reduction techniques. All numbers are multiples of 10^6.

	Basic hW	Pruning	PartR	ProdR
(a)	0.45	0.37 (*−16.7%*)	2.88 (*547.9%*)	2.88 (*547.4%*)
		...		
(b)	2.51	2.18 (*−13.3%*)	1.74 (*−30.6%*)	2.47 (*−1.8%*)
		...		
(c)	5.83	2.73 (*−53.1%*)	1.19 (*−79.6%*)	1.20 (*−79.4%*)
Mean	3.09	2.40 (*−22.5%*)	3.22 (*4.2%*)	3.36 (*8.8%*)
Stddev.	2.66	1.92	2.23	2.21

Moreover, since the sequences in a generated W can be entirely different from the previous W, these approaches benefit less from the dictionary (50% and 51% as opposed to 54% for pruning).

Table 5 compares the trace lengths for all three methods. From that table, we can conclude that pruning is a winning heuristic, that can be safely added to hW-inference. Conversely, the other two methods that recompute a new W-set from the conjecture provide disappointing results, and should not be considered

Table 6. Data for 40 inferences of Scanette with different seeds, sorted by trace length of the basic hW-inference. The samples in Tables 1, 2, 3, and 4 are marked with (a), (b), and (c).

Seed	Trace length/10^6 (diff. to basic hW)				#subinferences				$\|W\|$ ($\sum_{w\in W}\|w\|/\|W\|$)				$\|A\|$				Share of dictionary hits				#reduce W			
	Basic	Prune	PartR	ProdR	Basic	Prune	PartR	ProdR	Basic	Prune	PartR	ProdR	Basic	Prune	PartR	ProdR	Basic	Prune	PartR	ProdR	Basic	Prune	PartR	ProdR
23	0.33	0.28 (-16%)	2.65 (697%)	2.66 (698%)	17	17	39	39	7 (26)	4 (21)	22 (200)	22 (200)	10	10	18	18	45%	39%	67%	67%	0	4	6	6
13	0.45	0.37 (-17%)	2.08 (368%)	2.07 (366%)	18	18	32	32	6 (28)	3 (23)	16 (89)	16 (89)	19	19	18	18	21%	17%	53%	53%	0	3	6	6
24	0.45	0.37 (-17%)	2.42 (444%)	2.42 (444%)	18	18	36	36	6 (28)	3 (23)	16 (89)	16 (89)	19	19	18	18	21%	17%	55%	55%	0	3	6	6
6	0.45	0.37 (-17%)	3.23 (625%)	3.23 (625%)	18	18	44	44	6 (28)	3 (23)	18 (116)	18 (116)	19	19	18	18	21%	17%	62%	62%	0	3	6	6
(a) 16	0.45	0.37 (-17%)	2.88 (548%)	2.88 (547%)	18	18	39	39	6 (28)	3 (23)	24 (221)	24 (221)	19	19	18	18	21%	17%	68%	68%	0	3	6	6
26	0.69	1.99 (190%)	0.66 (-5%)	0.66 (-5%)	24	46	24	24	16 (69)	27 (342)	4 (11)	4 (11)	8	8	8	8	70%	80%	50%	50%	0	6	4	4
14	0.69	0.61 (-11%)	0.66 (-4%)	0.66 (-5%)	24	25	24	24	16 (69)	9 (39)	4 (11)	4 (11)	8	8	8	8	70%	57%	50%	50%	0	6	4	4
33	0.69	0.73 (6%)	0.66 (-4%)	0.66 (-5%)	24	28	24	24	16 (69)	10 (48)	4 (11)	4 (11)	8	8	8	8	70%	62%	50%	50%	0	7	4	4
36	0.98	0.88 (-10%)	4.33 (341%)	4.35 (342%)	26	28	56	56	17 (124)	15 (120)	21 (148)	21 (148)	10	10	18	18	73%	72%	75%	74%	0	4	6	6
10	1.22	1.17 (-8%)	1.05 (-14%)	0.92 (-24%)	23	31	20	19	11 (66)	4 (30)	8 (22)	7 (18)	30	17	22	22	35%	39%	26%	24%	0	4	7	7
7	1.51	1.39 (-8%)	3.27 (117%)	3.26 (116%)	35	35	45	45	25 (251)	22 (246)	24 (221)	24 (221)	10	10	18	18	80%	80%	68%	68%	0	4	6	6
3	1.59	1.41 (-11%)	2.73 (72%)	7.61 (380%)	35	36	38	66	24 (127)	10 (50)	10 (31)	10 (31)	15	15	25	25	74%	54%	48%	62%	0	5	8	6
18	1.60	1.27 (-20%)	1.78 (12%)	1.77 (11%)	42	52	60	60	32 (208)	19 (149)	19 (131)	19 (131)	9	9	12	12	84%	78%	70%	69%	0	11	16	16
31	1.94	1.60 (-18%)	2.49 (29%)	2.15 (11%)	24	23	31	28	12 (71)	7 (59)	13 (63)	13 (63)	37	37	27	27	37%	32%	36%	36%	0	4	4	4
37	2.07	1.68 (-19%)	1.51 (-27%)	1.92 (-7%)	31	39	27	30	19 (127)	13 (92)	11 (47)	10 (31)	30	17	22	22	57%	55%	37%	43%	0	4	7	8
17	2.18	1.94 (-11%)	1.56 (-28%)	4.69 (116%)	32	33	19	36	20 (127)	11 (78)	7 (15)	17 (102)	23	23	32	40	65%	55%	35%	35%	0	4	4	5
38	2.38	2.15 (-10%)	4.40 (85%)	2.72 (14%)	30	32	42	29	16 (105)	9 (84)	16 (101)	9 (27)	45	45	45	45	51%	39%	42%	30%	0	8	7	6
1	2.42	1.82 (-25%)	2.62 (8%)	2.49 (3%)	34	41	50	48	23 (156)	15 (117)	7 (17)	7 (17)	30	17	22	22	66%	59%	68%	60%	0	8	7	8
(b) 22	2.51	2.18 (-13%)	1.74 (-31%)	2.47 (-2%)	35	39	30	38	23 (143)	11 (64)	8 (20)	9 (25)	28	28	16	16	66%	56%	31%	43%	0	8	7	7
15	2.52	2.50 (-1%)	7.04 (179%)	6.94 (175%)	31	32	63	62	19 (117)	10 (47)	19 (117)	19 (117)	45	45	45	45	52%	37%	49%	50%	0	5	7	7
20	2.55	1.39 (-46%)	1.32 (-48%)	1.06 (-58%)	36	35	27	21	25 (144)	9 (54)	7 (17)	5 (15)	30	17	22	22	61%	48%	40%	28%	0	4	8	7
2	2.56	1.80 (-30%)	1.65 (-36%)	3.19 (25%)	35	41	35	42	23 (157)	15 (117)	13 (64)	5 (14)	30	17	22	22	65%	60%	58%	48%	0	4	7	8
21	2.72	2.35 (-13%)	3.69 (36%)	3.80 (40%)	30	33	32	33	17 (132)	15 (127)	18 (116)	18 (116)	22	22	33	33	53%	53%	42%	41%	0	6	5	5
39	2.75	2.38 (-13%)	4.65 (69%)	4.54 (65%)	33	38	46	46	19 (136)	7 (56)	5 (25)	5 (25)	45	45	45	45	48%	49%	48%	49%	0	8	7	7
34	2.76	2.31 (-13%)	2.86 (4%)	2.86 (4%)	45	46	46	46	32 (188)	13 (86)	14 (57)	14 (57)	18	18	18	18	78%	68%	59%	59%	0	9	8	8
29	2.90	1.97 (-32%)	1.46 (-50%)	1.36 (-53%)	38	43	25	24	26 (193)	17 (146)	8 (19)	8 (22)	30	17	22	22	68%	63%	31%	35%	0	4	7	7
30	3.02	2.30 (-24%)	1.44 (-52%)	3.53 (17%)	40	37	26	50	26 (167)	11 (54)	8 (20)	21 (180)	28	28	16	16	70%	52%	25%	62%	0	10	7	7
19	3.13	2.89 (-8%)	3.72 (19%)	3.77 (21%)	41	48	49	52	27 (162)	11 (61)	24 (240)	21 (180)	28	19	16	16	70%	60%	64%	61%	0	9	7	6
35	3.16	2.87 (-9%)	3.19 (1%)	3.22 (2%)	35	35	32	32	22 (164)	13 (90)	11 (33)	11 (33)	45	45	45	45	59%	44%	33%	34%	0	7	7	7
25	3.27	3.00 (-8%)	4.98 (52%)	5.10 (56%)	36	42	38	39	19 (177)	8 (78)	24 (221)	24 (221)	28	28	33	33	64%	56%	53%	52%	0	7	5	5
27	3.76	2.25 (-40%)	5.44 (45%)	1.65 (-56%)	49	45	25	30	37 (558)	11 (61)	5 (17)	5 (17)	13	14	17	17	79%	65%	30%	37%	0	7	6	6
28	4.41	3.94 (-11%)	5.47 (24%)	5.11 (16%)	39	40	53	50	25 (205)	20 (188)	22 (182)	22 (182)	37	37	27	27	89%	56%	54%	55%	0	5	5	5
5	4.44	4.75 (0%)	5.58 (18%)	1.74 (-63%)	44	51	61	34	31 (387)	8 (70)	28 (334)	28 (334)	45	45	45	45	72%	68%	67%	57%	0	5	5	5
40	5.24	5.18 (-1%)	3.79 (-28%)	4.14 (-21%)	49	54	42	39	35 (273)	15 (110)	15 (98)	10 (30)	45	45	45	45	67%	47%	48%	41%	0	7	6	6
(c) 9	5.83	2.73 (-53%)	1.19 (-80%)	1.20 (-79%)	61	51	23	22	49 (544)	25 (302)	8 (19)	10 (27)	30	17	22	22	90%	84%	74%	73%	0	4	8	7
6	7.57	5.20 (-31%)	3.29 (-57%)	3.34 (-56%)	76	64	30	31	62 (860)	32 (434)	16 (89)	16 (89)	28	28	33	33	88%	74%	37%	38%	0	10	5	5
12	9.16	7.22 (-21%)	7.30 (-20%)	7.65 (-17%)	70	69	62	65	58 (776)	14 (114)	15 (79)	14 (77)	45	45	45	45	83%	72%	68%	68%	0	6	6	6
4	9.32	3.08 (-67%)	7.45 (-20%)	6.08 (-35%)	70	39	62	71	56 (739)	10 (90)	29 (319)	28 (314)	45	45	45	45	81%	55%	62%	74%	0	7	7	6
32	12.22	9.93 (-19%)	11.44 (-6%)	11.30 (-8%)	86	91	106	105	62 (836)	12 (93)	18 (116)	18 (116)	45	45	45	45	84%	69%	72%	72%	0	4	6	6
Mean	3.09	2.40 (-23%)	3.22 (4%)	3.36 (9%)	38	40	41	42	26 (237)	12 (104)	14 (94)	14 (94)	27	25	26	26	62%	55%	50%	52%	0	6	7	6
Median	2.54	2.07 (-18%)	2.81 (11%)	3.03 (20%)	35	39	38	39	23 (150)	11 (74)	15 (72)	14 (70)	28	19	22	22	66%	56%	50%	51%	0	6	7	6
Stddev.	2.66	1.92 (-28%)	2.23 (-16%)	2.21 (-17%)	17	16	17	17	16 (240)	7 (90)	7 (88)	7 (87)	13	13	12	12	19%	18%	16%	15%	0	2	2	2

for hW-inference. However, they might have some value for other methods of testing or learning.

6 Conclusion

In this paper, we proposed three algorithms for computing reduced approximated W-sets on a conjectured model (itself an approximation of a system). In many testing or learning methods, the size of the set of sequences used to separate states can play a significant role on the length of testing or learning sequences. In the paper, we consider the impact on hW-inference, a learning algorithm, and assess it on a typical medium-sized model of a software system.

First, we observe that the trace length is proportional to the size of the W-set, even though heuristics such as dictionary caching are used in the learning algorithm. This provides solid ground for assessing the impact of the proposed reduction methods.

Using a reduced W-set can have conflicting effects. On the one hand, a shorter W-set will reduce the test cases (related to assessing a single transition's target state) where this set is used. On the other hand, since the W-set is only approximated, by reducing it, we may lose sequences that seem redundant on a conjecture, but that would actually separate states of the real system. Another adverse effect can come from the loss of cached test cases.

The results of our preliminary experiments show that reducing intermediate W-sets by simply pruning them is an efficient method when combined with hW-inference: we observe a 22% gain on average in our experiments on a representative case study. With the other two methods considered, the gain is often outweighed by the loss of cached responses and the increase in the number of rounds necessary to learn the whole system.

Based on those preliminary results, we propose to include the pruning heuristic as an additional improvement on hW-inference. This should be comforted on other types of case studies. As usual, this could be conducted on randomly generated machines of various sizes, but it is known that real systems have structures that may not be well reflected by random machines. A better testbed will be to use machines from the Radboud benchmark[3].

Although pruning improves the performance of hW-inference, it does not level the vast differences in trace length depending on the counterexamples provided by the oracles. A better understanding of how counterexamples facilitate a fast convergence to a characterizing W-set could alleviate this issue. One direction for future work would be to revise the counterexample processing in order to reduce the number of subinferences.

Finally, this preliminary study provides evidence for the proposed W-set reduction methods in the particular context of hW-inference. It might be interesting to assess those reduction methods in other testing or learning contexts.

Acknowledgments. The internship of the first author was funded by the French National Research Agency: ANR PHILAE project (ANR-18-CE25-0013). The second and the fifth authors were funded by Fundação de Amparo à Pesquisa do Estado de São Paulo (FAPESP: 2013/07375-0).

References

1. Angluin, D.: Learning regular sets from queries and counterexamples. Inf. Comput. **2**, 87–106 (1987)
2. Bennaceur, A., Hähnle, R., Meinke, K. (eds.): Machine Learning for Dynamic Software Analysis: Potentials and Limits – International Dagstuhl Seminar 16172, Dagstuhl Castle, Germany, April 24–27, 2016, Revised Papers, Volume 11026 of Lecture Notes in Computer Science. Springer, Cham (2018). https://doi.org/10.1007/978-3-319-96562-8
3. Bremond, N., Groz, R.: Case studies in learning models and testing without reset. In: 2019 IEEE International Conference on Software Testing, Verification and Validation Workshops, AMOST 2019, ICST Workshops 2019, Xi'an, China, 22 April 2019, pp. 40–45 (2019)
4. Fujiwara, S., von Bochmann, G., Khendek, F., Amalou, M., Ghedamsi, A.: Test selection based on finite state models. IEEE Trans. Softw. Eng. **17**(6), 591–603 (1991)

---

[3] http://automata.cs.ru.nl/Overview#Mealybenchmarks.

5. Gill, A.: Introduction to the Theory of Finite-State Machines. McGraw-Hill, New York (1962)
6. Groz, R., Bremond, N., Simao, A.: Using adaptive sequences for learning non-resettable FSMs. In: Unold, O., Dyrka, W., Wieczorek, W. (eds.) Proceedings of the 14th International Conference on Grammatical Inference 2018, Volume 93 of Proceedings of Machine Learning Research, pp. 30–43. PMLR, February 2019
7. Groz, R., Bremond, N., Simao, A., Oriat, C.: hW-inference: a heuristic approach to retrieve models through black box testing. J. Syst. Softw. **159**, 110426 (2020)
8. Irfan, M.N., Oriat, C., Groz, R.: Angluin style finite state machine inference with non-optimal counterexamples. In: MIIT, pp. 11–19. ACM, New York (2010)
9. Isberner, M., Howar, F., Steffen, B.: The TTT algorithm: a redundancy-free approach to active automata learning. In: Bonakdarpour, B., Smolka, S.A. (eds.) RV 2014. LNCS, vol. 8734, pp. 307–322. Springer, Cham (2014). https://doi.org/10.1007/978-3-319-11164-3_26
10. Lee, D., Yannakakis, M.: Principles and methods of testing finite state machines - a survey. Proc. IEEE **84**(8), 1090–1123 (1996)
11. Moore, E.F.: Gedanken-experiments on sequential machines. In: Shannon, C.E., McCarthy, J. (eds.) Automata Studies (AM-34), vol. 34, pp. 129–154. Princeton University Press (1956)
12. Niese, O.: An integrated approach to testing complex systems. Ph.D. thesis, University of Dortmund (2003)
13. Peled, D., Vardi, M.Y., Yannakakis, M.: Black box checking. In: Wu, J., Chanson, S.T., Gao, Q. (eds.) Formal Methods for Protocol Engineering and Distributed Systems. IAICT, vol. 28, pp. 225–240. Springer, Boston (1999). https://doi.org/10.1007/978-0-387-35578-8_13
14. Petrenko, A., Li, K., Groz, R., Hossen, K., Oriat, C.: Inferring approximated models for systems engineering. In: HASE 2014, Miami, Florida, USA, pp. 249–253 (2014)
15. Shahbaz, M., Groz, R.: Inferring mealy machines. In: Cavalcanti, A., Dams, D.R. (eds.) FM 2009. LNCS, vol. 5850, pp. 207–222. Springer, Heidelberg (2009). https://doi.org/10.1007/978-3-642-05089-3_14
16. Utting, M., Legeard, B., Dadeau, F., Tamagnan, F., Bouquet, F.: Identifying and generating missing tests using machine learning on execution traces. In: 2020 IEEE International Conference On Artificial Intelligence Testing (AITest), pp. 83–90 (2020)
17. Vaandrager, F.: Model learning. Commun. ACM **60**(2), 86–95 (2017)
18. Vasilievskii, M.P.: Failure diagnosis of automata. Cybern. Syst. Anal. **9**, 653–665 (1973). https://doi.org/10.1007/BF01068590

Using Ant Colony Optimisation to Select Features Having Associated Costs

Alfredo Ibias[✉][iD], Luis Llana[iD], and Manuel Núñez[iD]

Universidad Complutense de Madrid, Madrid 28040, Spain
{aibias,llana,manuelnu}@ucm.com

Abstract. Software Product Lines (SPLs) strongly facilitate the automation of software development processes. They combine features to create programs (called *products*) that fulfil certain properties. Testing SPLs is an intensive process where choosing the proper products to include in the testing process can be a critical task. In fact, selecting the *best* combination of features from an SPL is a complex problem that is frequently addressed in the literature. In this paper we use evolutionary algorithms to find a combination of features with low testing cost that include a target feature, to facilitate the integration testing of such feature. Specifically, we use an Ant Colony Optimisation algorithm to find one of the *cheapest* (in terms of testing) combination of features that contains a specific feature. Our results show that our framework overcomes the limitations of both brute force and random search algorithms.

Keywords: Software Product Lines · Integration testing · Ant Colony Optimisation · Feature selection

1 Introduction

Software Product Lines (SPLs) define generic software products, enabling mass customisation. Generally speaking, SPLs provide a systematic and disciplined approach to developing software. SPLs encode a set of similar (software) systems that can be constructed from a specific set of features. These features can be combined according to some specific rules defining which products (that is, which combinations of features) are valid. In this paper we use FODA [22] to represent SPLs. In order to formally reason about FODA diagrams, it is important to have a formal framework to represent FODA diagrams. In previous work, we introduced SPLA [1], an algebra that can provide a precise semantics to these diagrams. The original framework was extended to manage an important aspect of features: their costs. This is captured in the process algebra SPLA-CRIS [4]. In this work, these costs will represent the cost of testing a specific feature of the product. Testing SPLs is fundamental to ensure the quality and

This work has been supported by the Spanish MINECO/FEDER project FAME (RTI2018-093608-B-C31); the Region of Madrid project FORTE-CM (S2018/TCS-4314) co-funded by EIE Funds of the European Union; and the Santander - Complutense University of Madrid (grant number CT63/19-CT64/19).

D. Clark et al. (Eds.): ICTSS 2021, LNCS 13045, pp. 106–122, 2022.
https://doi.org/10.1007/978-3-031-04673-5_8

reliability of the products generated by them. When testing SPLs [26], it is crucial to distribute the testing resources between the different features of the line in a smart way. One way of distributing such resources is based on the probability of each feature being requested [18]. However, if we do not have such probabilities, we can consider the costs of testing each feature. The idea is that the products with the minimum cost will be easier to test and, therefore, will consume less resources. This situation is ideal when testing the integration of a specific feature into the SPL. For example, if we add a new feature to an existing SPL and we want to test that its integration with the other features does not produce any errors, then it is useful to have a product with lower testing cost because the integration testing process will be faster and/or cheaper.

We are going to focus on the problem of *Integration Testing of Software Components* [21]. Actually, software components can be seen as the features of an SPL. In fact, integration testing within an SPL has gained attention from researchers [7,29,33]. One important aspect of integration testing is its cost: although testing each variant of an SPL may be feasible, it is impossible to independently test all possible (maybe redundant) products [24]. In our approach, we are interested in getting the product that includes a particular feature having the smallest testing cost. Note that the order of the features may be relevant in the complexity and costs of the testing process [34].

In general, testing cost can refer to multiple concepts: from actual monetary cost of testing the integration of the feature into the product, to the necessary time to test such integration, passing through the amount of resources needed to test that integration. In our framework, we only need to know that such cost exists and that it represents the same along all individual costs of the same SPL. Therefore, along this paper we will be talking about testing cost in a broad sense and we will try to minimise it. Finally, regarding the origin of such costs, we will assume that they are provided together with the SPL. Ideally, such costs would be obtained through estimation, approximation or empirical methods and added to the SPL before using the solution presented in this paper.

It is important to clarify what we mean by computing a cheap (or expensive) product of an SPL. In our context, a cheap product is a product that has a low total testing cost compared to the cost of other products. For example, if the testing cost represents the estimated time needed to test such product, then a cheap product would be one whose aggregated time to test it is low compared with other products of the SPL (e.g. hours vs. weeks). Note that cheaper to test products will not necessarily be the ones with a smaller number of features.

Finally, we want to clarify that testing cost is not a proxy for fault detection effectiveness. We are not looking for the product that will arise more faults, but for the one that will be cheaper to test. This is so because our solution looks to fill a very specific need: we have a feature to add to an SPL and we want to cheaply test its integration into the SPL. The goal is not to find all the faults in the introduced feature, but instead ensure that it can be included into products of the SPL. This is specially useful when one has an SPL with hundreds or thousands of features and there is not enough time or resources to test all the possible combinations. Therefore, it is useful to test that the feature can be included into products and that there are no errors when used in combination with other features, what can be tested using any product. One example of such situation appears when adding a new database to a server SPL. It is necessary to test that the added database is correctly integrated with the other features of the SPL, but the tester only needs to test the integration in one product because all the productions might have the same integration faults.

In this paper we apply Ant Colony Optimisation algorithm (ACO) [9] to select a combination of features from an SPL with the minimum testing cost that contains a given feature. This combination will be later used to test the integration of such feature into the SPL. To the best of our knowledge, this is the first attempt to develop an efficient solution to this problem if we rely on a formal approach (in our case, a process algebra). To develop this algorithm we modify, enhance and extend our recently developed framework [18] so that we select feature combinations with low testing cost from SPLs including testing costs information, and so that we have the requirement of including a given feature in the generated product.

In order to evaluate the quality of the solutions obtained by our ACO-approach, we compare our framework with a brute force algorithm (computing all the combinations of features and choosing one with the lowest cost) and a random algorithm (randomly choosing features but such that they conform a valid product). We could not compare our algorithm to other alternatives as there were no previous proposals addressing our specific scenario. Our framework takes significantly less time to compute a solution than the brute force algorithm (around a 99% saving), while obtaining total testing costs that are not much higher (around a 25% increase). It also gets solutions with lower testing cost than the ones obtained by the random algorithm (around a 15% cheaper). In order to properly compare our ACO and the random approach, we allow the random approach to run an equal amount of time as the ACO one. In conclusion, our approach represents a preferable choice to these two alternatives.

The rest of the paper is organised as follows. In Sect. 2 we review related work. In Sect. 3 we present background concepts that we use in our paper. In Sect. 4 we introduce our feature selection framework. In Sect. 5 we present our experiments and discuss the results. In Sect. 6 we briefly review some threats to the validity of our results. In Sect. 7 we discuss some considerations concerning the different choices that we took when defining our algorithm. Finally, in Sect. 8, we give conclusions and outline some directions for future work.

2 Related Work

In this section we review previous work related to the research presented in this paper.

We have chosen FODA [22] to represent SPLs but there are other alternative approaches such as RSEB [12] and PLUSS [10]. We think that FODA represents several advantages: it is widely used and, more important, it is based on graphic models.

We are aware that we cannot compute the best, according to a given criteria, combination of features due to the combinatorial nature of the problem. In fact, we performed a small experiment to show that this is the case also in our framework. Therefore, we have to rely on an heuristic approach. Our previous work on applying heuristic approaches to testing [17,19,20] showed that Swarm Intelligence [36] was very suitable. Among the different approaches to implement a swarm, in this paper we have decided to consider the Ant Colony Optimisation algorithm (ACO) [9] because it allowed us to build on top of previous work, facilitating the implementation of the approach. ACO is inspired by the behaviour of real ant colonies in nature and has been successfully used in computationally hard classical optimisation problems such as the travelling salesman problem but, to the best of our knowledge, the research presented in this paper is a novel application of ACO. Although we have used ACO, other alternative approaches in the broad field of *evolutionary algorithms* could have been selected. Evolutionary algorithms are a family of meta-heuristics that base its intelligent behaviour in the evolution of its population. Some approaches in the broad field of Artificial Intelligence consider the combination of many individuals, usually with limited intelligence, that work as a collective to either reach a goal or find a *good enough* solution to a certain problem. In particular, there are several applications of these algorithms in testing [3,5,30].

We have used an evolutionary computation approach to find cheap to test products but a framework supporting constraint propagation could be used. In this case, we could rely on tools like FaMa [2] and FeatureIDE [35]. However, we prefer to use the combination of a process algebra and an evolutionary computation technique because they allow us to work with a precise semantic description of each product, facilitating the task of deciding the equivalence, up to a certain criterion, of different products.

There exist evolutionary approaches for test case selection and prioritisation in SPLs [13,25]. Despite working on testing, these solutions cannot be easily adapted to cope with our problem because we do not select/generate test cases: we select a set of features such that testing the resulting product is as cheap as possible.

Finally, more related to our work, there are evolutionary computation approaches to select features. A study [31] showed that the *Indicator-Based Evolutionary Algorithm* (IBEA) was better than other evolutionary approaches dealing with high complexity in the decision objective spaces. We cannot use this algorithm to solve our problem because IBEA strongly depends on user preferences (we do not have them). In addition, it seems like this algorithm performs better in a multi-objective optimisation problem: we think that a simpler approach, like ours, might work better in our single-objective optimisation problem but further experiments are needed to support this claim. Finally, another important difference is that they define the set of rules from the SPL as an objective of the optimisation problem because their solution can create non-valid products. In our case, we use a process algebra as the search space to ensure the correctness of the generated products. Another related study [14] proposed the SIP method, which improved previous proposals beating even the IBEA algorithm. The approach mainly focused on enhancing the search through a novel representation that hard-codified some constraints and through optimising first the constraints related to the generation of valid products. They also used their approach over real-world SPLs. However, this approach has the same concerns than the previous one: its problem is based on user preferences, it is focused on multi-objective optimisation, and, furthermore, it can produce non-valid products. All these differences make hard to adapt this kind of algorithms to our problem, as they rely on some assumptions that we do not consider and they can generate non-valid products that our approach cannot generate.

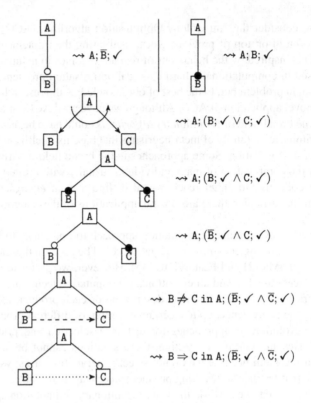

Fig. 1. Translation of FODA diagrams into SPLA.

3 Preliminaries

In this section we present notation and introduce concepts related to the main two lines that we use in this paper: specification of Software Product Lines with costs and the Ant Colony Optimisation algorithm.

3.1 SPLA-CRIS: SPLs with Costs

In this section we briefly review the formal language SPLA-CRIS. The interested reader is referred to the original work [4] for more details.

Definition 1. *We will assume that we have a finite set of features* $\mathcal{F}$ *and we will use* A, B, C... *to denote single features. A* Software Product Line *is a term generated by the following Extended BNF-like expression:*

$$P ::= \checkmark \mid \text{nil} \mid A; P \mid \overline{A}; P \mid P \vee Q \mid P \wedge Q$$
$$A \not\Rightarrow B \text{ in } P \mid A \Rightarrow B \text{ in } P$$

where $A, B \in \mathcal{F}$. *We denote the set of terms of this algebra by* SPLA.

Next we describe the operators of the algebra. The term nil *represents an SPL with no products, while* $\checkmark$ *is an SPL that has only the empty product; they are the terminal elements of the syntax. Then the we have the mandatory prefix operator* A; P *(feature* A *is mandatory) and the optional prefix operator* $\overline{A}$; P *(*A *is optional). The binary operator* $P \vee Q$ *represents the* choose-one. *The binary operator* $P \wedge Q$ *represents the* conjunction *operator. These operators are associative and commutative, so they can be extended as n-ary operators. The operator* A $\Rightarrow$ B *in* P *represents the* require *constraint. The operator* A $\not\Rightarrow$ B *in* P *represents the* exclusion *constraint. Figure 1 shows the relation between these operators and FODA diagrams.*

We can define an operational semantics. *Given* A $\in \mathcal{F} \cup \{\checkmark\}$, *we will write* $P \xrightarrow{A} Q$ *if we can evolve from* P *to* Q *using the defined operational rules. It is important to remark that* $\checkmark$ *is not a feature and, as such, it is not included in the product. This semantics is given as a set of SOS rules and the interested reader can find them, as well as detailed explanations, in our previous work [1,4].*

Single transitions can be sequentially executed to produce traces. *We use* ϵ *to denote an empty trace and consider the usual concatenation operator* $s_1 \cdot s_2$. *Abusing the notation, we will write* A $\in s$ *is* A *appears in* s. *Traces ending with* $\checkmark$, *that we call* successful, *are the only ones associated with valid products. It is irrelevant the order in which the features of a trace are obtained. Given a successful trace* s, $[s]$ *denotes the set obtained from the elements of* s.

Finally, given $P \in$ SPLA, *we define the products of* P, *denoted by* prod (P), *as* prod $(P) = \{[s] \mid s \in \text{tr}(P)\}$. $\square$

In order to define a cost model, we will have a cost function such that given a sequence of features (representing the part of the product that we have defined so far) and a single feature (representing the new feature that we would like to add), returns the cost of testing this new feature in the given product. This cost can represent either time and/or resources needed to perform the (integration) testing of this new feature, given the previous ones. In our framework, we assume that costs can be represented by natural numbers. Sometimes, we will not be able to compute the testing cost of integrating a new feature with the ones already chosen. For instance, if the new one is incompatible with the existing features or there are missing dependencies. Therefore, we extend the set of costs with a new symbol $\perp$ to represent *indefiniteness.*

Definition 2. *The set of costs is given by* $N_\perp = N \cup \{\perp\}$. *We extend arithmetic operations in the expected way: for any* $x \in N_\perp$ *we have* $x + \perp = \perp + x = \perp$ *and* $x \leq \perp$.

A cost function is a function c : $\mathcal{F}^* \times \mathcal{F} \mapsto N_\perp$. $\square$

In order to compute the cost associated with a product we need to extend the operational semantics (see our previous work [4] for a complete definition). Intuitively, let $P \in$ SPLA be a process, c be a cost function and s be a successful trace of P. We denote by tc(P, s) the cost associated with the set of features included in s according to c.

Finally, let us remind that the position of the features in the trace is not relevant to define a product although it may have an impact in its costs. Therefore, different traces can produce the same product but with different costs. As a consequence, we need to

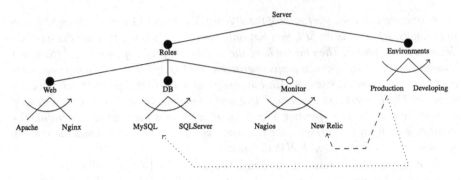

Fig. 2. FODA app server feature diagram.

$Server =$
  $P \Rightarrow MS$ in (
    $P \not\Rightarrow NE$ in (
      S; (
        R; (
          W; (AP; ✓ ∨ NG; ✓)
          ∧
          D; (MS; ✓ ∨ SS; ✓)
          ∧
          $\overline{M}$; (NA; ✓ ∨ NR; ✓)
)
        ∧
        E; (P; ✓ ∨ Dv; ✓)
)
)
)
)

P	$itc(P)$
$\{S, R, E, W, D, P, AP, MS\}$	2.10
$\{S, R, E, W, D, P, NG, MS\}$	2.40
$\{S, R, E, W, D, Dv, AP, MS\}$	1.10
$\{S, R, E, W, D, Dv, NG, MS\}$	1.30
$\{S, R, E, W, D, Dv, AP, SS\}$	1.20
$\{S, R, E, W, D, Dv, NG, SS\}$	1.00
$\{S, R, E, W, D, P, M, NA, AP, MS\}$	2.50
$\{S, R, E, W, D, Dv, M, NA, AP, MS\}$	2.30
$\{S, R, E, W, D, Dv, M, NE, AP, MS\}$	2.20
$\{S, R, E, W, D, Dv, M, NA, AP, SS\}$	2.20
$\{S, R, E, W, D, Dv, M, NE, AP, SS\}$	2.10
$\{S, R, E, W, D, P, M, NA, NG, MS\}$	2.80
$\{S, R, E, W, D, Dv, M, NA, NG, MS\}$	2, 40
$\{S, R, E, W, D, Dv, M, NE, NG, MS\}$	2.30
$\{S, R, E, W, D, Dv, M, NA, NG, SS\}$	2.20
$\{S, R, E, W, D, Dv, M, NE, NG, SS\}$	2.10

Legend:
S : Server
R : Roles
E : Environments
P : Production
Dv : Developing
W : Web server
D : Database Server
M : Monitoring service
AP : Apache
NG : Nginx
MS : MySQL
SS : SQLServer
NA : Nagios
NE : New Relic

Fig. 3. SPLA term.

consider a set of costs for each product, because a product will be *equivalent* to a set of sequences.

Definition 3. *Let* c *be a cost function. We consider the function* c_{SPLA} : SPLA × $\mathcal{P}(\mathcal{F}^*) \mapsto \mathcal{P}(N_\perp)$ *defined as follows:*

$$c_{SPLA}(P, p) = \{tc(P, s) \in N_\perp | \exists s \text{ trace of } P : [s] = p\}$$

□

Example. Let us illustrate the previous definitions with an example. Let us consider a *Server* consisting of a Web Server and a Database. There are two possible environments for the running server: the *production* environment and the *developing* environment. There are two possibilities for the database: MySQL or SQLServer. For the Web server we can use either Apache Web Server or Nginx. There are also two restrictions in the case of the Production environment: First, the use of the New Relic monitor system is forbidden. Second, the use of MySQL is mandatory. Figure 2 show the FODA diagram corresponding to this description. This FODA diagram is translated to the SPLA term in Fig. 3 (left) to handle the system formally. The Integration Test costs appears in the centre of Fig. 3. Formally, the cost function is defined as follows: for $s \in \mathcal{F}^*$ and $A \in \mathcal{F}$, $c(s, A) = itc([sA])$ if the product $[sA]$ is listed in table and $c(s, A) = 0$ otherwise.

3.2   Ant Colony Optimisation

The Ant Colony Optimisation algorithm (ACO) [9] is a well-known algorithm in the evolutionary algorithms field. It is a distributed algorithm to explore a graph-like search space associated with a combinatorial optimisation problem. It consists of a set of *ants*, which are the agents that explore the search space. Each ant looks for the shortest path from the initial node to the target node, choosing their next move based on a random choice modified by the weigh of each path and the *pheromones* released by other ants that previously performed that move.

Definition 4. *A model P of a combinatorial optimisation problem is a tuple $(\mathbf{S}, \Omega, f)$, where $\mathbf{S}$ is a search space defined over a finite set $X_1, \ldots, X_n$ of discrete decision variables, Ω is a set of constraints over the variables, and $f : \mathbf{S} \to R_0^+$ is the objective function to be minimised.*

Each generic variable X_i takes values in $D_i = \{v_i^1, \ldots, v_i^{|D_i|}\}$. A feasible solution $s \in \mathbf{S}$ is a complete assignment of values to variables such that all the constraints in Ω are satisfied. A feasible solution $s^* \in \mathbf{S}$ is called a global optimum if and only if for all $s \in \mathbf{S}$ we have $f(s^*) \leq f(s)$. ☐

Once we have a model of the problem that we would like to solve, we can generate a *construction graph*. Artificial ants move from vertex to vertex along the edges of this graph, incrementally building a partial solution. During this traversal of the graph, the ants deposit a certain amount of pheromone on the edges that they traverse. The amount of pheromone deposited by each artificial ant usually depends on the *quality* of the solution reached after that specific traversal. The idea underlying ACO and the simulation of pheromone is that other ants will use the information concerning the concentration of pheromone as a hint to further explore promising regions of the search space.

The *ACO general scheme* proceeds as follows. After a preliminary step, where the main parameters and the pheromone trails are initialised, we have a main loop that iterates until we reach the termination criterion. This criterion may be based on the numbers of iterations of the loop or on the quality of the obtained solution. In each iteration of the loop, each ant generates a solution. Then, the global state updates the pheromones left by the ants in their solution path. This task consists of two main consecutive steps.

First Step of the Loop: Construct Ant Solutions. In each iteration, m ants generate solutions from a finite set of available solution components C. The construction starts from an empty solution set $s^P = \emptyset$ and, in each step, the ant extends its partial solution by adding a feasible solution element from the set of elements of C that can be added to the partial solution s^P without violating any constraint in Ω. The choice of a solution component from this set is guided by a stochastic mechanism, which is biased by the pheromone associated with each of the elements in it. The rule for the stochastic choice of solution components varies across different ACO algorithms but they are always inspired by the behaviour of real ants. This process can be seen as a traversal of the *construction graph.*

Second Step of the Loop: Update Pheromones. The pheromone update aims to increase the pheromone values associated with good or promising solutions and, in turn, decrease those associated with bad ones. Usually, this is achieved by decreasing all the pheromone values through *pheromone evaporation* and by increasing the pheromone levels associated with a chosen set of good solutions.

4 ACO for Feature Selection Taking into Account Testing Costs

Our feature selection framework finds, for a given SPL and a selected feature, a combination of features that contains said feature and such that the cost (in time and/or resources) of testing the generated product is as low as possible. We will consider that the SPL is formally defined as an SPLA-CRIS term. We use an ACO algorithm because it is the most suitable one for this problem. A comprehensive discussion about this choice can be found in Sect. 7. Next, we briefly describe the main components of our framework:

- An SPL represented as an SPLA-CRIS expression.
- An SPLA-CRIS interpreter that allows us to explore the search space generated by the SPLA-CRIS expression without fully computing it.
- An ACO to lead the search for a feature combination with low cost.

We combine these three components as follows. We consider an SPLA-CRIS expression and derive the structure needed to execute our ACO over it with the goal of finding a *cheap* to test product. However, we cannot compute the testing cost of all the possible combinations of features of the SPLA-CRIS expression. We will rely on an interpreter to compute the added testing cost after adding a new feature to the current selection, but without constructing the full SPLA-CRIS expression tree.

As usual, our ACO needs to have a representation of our setting as a combinatorial optimisation problem. We will define this problem as follows:

- Search space **S**. This is the full SPLA-CRIS tree. In addition, the associated decision variables are associated to the feature that we have to choose next.
- Set of constraints Ω. We have three constraints.
  - A constraint stating that the last symbol of a valid path must be $\checkmark$. Remind that this is the special symbol that we use to denote successful termination, that is, the last symbol of a successful trace.
  - A constraint stating that a valid feature combination should contain the previously selected feature.
  - A constraint stating that a valid path can be generated by the definition of the SPLA-CRIS expression that we are considering.
- Objective function f. This function assigns its cost to each set of features that can be produced from the SPLA-CRIS expression. The goal of our ACO is to minimise the value of this function.

Once we have our problem redefined as a combinatorial optimisation problem, our ACO follows the general scheme presented in Sect. 3.2. The only adaption with respect to this general scheme is that our ants generate *on the fly* the search space while exploring it, instead of having all the information stored beforehand. Thus, our ACO has to work together with our SPLA-CRIS interpreter in order to obtain the associated costs.

It is important to note that our algorithm does not use any additional heuristic optimisation. In the literature there are some common heuristics, like removing mandatory features (i.e. computing atomic sets), that are usually used to simplify the problem at hand. In our case, as the goal is to have a lower testing cost, we cannot consider such heuristic optimisation as they would modify the obtained testing costs. For example, in the case of removing the mandatory features, that heuristic would produce testing costs that do not consider the additional testing costs that each mandatory feature would add with each added feature, costs that are not constant neither uniform between different features.

5   Experimental Results

In order to evaluate the usefulness of our ACO to find *cheap* (in terms of testing) combinations of features, according to a certain set of constraints defined by the corresponding SPL, we decided to initially compare it with a *brute force* algorithm. The brute force algorithm will effectively compute a feature combination with the lowest testing cost at the expense of a long execution time. In contrast, we will show that our framework can give feature combinations with slightly higher testing costs but having (much) shorter execution times.

We set our ACO algorithm with the following parameters:

- Number of ants: 10.
- Number of maximum iterations: 100.
- Pheromone constant: 1000.
- Pheromone evaporation coefficient: 0.4.
- α coefficient: 0.5.
- β coefficient: 1.2.

These parameters are typical parameters in the literature and they worked very well in our previous work [18]. Moreover, we did small experiments to tune the parameters and none of them show better performance than these ones.

For our experiments, we used 75 SPLA-CRIS expressions with between 10 and 85 features. These SPLA-CRIS expressions were generated using previous work with SPLA-CRIS [4], automatically generating them using the BeTTy tool [32] and storing them in an fodaA format in .xml files. The costs in these expressions are also automatically generated, and thus we consider that they represent the additional testing costs that a feature will add to the product if included in it.

In our first experiment we evaluated these expressions through our SPLA-CRIS interpreter. Using this interpreter, we executed a brute force algorithm to compute all the possible feature combinations as well as their costs. We also executed our ACO algorithm using the SPLA-CRIS interpreter to obtain a feature combination with low

Table 1. Comparing our approach and brute force (time is measured in seconds).

Trial number	Brute force cost	ACO cost	Cost increase	Brute force time	ACO time	Time saving
1	27	36	33.33%	1.1713	4.5798	−291.01%
2	18	27	53.33%	6.5209	8.9389	−37.08%
3	36	45	25.00%	20.5985	9.8473	52.19%
4	63	72	14.29%	4,434.4519	14.8687	99.66%
Average	**36**	**45**	**25.42%**	**1,115.6856**	**9.5587**	**99.14%**

cost. Due to the randomisation involved in the ACO algorithm, we executed both algorithms 15 times for each SPLA-CRIS expression and measured the mean of the results of all the computations. Unfortunately, after running during 20 h the brute force algorithm was able to compute the solution only for four expressions (note that the longest time used by our ACO was less than 15 s). In Table 1 we compare the cost and computation time for these expressions.

As expected, the brute force algorithm was unable to compute, in a reasonable time, the best feature selection for most of the experiments (in fact, it was only able to compute it for the smaller expressions, the ones with less than 13 features) due to the combinatorial explosion underlying feature selection, aggravated with minimising the cost. This leaves us with only four values to compare our ACO with the brute force algorithm. In this comparison we can see that our algorithm obtains, on average, a solution that it is 25.42% more expensive than the best features combination (computed by the brute force algorithm). In contrast, it needs on average 99.14% less time to produce this solution.

Here, it is important to note that for the simplest cases, the brute force algorithm needs less time than our ACO algorithm. The reason is that the expressions are so simple that our ACO algorithm is overpowered for this task. That means that, as the expression is so small, brute force computes all the combinations quickly (because there are so few) while the ACO algorithm not only has to explore the expression, but it also needs to achieve convergence (what will take a while due to the required iterations). However, as we increase the complexity of the expressions, the brute force algorithm quickly raises its execution time a lot (due to its exponential nature), while our ACO algorithm keeps its execution time in a reasonable value.

The comparison with the brute force algorithm leaves us with so few results that we decided to perform a second experiment and compare our framework with a random algorithm. This random algorithm will give us the feature combination with lowest costs of a set of randomly generated feature combinations that represent valid products. The number of feature combinations on this set of randomly generated feature combinations will depend on how much time the algorithm is running. In our experiment, we first run the ACO algorithm and then we run the random algorithm until it overcomes the execution time the ACO algorithm needed. This way, the random algorithm always has the same (or more) time to execute as our ACO and we compare the algorithms performance, that is, the feature combination costs obtained.

Table 2. Results of the experiment comparing with respect to random.

Trial Number	Random Cost	ACO Cost	Cost Saving (%)	Trial Number	Random Cost	ACO Cost	Cost Saving (%)	Trial Number	Random Cost	ACO Cost	Cost Saving (%)
1	52.2	52.2	0.00	26	131.4	102.6	21.92	51	221.4	159.6	27.91
2	36.0	34.8	3.33	27	120.6	98.4	18.41	52	136.8	120.6	11.84
3	50.4	50.4	0.00	28	147.6	115.8	21.54	53	176.4	142.8	19.05
4	73.8	73.8	0.00	29	109.2	94.8	13.19	54	151.2	123.0	18.65
5	63.6	63.6	0.00	30	115.8	102.0	11.92	55	142.2	96.0	32.49
6	70.2	69.0	1.71	31	161.4	128.4	20.45	56	208.8	176.4	15.52
7	63.6	61.2	3.77	32	114.6	82.8	27.75	57	166.8	139.8	16.19
8	73.2	70.8	3.28	33	130.2	117.0	10.14	58	145.2	105.0	27.69
9	67.8	67.2	0.88	34	157.2	148.8	5.34	59	166.8	135.0	19.06
10	75.0	70.8	5.60	35	78.0	70.2	10.00	60	175.2	135.0	22.95
11	63.6	63.6	0.00	36	93.0	78.0	16.13	61	178.2	139.2	21.89
12	62.4	57.0	8.65	37	100.8	97.2	3.57	62	185.4	167.4	9.71
13	91.8	87.0	5.23	38	149.4	133.2	10.84	63	199.2	171.0	14.16
14	81.6	77.4	5.15	39	122.4	101.4	17.16	64	254.4	171.6	32.55
15	70.8	66.0	6.78	40	166.8	142.2	14.75	65	168.6	121.2	28.11
16	58.2	54.0	7.22	41	147.0	138.0	6.12	66	173.4	146.4	15.57
17	83.4	79.2	5.04	42	159.0	146.4	7.92	67	238.8	187.8	21.36
18	99.6	79.8	19.88	43	115.2	89.4	22.40	68	210.0	191.4	8.86
19	78.0	76.8	1.54	44	148.8	135.6	8.87	69	226.2	129.0	42.97
20	99.0	81.0	18.18	45	168.0	132.0	21.43	70	201.0	133.2	33.73
21	80.4	79.2	1.49	46	156.0	134.4	13.85	71	209.4	163.8	21.78
22	111.0	96.6	12.97	47	118.2	98.4	16.75	72	309.6	196.8	36.43
23	70.8	67.8	4.24	48	189.6	144.6	23.73	73	340.8	207.0	39.26
24	96.0	80.4	16.25	49	175.8	168.0	4.44	74	285.6	150.6	47.27
25	76.8	69.0	10.16	50	201.6	175.8	12.8	75	197.4	143.4	27.36

We started with the same set of 75 SPLA-CRIS expressions and evaluated them using our SPLA-CRIS interpreter. For each SPLA-CRIS expression, we also used this interpreter to execute 15 times both our ACO algorithm and the random algorithm. We computed mean costs and compared them (see Table 2).

In order to present an easy visualisation of all the results, we sorted the obtained costs for the ACO approach, from lowest to highest, and produced the graphic shown in Fig. 4. We also obtained the sorted percentage cost saving of the ACO algorithm with respect to the random algorithm (see Fig. 5). In order to compute the cost saving of our approach with respect to the random algorithm, we proceeded as follows. For each SPLA-CRIS expression, we computed the cost using both our ACO and the random algorithm and computed the percentage difference of the ACO with respect to the random algorithm. For example, if the cost associated with the selected product by the ACO is equal to 135.0 and the cost obtained by the random algorithm, most likely for a different product but also fulfilling the constraints associated to the SPL, is 175.2, then the cost saving is equal to $100 \cdot \left(1 - \frac{135.0}{175.2}\right) \approx 22.95$.

The analysis of the results shows that our ACO algorithm always finds feature combinations with lower costs than the random algorithm (or equal cost in the worst cases). Therefore, our algorithm performs better than the random algorithm. On average, our ACO computes solutions that are 14.87% cheaper.

We performed a statistical hypothesis test over the results, whose null hypothesis was that the random algorithm and our framework give similar results, that is, both obtain similar costs. We applied a one-way ANOVA test where we tested whether the results of both algorithms are similar in average. Then, we computed the p-value for the experiment, obtaining a p-value of 0.0037. This represents that there is a 00.37%

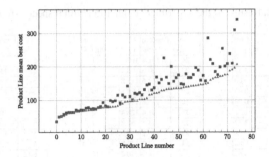

Fig. 4. Sorted obtained costs (blue = random, red = ACO). (Color figure online)

of probability that the null hypothesis is fulfilled. Therefore, we can reject the null hypothesis for the experiment with a confidence higher than 99%, as its p-value is lower than 0.01. In order to double-check our results, we also performed a t-test and obtained the same p-value. Thus, the conclusion is that the performance of our ACO algorithm is better than the random algorithm.

6 Threats to Validity

Threats to *internal validity* refer to uncontrolled factors that can affect the output of the experiments, either in favour or against our hypothesis. The main threat in this category is the possibility of having faults in the code of the experiments. We diminished this threat by carefully testing the code, even using small examples for which we knew the expected results. Additionally, in order to reduce the impact of the randomness associated with our methodology, we repeated the experiments several times.

Threats to *external validity* refer to the generality of our findings to other situations. The main threat in this category is given by the different possible SPLs to which we could apply our framework. As the population of SPLs is unknown, this threat is not fully addressable. In order to diminish this risk, we considered different SPLs in the experiments.

Finally, threats to *construct validity* refer to the relevance of the properties we are measuring for the extrapolation of the results to real-world examples. The main threat in this category is what would happen if we use our framework with real-world SPLs and/or with much more complex SPLs, which is a matter of future work.

7 Discussion About the Suitability of ACO

We have shown that our ACO achieves good solutions for this task. However, it is possible that other heuristics could work better than ACO in this specific framework. Although this comparison should be further investigated, and it will be indeed a matter of future work, we would like to briefly justify why we decided to use an ACO algorithm.

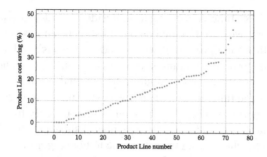

Fig. 5. Sorted cost *saving*.

Our main concern when developing the algorithm was that we needed to provide a much faster solution than brute force while, at the same time, being able to obtain good enough results. Therefore, we classified our problem as an *exploratory problem*. We are aware that there are many evolutionary algorithms that usually work better than a random based search. In our case, we needed a proposal able to *search* in a SPLA-CRIS expression. Fortunately, this kind of syntactical expressions can be transformed into a graph whose *final states* represent all the possible feature combinations that fulfil the expression restrictions. Since this graph can have cycles, we need to perform an extra step to unfold these cycles in order to be able to use a Genetic Programming based algorithm to search for feature combinations inside this graph. This operation would increase the complexity of the approach. In addition, since we are working with a search space based on a graph structure, an approach such as particle swarm optimisation algorithms would suffer because it needs extra adaptation phases that also will increase the complexity of the algorithm. In contrast, ACO can be easily applied to this scenario because our search space is represented as a graph where we are looking for a path from the root to a *final state*, representing a valid feature combination, with a cost as low as possible. So, in order to put into practice our approach we only needed an available interpreter [4] that transform the SPLA-CRIS expressions into appropriate graphs.

8   Conclusions and Future Work

Software Product Lines are a useful tool for developing software systems in an automatic way and testing them is a must. Integration testing is a process that SPLs should overcome: we test how well a new feature is integrated with the already existing features of the SPL. If we have the costs of testing each feature of the SPL, then we can select the product that contains the new feature that has a lower testing cost, so we can test its integration with the other features of the SPL in a quicker and/or cheaper way.

In this paper we have proposed a new framework for feature selection in SPLs having testing costs associated with the combination of features. This feature selection generates a product with low cost and a given feature. We have adapted ACO to deal with an *a priory* unknown search space. Therefore, our framework is able to obtain new feature combinations for a given SPL without computing all the possible feature combinations, which is a time-consuming task. Besides, in order to assess the usefulness of the new framework, we have reported on our most representative experiments. These experiments show that our algorithm is well suited for this task and that it is preferable than other simpler algorithms. Finding sub-optimal solutions in a shorter time can be fundamental in some scenarios, as computing the optimal solution can require a huge amount of resources and time. In fact, in our own experiments we were able to compute the exact solution, by computing all the possible solutions, only for SPLs with a very small number of features. In addition, our experiments show that our algorithm is better than a random search, when giving the same time to both algorithms.

We have identified several research directions concerning applicability, scalability, suitability and adaptability of our framework. Concerning scalability, we will consider more complex SPLs and check whether our technique scales well. Although we will not be able to compare our ACO with brute force, because the latter will not compute the best solution, we want to explore the *limit* of our approach. In addition, we would like to use current mutation testing approaches [11,28] to efficiently generate and process big amount of mutants representing either non-optimal or faulty selections of features.

With respect to suitability, we will consider two unrelated lines of work. First, although our ACO is well suited for this task, we would like to compare it with other heuristics that could work better than our proposal in this specific framework. Specifically, we would like to compare our ACO approach with other meta-heuristics based on Bee Swarm [23]. A second line of work to analyse the suitability of our framework is to consider SPLs with existing feature selections, produced by an expert, and compare their costs and the ones produced by our framework. In addition, as suggested by a reviewer, it would be interesting to take into account that products including features interacting with the new feature will be more likely to expose bugs, than products running the feature in isolation. Finally, concerning adaptability, we would like to assess the usefulness of our methodology in other frameworks. First, we would like to apply our framework to study formal models of cloud [6,27] and distributed [15,16] systems. We choose this type of systems because we are familiar with them and, more importantly, because they are highly configurable and, therefore, will induce SPLs with many features. Finally, we would like to evaluate whether it is possible to integrate our feature selection framework in existing tools like ProFeat [8].

Acknowledgements. We would like to thank the anonymous reviewers for the careful reading, the many constructive comments and the useful suggestions, which have helped us to further strengthen the paper.

References

1. Andrés, C., Camacho, C., Llana, L.: A formal framework for software product lines. Inf. Softw. Technol. **55**(11), 1925–1947 (2013)
2. Benavides, D., Trinidad, P., Ruiz Cortés, A., Segura, S.: FaMa. In: Capilla, R., Bosch, J., Kang, K.C. (eds.) Systems and Software Variability Management - Concepts, Tools and Experiences, pp. 163–171. Springer, Heidelberg (2013). https://doi.org/10.1007/978-3-642-36583-6_11

3. Benito-Parejo, M., Merayo, M.G.: An evolutionary algorithm for selection of test cases. In: 22nd IEEE Congress on Evolutionary Computation, CEC 2020, pp. E-24535: 1–8. IEEE Computer Society (2020)
4. Camacho, C., Llana, L., Núñez, A.: Cost-related interface for software product lines. J. Log. Algebraic Methods Program. **85**(1), 227–244 (2016)
5. Campos, J., Ge, Y., Albunian, N., Fraser, G., Eler, M., Arcuri, A.: An empirical evaluation of evolutionary algorithms for unit test suite generation. Inf. Softw. Technol. **104**, 207–235 (2018)
6. Cañizares, P.C., Núñez, A., de Lara, J., Llana, L.: MT-EA4Cloud: a methodology for testing and optimising energy-aware cloud systems. J. Syst. Softw. **163**, 110522:1–25 (2020)
7. do Carmo Machado, I., da Mota Silveira Neto, P.A., Santana de Almeida, E.: Towards an integration testing approach for software product lines. In: IEEE 13th International Conference on Information Reuse & Integration, IRI 2012, pp. 616–623. IEEE (2012)
8. Chrszon, P., Dubslaff, C., Klüppelholz, S., Baier, C.: ProFeat: feature-oriented engineering for family-based probabilistic model checking. Formal Aspects Comput. **30**(1), 45–75 (2017). https://doi.org/10.1007/s00165-017-0432-4
9. Dorigo, M., Stützle, T.: Ant Colony Optimization. MIT Press, Cambridge (2004)
10. Eriksson, M., Börstler, J., Borg, K.: The PLUSS approach – domain modeling with features, use cases and use case realizations. In: Obbink, H., Pohl, K. (eds.) SPLC 2005. LNCS, vol. 3714, pp. 33–44. Springer, Heidelberg (2005). https://doi.org/10.1007/11554844_5
11. Gómez-Abajo, P., Guerra, E., Lara, J., Merayo, M.G.: Wodel-test: a model-based framework for language-independent mutation testing. Softw. Syst. Model. **20**(3), 767–793 (2020). https://doi.org/10.1007/s10270-020-00827-0
12. Griss, M., Favaro, J., D'Alessandro, M.: Integrating feature modeling with the RSEB. In: 5th International Conference on Software Reuse, ICSR 1998, pp. 76–85. IEEE Computer Society (1998)
13. Henard, C., Papadakis, M., Perrouin, G., Klein, J., Heymans, P., Le Traon, Y.: Bypassing the combinatorial explosion: using similarity to generate and prioritize T-Wise test configurations for software product lines. IEEE Trans. Softw. Eng. **40**(7), 650–670 (2014)
14. Hierons, R.M., Li, M., Liu, X., Segura, S., Zheng, W.: SIP: optimal product selection from feature models using many-objective evolutionary optimization. ACM Trans. Softw. Eng. Methodol. **25**(2), 17:1–17:39 (2016)
15. Hierons, R.M., Merayo, M.G., Núñez, M.: Bounded reordering in the distributed test architecture. IEEE Trans. Reliab. **67**(2), 522–537 (2018)
16. Hierons, R.M., Núñez, M.: Implementation relations and probabilistic schedulers in the distributed test architecture. J. Syst. Softw. **132**, 319–335 (2017)
17. Ibias, A., Griñán, D., Núñez, M.: GPTSG: a genetic programming test suite generator using information theory measures. In: Rojas, I., Joya, G., Catala, A. (eds.) IWANN 2019. LNCS, vol. 11506, pp. 716–728. Springer, Cham (2019). https://doi.org/10.1007/978-3-030-20521-8_59
18. Ibias, A., Llana, L.: Feature selection using evolutionary computation techniques for software product line testing. In: 22nd IEEE Congress on Evolutionary Computation, CEC 2020, pp. E-24502:1–8. IEEE Computer Society (2020)
19. Ibias, A., Núñez, M.: Using a swarm to detect hard-to-kill mutants. In: 2020 IEEE International Conference on Systems, Man and Cybernetics, SMC 2020, pp. 2190–2195. IEEE Computer Society (2020)
20. Ibias, A., Vazquez-Gomis, P., Benito-Parejo, M.: Coverage-based grammar-guided genetic programming generation of test suites. In: 23rd IEEE Congress on Evolutionary Computation, CEC 2021, pp. 2411–2418. IEEE (2021)

21. Jaffar-ur Rehman, M., Jabeen, F., Bertolino, A., Polini, A.: Testing software components for integration: a survey of issues and techniques. Softw. Test. Verification Reliab. **17**(2), 95–133 (2007)
22. Kang, K.C., Cohen, S.G., Hess, J.A., Novak, W.E., Peterson, A.S.: Feature-oriented domain analysis (FODA) feasibility study. Technical report CMU/SEI-90-TR-21, Carnegie Mellon University (1990)
23. Karaboga, D., Akay, B.: A survey: algorithms simulating bee swarm intelligence. Artif. Intell. Rev. **31**(1), 61–85 (2009). https://doi.org/10.1007/s10462-009-9127-4
24. Lachmann, R., Beddig, S., Lity, S., Schulze, S., Schaefer, I.: Risk-based integration testing of software product lines. In: 11th International Workshop on Variability Modelling of Software-Intensive Systems, VaMoS 2017, pp. 52–59. ACM Press (2017)
25. Lopez-Herrejon, R.E., Ferrer, J., Chicano, F., Egyed, A., Alba, E.: Comparative analysis of classical multi-objective evolutionary algorithms and seeding strategies for pairwise testing of software product lines. In: 16th IEEE Congress on Evolutionary Computation, CEC 2014, pp. 387–396. IEEE (2014)
26. McGregor, J.D.: Testing a software product line. In: Borba, P., Cavalcanti, A., Sampaio, A., Woodcook, J. (eds.) PSSE 2007. LNCS, vol. 6153, pp. 104–140. Springer, Heidelberg (2010). https://doi.org/10.1007/978-3-642-14335-9_4
27. Núñez, A., Cañizares, P.C., Núñez, M., Hierons, R.M.: TEA-Cloud: a formal framework for testing cloud computing systems. IEEE Trans. Reliab. **70**(1), 261–284 (2021)
28. Papadakis, M., Kintis, M., Zhang, J., Jia, Y., Traon, Y.L., Harman, M.: Mutation testing advances: an analysis and survey. In: Volume 112 of Advances in Computers, pp. 275–378. Elsevier (2019)
29. Reis, S., Metzger, A., Pohl, K.: Integration testing in software product line engineering: a model-based technique. In: Dwyer, M.B., Lopes, A. (eds.) FASE 2007. LNCS, vol. 4422, pp. 321–335. Springer, Heidelberg (2007). https://doi.org/10.1007/978-3-540-71289-3_25
30. Rodrigues, D.S., Delamaro, M.E., Corrêa, C.G., Nunes, F.L.S.: Using genetic algorithms in test data generation: a critical systematic mapping. ACM Comput. Surv. **51**(2), 1–23 (2018). Article 41
31. Sayyad, A.S., Ingram, J., Menzies, T., Ammar, H.H.: Optimum feature selection in software product lines: let your model and values guide your search. In: 1st International Workshop on Combining Modelling and Search-Based Software Engineering, CMSBSE 2013, pp. 22–27. IEEE Computer Society (2013)
32. Segura, S., Galindo, J.A., Benavides, D., Parejo, J.A., Ruiz-Cortés, A.: BeTTy: benchmarking and testing on the automated analysis of feature models. In: 6th International Workshop on Variability Modeling of Software-Intensive Systems, VaMoS 2012, pp. 63–71 (2012)
33. Shi, J., Cohen, M.B., Dwyer, M.B.: Integration testing of software product lines using compositional symbolic execution. In: de Lara, J., Zisman, A. (eds.) FASE 2012. LNCS, vol. 7212, pp. 270–284. Springer, Heidelberg (2012). https://doi.org/10.1007/978-3-642-28872-2_19
34. Steindl, M., Mottok, J.: Optimizing software integration by considering integration test complexity and test effort. In: 10th International Workshop on Intelligent Solutions in Embedded Systems, WISES 2012, pp. 63–68. IEEE Computer Society (2012)
35. Thüm, T., Kästner, C., Benduhn, F., Meinicke, J., Saake, G., Leich, T.: FeatureIDE: an extensible framework for feature-oriented software development. Sci. Comput. Program. **79**, 70–85 (2014)
36. Wang, D., Tan, D., Liu, L.: Particle swarm optimization algorithm: an overview. Soft. Comput. **22**(2), 387–408 (2017). https://doi.org/10.1007/s00500-016-2474-6

Initial Results on Counting Test Orders for Order-Dependent Flaky Tests Using Alloy

Wenxi Wang[1](✉), Pu Yi[2], Sarfraz Khurshid[1], and Darko Marinov[3]

[1] The University of Texas at Austin, Austin, USA
wenxiw@utexas.edu
[2] Peking University, Beijing, China
[3] University of Illinois Urbana-Champaign, Champaign, USA

Abstract. Flaky tests can seemingly nondeterministically pass or fail for the same code under test. Flaky tests are detrimental to regression testing because tests that pass before code changes and fail after code changes do not reliably indicate problems in code changes. An important category of flaky tests is order-dependent tests that pass or fail based on the order of tests in the test suite. Prior work has considered the problem of counting test orders that pass or fail, given relationships of tests within a test suite. However, prior work has not addressed the most general case of these relationships. This paper shows how to encode the problem of counting test orders in the Alloy modeling language and how to use propositional model counters to obtain the count for test orders. We illustrate that Alloy makes it easy to handle even the most general case. The results show that this problem produces challenging propositional formulas for the state-of-the-art model counters.

1 Introduction

Flaky tests [15] can seemingly nondeterministically pass or fail for the same code under test. Flaky tests are detrimental to regression testing because tests that pass before code changes and fail after code changes do not reliably indicate problems in code changes. For example, Harman and O'Hearn point out problems of flaky tests at Facebook [5], and several other companies point out similar problems, including Apple [11], Google [4,16,22], Huawei [9], and Microsoft [6,7,13,14].

An important category of flaky tests is order-dependent tests that pass or fail based on the order of tests in the test suite. More specifically, the tests deterministicaly fail in some test orders and deterministically pass in other test orders. Before establishing that the tests depend just on the order, the developers may view them as nondeterministically passing or failing in various runs.

Shi et al. [17] have categorized several roles for order-dependent tests. Each order-dependent test itself can be either a *victim*, which passes when run by itself but fails when run after some other tests in the test suite, or a *brittle*, which fails when run by itself but passes when run after some other test in the test suite. Each victim test fails when run after (not necessarily immediately after)

© IFIP International Federation for Information Processing 2022
Published by Springer Nature Switzerland AG 2022
D. Clark et al. (Eds.): ICTSS 2021, LNCS 13045, pp. 123–130, 2022.
https://doi.org/10.1007/978-3-031-04673-5_9

a *polluter* test, unless a *cleaner* test runs between the polluter and the victim. Each brittle test passes when run after (not necessarily immediately after) a *state-setter* test. We focus on victim tests, because the analysis for brittle tests comes out as a special case.

Wei et al. [20] have recently considered the problem of counting the number of test orders for which a victim fails. This problem is important because it allows computing the *flake rate*, i.e., the probability that a test fails if the test order is a uniformly sampled permutation of the test suite. In turn, the flake rate allows developers to determine whether to fix the test or not, and it allows researchers to compare various algorithms for detecting order-dependent tests [20]. Wei et al. [20] have derived analytical formulas for some cases of victims, namely when all polluters have the same set of cleaners, but have not addressed the most general case, namely when two or more polluters have a different set of cleaners.

We show how to encode the problem of counting test orders in the Alloy modeling language [8], and we use propositional model counters [12,18] to count the test orders. Alloy has been used for many software analysis and testing tasks [3,10], and model counters have seen wide applications in various domains [1,2]. The Alloy toolset automatically translates the Alloy models into propositional formulas that are fed into model counters to solve the counting problems. Yang et al. [21] have presented AlloyMC that connects Alloy with model counters. However, no prior work has used Alloy to count test orders.

We illustrate how Alloy makes it easy to handle even the most general case of victims with polluters that may have different cleaners. We show a general *skeleton* model to encode the problem of counting test orders; the skeleton can be instantiated with the specific sets of polluters and cleaners. To evaluate correctness and scalability of our approach, we use 24 propositional formulas as our benchmarks. The benchmarks consider a real scenario from the flaky test dataset published by Wei et al. [20] with two polluters where one has a subset of cleaners of the other. We instantiate our skeleton with an increasing number of cleaners. We choose Alloy to translate this difficult problem into SAT formula, because the Alloy analyzer employs the heavily optimized constraint solver Kodkod [19], which efficiently translates Alloy specifications into simplified SAT formulas. The SAT formulas can be counted using any off-the-shelf model counters. We apply state-of-the-art model counters for both exact counting (ProjMC [12]) and approximate counting (ApproxMC4 [18]).

The results show that the problem of counting test orders provides *challenging* propositional formulas for model counters. In addition, we found that the exact counter generally runs *faster* than the approximate counter for all our non-trivial benchmarks, which is a surprising result because it is unusual that an exact model counter outperforms an approximate model counter [18].

In summary, this paper makes the following contributions:

- **Encoding:** We show how to encode the problem of test orders in Alloy.
- **Evaluation:** We evaluate our encoding on a number of challenging problems. The initial results are promising but point out to scalability issues.
- **Challenges:** We obtain a number of interesting and challenging problems for propositional model counters.

```
1.  open util/ordering[Test]

2.  abstract sig Test {}
3.  one sig Victim extends Test {}
4.  abstract sig Cleaner extends Test {}
5.  abstract sig Polluter extends Test { cleaners: set Cleaner }
6.  fact { Polluter.cleaners = Cleaner }
7.  pred Pollutes[p: Polluter] {
8.      p in prevs[Victim]
9.      and no p.cleaners & prevs[Victim] & nexts[p] }
10. pred Fail[] {
11.     some p: Polluter | Pollutes[p]
12.     and no p': nexts[p] & prevs[Victim] & Polluter | Pollutes[p'] }
13. pred Pass[] {
14.     !Fail[] }
15. pred Pass2[] {
16.     all p: Polluter & prevs[Victim] |
17.         some p.cleaners & prevs[Victim] & nexts[p] }

18. one sig c_1, c_2, c_3 extends Cleaner {}
19. one sig p_1, p_2 extends Polluter {}
20. fact Matrix {
21.     p_1.cleaners = c_1 + c_2
22.     p_2.cleaners = c_1 + c_2 + c_3 }

23. run Fail
24. run Pass
25. run Pass2
```

Fig. 1. An example of modeling flaky test orders in Alloy

2 Modeling Flaky Test Orders Using Alloy

We illustrate our approach for modeling flaky test orders in Alloy using an example. Through the example we also introduce the aspects of the Alloy language required to understand the modeling. Figure 1 shows an example Alloy model which encodes the problem of counting test orders.

We model the order of tests in a test suite using the Alloy library util/ordering, which defines a linear order (line 1). The signature (sig) Test declares a set of atoms that represent tests (line 2). The set of tests is partitioned (using keyword extends) into three subsets: a singleton (one) set for the victim (line 3), a set of cleaners (line 4), and a set of polluters (line 5). Note that we do not model neutral tests which do not have any impact on the the victim, because their presence has no impact on the flake rate. The *field* cleaners in sig Polluter introduces a binary relation cleaners: Polluter x Cleaner to represent the matrix that relate polluters to cleaners (line 5). A fact introduces a constraint that must be satisfied in all models; the stated fact uses relational composition ('.') to require that the relational image of Polluter under the relation `cleaners` equals the set of all cleaners, i.e., models have no extraneous cleaners (line 6).

A predicate (`pred`) introduces a parameterized formula that can be *invoked* elsewhere. The predicate `Pollutes` enforces two constraints on its parameter p that is a polluter (lines 7–9). One, p appears before the victim in the test order; `prevs[i]` (likewise, `nexts[i]`) is a library function that represents the set of atoms in the linear order before (likewise, after) i, and `in` is the subset operator. Two, no cleaner for p is between p and the victim; the quantifier `no` is the negation of existential quantifier `some`, and '`&`' is set intersection. A vertical bar "—" indicates the start of a sequence of constraints. The predicate `Fail` defines the failing test order using the existential quantification: there is some atom in the set of polluters such that it pollutes (lines 10–12). The additional constraint (line 12) requires that p be the *last* such test before the victim, which rules out duplicate solutions where the difference is not based on the test order but based on which polluter is a *witness* to failure. (More formally, this constraint ignores from the model the new variable arising from Skolemization.) The predicate `Pass` defines the passing test order as the negation of the constraints for failing test order (lines 13–14). We also evaluate the predicate `Pass2` that defines another encoding for the passing test order, stating more directly that all polluters before the victim have a cleaner between the polluter and the victim; we expect this encoding to enable faster model counting.

The test suites in a general model contain 1 victim, n polluters, and k cleaners. Figure 1 (lines 18–22) shows one example containing 2 polluters and 3 cleaners. The `Matrix` (`fact`) states the cleaners for each polluter. In this example, polluter p_1 has two cleaners c_1 and c_2, and polluter p_2 has three cleaners c_1, c_2, and c_3. We can change the number of polluters and cleaners simply by changing the declarations in lines 18–19, and change the relations between polluters and cleaners by changing the `Matrix`. The `run` command defines the constraint-solving problem, which is to solve the predicate `Fail/Pass/Pass2` subject to all applicable constraints on the sets and relations declared in the Alloy model (lines 23–25). Each model represents one test order, and counting the number of models thus counts the number of test orders.

3   Experimental Evaluation

```
18. one sig c_1, c_2, ..., c_k extends Cleaner {}
19. one sig p_1, p_2 extends Polluter {}
20. fact Matrix {
21.     p_1.cleaners = c_1 + c_2 + ... + c_(k/2)
22.     p_2.cleaners = c_1 + c_2 + ... + c_k }
```

Fig. 2. The template for our benchmark generation

Table 1. Counting results of our benchmarks ('-' denotes not applicable)

Benchmarks	ProjMC		ApproxMC		
	Time	Count	Time	Count	Error (%)
k = 1, Fail	0.01	15	0.00	15	0.00
k = 2, Fail	0.02	56	0.01	56	0.00
k = 3, Fail	0.09	270	0.21	260	3.85
k = 4, Fail	0.87	1800	1.22	1856	3.11
k = 5, Fail	6.79	12096	15.27	13056	7.94
k = 6, Fail	93.21	104832	204.67	110592	5.49
k = 7, Fail	937.31	907200	1040.32	884736	2.54
k = 1, Pass	0.01	9	0.00	9	0.00
k = 2, Pass	0.02	64	0.01	64	0.00
k = 3, Pass	0.13	450	0.45	496	10.22
k = 4, Pass	1.23	3240	5.21	3456	6.67
k = 5, Pass	13.71	28224	72.8	31744	12.47
k = 6, Pass	256.93	258048	547.6	278528	7.94
k = 7, Pass	3197.09	2721600	>5000	–	–
k = 1, Pass2	0.01	9	0.00	9	0.00
k = 2, Pass2	0.02	64	0.01	64	0.00
k = 3, Pass2	0.14	450	0.44	496	10.22
k = 4, Pass2	1.22	3240	4.74	3456	6.67
k = 5, Pass2	12.33	28224	80.05	31744	12.47
k = 6, Pass2	217.80	258048	555.24	278528	7.94
k = 7, Pass2	2905.76	2721600	4700.48	2359296	15.36

3.1 Setup

Model Counters. We study how both exact model counting and approximate model counting perform on the generated propositional formulas. We apply ProjMC [12], which is the state-of-the-art exact model counter, and ApproxMC4 [18], which is the state-of-the-art approximate model counter.

Benchmarks. As our benchmark, we want to generate propositional formulas for Fail, Pass, and Pass2 predicates introduced in the above Alloy model (Fig. 1) with various test combinations. To do so, we replace lines 18–22 of our Alloy model with a simple template shown in Fig. 2. The template introduces 2 polluters and k cleaners: the first polluter has half of all cleaners as its cleaners, and the second polluter has all the cleaners as its cleaners. In our experiments, we range k from 1 to 8, generating 8 propositional formulas for each predicate. In total, we generate 24 benchmarks for our evaluation. We choose to use this template because it is the most complicated case that exists in the real-world flaky test dataset published by Wei et al. [20]. Therefore, we think it represents the most complicated model we can encounter in a real-life setting.

Metrics. The two key metrics we use in our evaluation are the model counts and the actual wall time to compute them. In line with ApproxMC, we report the error rate of the approximate model counting as $max(\frac{approx}{exact}, \frac{exact}{approx}) - 1$, based on multiplicative guarantees. We use timeout of 5000 s, as commonly done in work on model counting [18].

Platform. All the experiments are conducted on a machine with Intel Core i7-8700k CPU (12 logical cores in total) and 32-GB RAM.

3.2   Results

We apply both model counters on all the generated propositional formulas (with k ranging from 1 to 8) for all the three predicates (i.e., Fail, Pass, and Pass2). Our experimental results show that the limit of ProjMC for all three predicates is $k = 7$; the limit of ApproxMC for Fail and Pass2 is $k = 7$ and for Pass is $k = 6$. Thus, the propositional formulas generated with our Alloy model are generally difficult, providing a challenging dataset for future work on model counters. For formulas in many other domains, model counters can handle orders of magnitude more models [18]. For formulas in many other domains, model counters can handle many more models with orders of magnitude [18].

The detailed results of the benchmarks encoding all the three predicates with k up to 7 are shown in Table 1. Our results provide a way to sanity check the correctness of our proposed Alloy model: the exact counts of Pass/Pass2 should be the same, and the sum of the exact count of Fail and the exact count of Pass/Pass2 should be the total number of permutations of all the tests (i.e., k cleaners, 2 polluters, and 1 victim), i.e., $(k+3)!$. With the exact counts reported by ProjMC, we confirm that our proposed model passes the sanity check. We also manually check that correct models (not just count) are generated for $k = 1$.

Moreover, the results show that ProjMC generally runs *faster* than ApproxMC for all the non-trivial benchmarks (where $k \geq 3$), which is quite a surprising result. It is unusual that an exact model counter outperforms an approximate model counter. Hence, our non-trivial benchmarks pose additional value for model counting community. Our intuitive explanation for this phenomenon is that the problem of counting the test orders for order dependent flaky tests is generally hard and has little space for the optimization, which may not favor the fancy tricks operated by the approximate model counters as ApproxMC. We also did some preliminary experiments using the SAT encoding, this phenomenon still exists. Therefore, we do not think it is the encoding Alloy provides that causes this interesting results. Besides, we can also observe that ApproxMC sometimes over-approximates and sometimes under-approximates, with the error rate ranging from 0.00% to 15.36%; interestingly, ApproxMC approximates with lower error for the Fail predicate than for the Pass/Pass2 predicates. Lastly, the results show that the Pass predicate is easier for both counters to solve, compared to the `Pass2` predicate. Therefore, we confirm that different encoding for the same problem can result in different counting efficiency.

4   Conclusions

This paper presents a general way of encoding the problem of counting flaky test orders using the Alloy modeling language. We illustrate how Alloy makes it easy to handle even the most general case of victims with polluters that have different cleaners. We provide a general skeleton Alloy model that can be instantiated with the specific sets of polluters and cleaners. To evaluate our encoding, we generate 24 problems with various test combinations of different sizes. The results show that our Alloy encoding provides interesting and challenging propositional formulas that can be a useful resource to advance development of the state-of-the-art model counters.

Our future work is to evaluate more encodings of passing and failing test orders to try to improve scalability of the approach. We hope that we can push the approach to $k = 10$. Such values would cover many real cases [20] and also provide inspiration to develop analytical formulas for the number of test orders.

Acknowledgment. We thank Wing Lam and Anjiang Wei for discussions on counting test orders. This work was partially supported by NSF grants CCF-1763788. We also acknowledge support for research on flaky tests from Facebook and Google.

References

1. Aydin, A., Bang, L., Bultan, T.: Automata-based model counting for string constraints. In: Kroening, D., Păsăreanu, C.S. (eds.) CAV 2015, Part I. LNCS, vol. 9206, pp. 255–272. Springer, Cham (2015). https://doi.org/10.1007/978-3-319-21690-4_15
2. Bacchus, F., Dalmao, S., Pitassi, T.: Algorithms and complexity results for # SAT and Bayesian inference. In: FOCS (2003)
3. Büttner, F., Egea, M., Cabot, J., Gogolla, M.: Verification of ATL transformations using transformation models and model finders. In: Aoki, T., Taguchi, K. (eds.) ICFEM 2012. LNCS, vol. 7635, pp. 198–213. Springer, Heidelberg (2012). https://doi.org/10.1007/978-3-642-34281-3_16
4. Google: Avoiding flakey tests (2008). http://googletesting.blogspot.com/2008/04/tott-avoiding-flakey-tests.html
5. Harman, M., O'Hearn, P.: From start-ups to scale-ups: opportunities and open problems for static and dynamic program analysis. In: SCAM (2018)
6. Herzig, K., Greiler, M., Czerwonka, J., Murphy, B.: The art of testing less without sacrificing quality. In: ICSE (2015)
7. Herzig, K., Nagappan, N.: Empirically detecting false test alarms using association rules. In: ICSE (2015)
8. Jackson, D.: Software Abstractions: Logic, Language, and Analysis. The MIT Press, Cambridge (2006)
9. Jiang, H., Li, X., Yang, Z., Xuan, J.: What causes my test alarm? Automatic cause analysis for test alarms in system and integration testing. In: ICSE (2017)

10. Kang, E., Jackson, D.: Formal modeling and analysis of a flash filesystem in alloy. In: Börger, E., Butler, M., Bowen, J.P., Boca, P. (eds.) ABZ 2008. LNCS, vol. 5238, pp. 294–308. Springer, Heidelberg (2008). https://doi.org/10.1007/978-3-540-87603-8_23

11. Kowalczyk, E., Nair, K., Gao, Z., Silberstein, L., Long, T., Memon, A.: Modeling and ranking flaky tests at Apple. In: ICSE-SEIP (2020)

12. Lagniez, J.-M., Marquis, P.: A recursive algorithm for projected model counting. In: AAAI, vol. 33, pp. 1536–1543 (2019)

13. Lam, W., Godefroid, P., Nath, S., Santhiar, A., Thummalapenta, S.: Root causing flaky tests in a large-scale industrial setting. In: ISSTA (2019)

14. Lam, W., Muşlu, K., Sajnani, H., Thummalapenta, S.: A study on the lifecycle of flaky tests. In: ICSE (2020)

15. Luo, Q., Hariri, F., Eloussi, L., Marinov, D.: An empirical analysis of flaky tests. In: FSE (2014)

16. Memon, A., Gao, Z., Nguyen, B., Dhanda, S., Siemborski, R., Micco, J.: Taming Google-scale continuous testing. In: ICSE-SEIP, Eric Nickell (2017)

17. Shi, A., Lam, W., Oei, R., Xie, T., Marinov, D.: iFixFlakies: a framework for automatically fixing order-dependent flaky tests. In: FSE (2019)

18. Soos, M., Gocht, S., Meel, K.S.: Tinted, detached, and lazy CNF-XOR SOLVING and its applications to counting and sampling. In: Lahiri, S.K., Wang, C. (eds.) CAV 2020, Part I. LNCS, vol. 12224, pp. 463–484. Springer, Cham (2020). https://doi.org/10.1007/978-3-030-53288-8_22

19. Torlak, E., Jackson, D.: Kodkod: a relational model finder. In: Grumberg, O., Huth, M. (eds.) TACAS 2007. LNCS, vol. 4424, pp. 632–647. Springer, Heidelberg (2007). https://doi.org/10.1007/978-3-540-71209-1_49

20. Wei, A., Yi, P., Xie, T., Marinov, D., Lam, W.: Probabilistic and systematic coverage of consecutive test-method pairs for detecting order-dependent flaky tests. In: TACAS 2021, Part I. LNCS, vol. 12651, pp. 270–287. Springer, Cham (2021). https://doi.org/10.1007/978-3-030-72016-2_15

21. Yang, J., Wang, W., Marinov, D., Khurshid, S.: Alloy meets model counting. In: FSE, AlloyMC (2020)

22. Ziftci, C., Reardon. J.: Who broke the build? Automatically identifying changes that induce test failures in continuous integration at Google scale. In: ICSE (2017)

Metamorphic Testing of Logic Theorem Prover

Oliver A. Tazl and Franz Wotawa[✉]

Institute for Software Technology, Graz University of Technology, Graz, Austria
{oliver.tazl,wotawa}@ist.tugraz.at

Abstract. The use of Artificial Intelligence methodologies including machine learning for object recognition and other tasks as well as reasoning has recently gained more attention. This is due to the fact of applications like autonomous driving but also apps for providing recommendations or schedules. In this paper, we focus on testing applications utilizing logic theorem proving for implementing their functionalities. Testing logic theorem prover is important in order to assure that the obtained results are correct and complete as specified. We show how metamorphic testing can be used in this context. In particular, the proposed method takes a logic sentence and modifies it without changing its logical status, i.e., satisfiability. The testing method can be applied to assure the correctness of reasoning via generating logic sentences of arbitrary sizes, but also for performance testing. We applied the presented testing method to 2 different theorem provers and report on obtained results.

Keywords: Test automation · Theorem prover testing · Metamorphic testing · Test case generation

1 Introduction

With the increasing interest in Artificial Intelligence (AI) and its sub-fields like machine learning (ML) or knowledge-based reasoning (KBR), there is a need for assuring that the implemented AI meets its requirements. This allows for gaining trust in the implementation, which is the basis for successful and widely used applications. For example, let us consider a decision support system for medical doctors to be used in diagnostics. In any case, such a system must deliver a reasonable diagnosis that does not harm the patient. Or let us have a look at a

---

ArchitectECA2030 receives funding within the Electronic Components and Systems For European Leadership Joint Undertaking (ESCEL JU) in collaboration with the European Union's Horizon2020 Framework Programme and National Authorities, under grant agreement n° 877539. The work was partially funded by the Austrian Federal Ministry of Climate Action, Environment, Energy, Mobility, Innovation and Technology (BMK) under the program "ICT of the Future" project 877587.

ⓒ IFIP International Federation for Information Processing 2022
Published by Springer Nature Switzerland AG 2022
D. Clark et al. (Eds.): ICTSS 2021, LNCS 13045, pp. 131–137, 2022.
https://doi.org/10.1007/978-3-031-04673-5_10

car equipped with a diagnosis system that can adapt the vehicle's behavior for compensating a fault. A wrong diagnosis result, in this case, may cause severe danger for the car's passengers or other cars in close proximity. In any of these cases, we have to assure that the AI part is working as expected without any doubt.

In this paper, we contribute to testing AI-based systems focusing on KBR, which relies on theorem proving. KBR has been successfully used for various applications including recommender systems [5,6], to expert systems [11], and diagnosis [3,12]. In particular, we introduce the application of metamorphic testing [1,2] for generating tests in the context of theorem proving. In metamorphic testing relations between two inputs are used to identify the correctness of an implementation. For example, it is well known that $\sin(x) = \sin(x + 2\pi)$ holds for all values of x. Such metamorphic relations can be used as properties that must always hold, i.e., to work as test oracles, or for generating new test cases. Once, we know that the value of $\sin(x)$ is y, we can generate a new test case using $x + 2\pi$ as input and y as expected output.

The proposed metamorphic testing approach applied to theorem proving makes use of the following underlying idea. If we have a theory Th, i.e., a logic sentence representing knowledge, then we only need to apply change operators that do not influence the status of the theory. In logic, every sentence can be either satisfiable, i.e., there is an interpretation making the sentence true, or contradicting, i.e., there is no such interpretation. Let us discuss the idea using the following sentence: "*It is raining, and if it is raining, then the streets are wet.*". Obviously, this sentence is satisfiable. If we assume that it is raining and the streets are wet, the sentence must be true. When adding "*If it is raining, then it is raining.*", the whole theory comprising both sentences is still satisfiable.

In case of a contradiction, we observe the same outcome. When adding "*If it is raining, then it is raining.*" to the sentence "*It is raining, and if it is raining, then the streets are wet, and the streets are not wet*", which is obviously leading to a contradiction, the resulting sentence is still not satisfiable, i.e., in contradiction. Hence, this modification has no influence on the logic characterization of the given theory. This idea can be used to come up with new test cases, i.e., theories we want to check using a theorem prover. We only need to apply modifications to a given sentences that are neutral with respect to the logic characterization.

The use of metamorphic testing in the domain of theorem prover testing is not new. Wotawa [13] introduce the use of metamorphic testing in combination with combinatorial testing [8,9] for checking that the theorem prover's computed result is not depending on the sequence of sentences added, e.g., that when adding "*it is raining*" before adding "*if it is raining, then the streets are wet.*" to the theorem prover delivers the same outcome than when adding the last sentence first. This objective is different from ours where we want to extend any logic theory such that we obtain new test cases. Using this approach, we are able to check for faults that would only be visible when making use of large logic theories, which are hard to obtain in practice. In addition, such theories can be used for other purposes like testing the performance of theorem prover implementations as a function of the size of the theory.

This paper is organized as follows: In Sect. 2, we discuss the foundations behind theorem proving focusing on propositional horn clause logic. Afterwards, we summarize our approach and introduce the underlying modification rules in Sect. 3. This is followed by a discussion regarding results obtained from an initial experimental evaluation in Sect. 4. Finally, we summarize the content of this paper.

2   Basic Foundations

To be self-contained, we briefly outline the underlying foundations behind logic and metamorphic testing. In case of logic, we restrict our view to propositional horn clause logic (PHCL). In propositional logic atomic entities are propositions that represent some information like *"The streets are wet"* that is either true or false in a particular world. In addition to propositions, we have operators like negation ($\neg$), conjunction ($\wedge$, i.e., logic *and*), disjunction ($\vee$, i.e., logic *or*), implications ($\rightarrow$), or equivalence ($\leftrightarrow$) to combine propositions for coming up with logic sentences. For example, using propositional logic, we are able to formalize English sentences like *"If it is raining, then the streets are wet"* as follows: $raining \rightarrow wet\_streets$, where $raining$ and $wet\_streets$ are propositions representing *"it is raining"* and *"the streets are wet"* respectively.

We now formally, define PHCL, where we only consider set of facts and rules. A PHCL is a tuple (P, Th) where P is a finite set of propositions, and Th a finite set of facts and rules defined as follows:

1. If $p \in P$ is element of Th, then p is a fact, i.e., a proposition that is always true.
2. If $p_1, \ldots, p_{n+1} \in P$, then any rule in Th is either of the form $p_1 \wedge \ldots \wedge p_n \rightarrow p_{n+1}$ or $p_1 \wedge \ldots \wedge p_n \rightarrow \perp$, where $\perp$ represents the contradiction, i.e., a proposition that is always false. Note that $\perp$ is not element of P.

We now formally define inference for a particular PHCL (P, Th). In particular, we want to infer a proposition in P from the theory Th. For this purpose, we use the following inference rule. If $p_1, \ldots, p_n$ are facts, i.e., $p_1, \ldots, p_n \in Th$, and $p_1 \wedge \ldots \wedge p_n \rightarrow p \in Th$ where $p \in P$ or $p \equiv \perp$, then we can infer p from the theory Th. In this case, we write $Th \vdash p$. In order to infer all possible facts, we have to apply $\vdash$ on Th, add the inferred fact to Th and continue the process until no more facts can be derived. This can be expressed using the fix-point equation $Th = Th \cup \{p | Th \vdash p, p \in P \cup \{\perp\}\}$. Note that there must be a fix-point because P is finite. This fix-point has also to be unique, because we consider all possible inferences.

In the following we call the fix-point $I(Th)$. If $\perp \in I(Th)$ we call Th to be contradictory. Otherwise, Th is satisfiable. Furthermore, we introduce a function $facts$ mapping fix-points to the set comprising all propositions or $\perp$ that can be inferred. Note that from here on, we write $Th \vdash p$ if $p \in facts(I(Th))$ for simplification.

$$\frac{x \notin P}{P \cup \{x\}, Th \cup \{x\}} \tag{1}$$

$$\frac{x \in Th}{P, Th \cup \{x \to x\}} \tag{2}$$

$$\frac{r = (p_1 \wedge \ldots \wedge p_i \wedge \ldots \wedge p_j \wedge \ldots \wedge p_n \to p_{n+1}) \in Th \wedge 1 \le i < j \le n}{P, Th \setminus \{r\} \cup \{p_1 \wedge \ldots \wedge p_j \wedge \ldots \wedge p_i \wedge \ldots \wedge p_n \to p_{n+1}\}} \tag{3}$$

$$\frac{x \in Th \wedge r = (p_1 \wedge \ldots \wedge p_n \to p_{n+1}) \in Th \wedge \forall i \in \{1, \ldots, n+1\} x \ne p_i}{P, Th \setminus \{r\} \cup \{x \wedge p_1 \wedge \ldots \wedge p_n \to p_{n+1}\}} \tag{4}$$

$$\frac{x \notin P \wedge r = (p_1 \wedge \ldots \wedge p_n \to p_{n+1}) \in Th}{P \cup \{x\}, Th \setminus \{r\} \cup \{p_1 \wedge \ldots \wedge p_n \to x, x \to p_{n+1}\}} \tag{5}$$

$$\frac{x, y \notin P \wedge r = (p_1 \wedge \ldots \wedge p_n \to p_{n+1}) \in Th \wedge 1 < k < n}{P \cup \{x, y\}, Th \setminus \{r\} \cup \left\{ \begin{array}{l} p_1 \wedge \ldots \wedge p_k \to x \\ p_{k+1} \wedge \ldots \wedge p_n \to y \\ x \wedge y \to p_{n+1} \end{array} \right\}} \tag{6}$$

Fig. 1. The modification rules for propositional theories.

Using the definition inference and the PHCL ($\{raining, wet\_streets\}$, $\{raining, raining \to wet\_streets\}$), we are able to compute the fixpoint $I = \{raining, raining \to wet\_streets, wet\_streets\}$ and the facts $\{raining, wet\_streets\}$ that can be inferred.

Note that there are many algorithms available for checking satisfiability of general theories, which is known to be NP-complete, e.g., the famous Davis-Putnam-Logemann-Loveland (DPLL) algorithm [4]. For the restricted propositional horn clause logic, it is worth mentioning Minoux's algorithm [10], which has a linear runtime.

3   Metamorphic Theorem Prover Testing

As outlined in the previous section, a theorem prover takes a logic theory like a PHCL (P, Th) and answers the question whether Th is contradictory or satisfiable, i.e., $Th \vdash \bot$ or $Th \nvdash \bot$ respectively. In order to test a theorem prover using metamorphic testing, we have to define metamorphic relations for theories. In particular, we are interested in changing the theory, e.g., adding or modifying facts or rule, such that the computed outcome, i.e., being able to derive $\bot$ or not, should not be changed.

Hence, we want to have (P', Th') obtained from (P, Th) such that $Th' \vdash \bot$ if and only if $Th \vdash \bot$. In the following, we discuss some rules modifying the set of propositions and theories, where this metamorphic relation holds.

In Fig. 1 we summarize the modification rules. Modification Rule 1 formalizes adding new facts to the theory. For this purpose a new proposition is generated, and added to P and Th. In modification rule 2 a given fact x is chosen, and a rule $x \rightarrow x$ is added. Obviously, $x \rightarrow x$ does not change the status of the theory, which is either contradiction or satisfiability. Modification rule 3 is introduced for stating that arbitrary propositions occurring left from $\rightarrow$ can be interchanged, i.e., the order of propositions on the left side of a rule does not influence inference.

Modification rule 4 introduces the case of adding a new fact to the left side of a rule. Obviously, when adding a fact, we do not change the inference abilities of a rule. A similar modification rule is 5, where we add a new proposition x and use it to separate one rule into two. Again because of construction this does not change the ability to infer p_{n+1}. The final modification rule 6 is an extension considering the separation of one rule into three rules. Because the propositions x and y are required to be new, the inference of p_{n+1} is not influenced.

It is worth noting, that the modification rules change the proposition set and the theory. Therefore, they change the set of facts to be able to be derived. But the modification rules do not change the ability to derive $\perp$.

After the definition of the metamorphic relations, we iterate to the next two steps of a metamorphic testing approach, namely test generation and test execution. Therefore, we use the algorithm MMTTP as shown in Algorithm 1. This algorithm implements our whole test generation and execution approach. The process starts with an initially empty test suite and executes the unmodified logic theory against the system under test (SUT), i.e., the theorem prover implementation. The result of this execution is then recorded and functions as the reference output we rely on later. Next, the process selects a metamorphic relation from the available set and applies it to the theory. This theory is executed and its result is compared to the result of the initial theory. In case of a divergent result, the newly created theory is stored in the test suite. Otherwise,

---

Algorithm 1. MMTTP (Ops, Th)

Require: *A set of modification operators Ops (i.e., metamorphic relations), and a logic theory Th.*
Ensure: *A test suite comprising a set of theories that are considered failing test cases.*

1: Let TS be the empty set.
2: Call TP(Th) and store the result in r.
3: **repeat**
4:     Let o be any modification operator (randomly) selected from Ops.
5:     Let $Th' = o(Th)$.
6:     Call TP(Th') and store the result in r'.
7:     **if** $r \neq r'$ **then**
8:         Add Th' to TS
9:     **end if**
10:     Let $Th = Th'$
11: **until** A stop criterion SC is fulfilled
12: **return** TS

---

this theory becomes the basis for the next iteration of the process. The process is iterated until a stop criterion SC is fulfilled.

For our experiments the defined stop criterion is a counter of the applied relations on the initial theory. After the repetitions, the process ends and provides the theories with divergent results. This algorithm is used in our experiments. In the next section, we discuss the obtain evaluation results.

4   Experimental Evaluation

In this section, we report on an initial evaluation of the proposed metamorphic testing approach for theorem provers. We evaluated the approach using two different logic theorem provers. The first prover is a propositional logic theorem prover (PLTP) (implementing the algorithm of Minoux [10]), and the second one is an assumption-based truth maintenance system (ATMS) [7]. Both implementations are using Java as their programming language.

The implementations were executed on the AdoptJDK 16.0.1+9 Hotspot JVM. All results of this study were obtained on an Apple MacBook Pro (2016) with a 2.6 GHz Intel i7 Quad-Core processor and 16 GB RAM running macOS Big Sur 11.4. For testing both theorem provers we used five different base test cases of varying complexities. We used an implementation of the **MMTTP** algorithm and the metamorphic relations described previously for the initial experimental evaluation. As a stop criterion, we used 1,000 as the maximum number of iterations.

For the two theorem provers, we obtained the following *results* of metamorphic testing:

- Both theorem prover implementations did not respond unexpectedly. Hence, we were not able to generate failing test cases in this study.
- The only limitation, we faced when carrying out the evaluation, was a stack overflow that was caused by the recursive nature of the implementations.

Hence, the experimental evaluation showed that the presented metamorphic testing approach can be applied to theorem prover testing. The reason for not being able to detect faults in the two implementations may be due to the simplicity of the implementations. However, we also showed that metamorphic testing in could find runtime limitations in the theorem provers. Hence, metamorphic testing of theorem provers might be used for testing the performance and robustness.

5   Conclusions

In this paper, we addressed the topic of testing logic theorem provers. For this purpose, we introduced a metamorphic testing approach that allows generating modifications of logic sentences that do not change the logic state of the sentence to be passed to the theorem prover. Furthermore, we discussed the outcome of an initial experimental evaluation showing the applicability of metamorphic testing for theorem provers. Future research will include extending the study to cover other more complex theorem provers and constraint solvers.

References

1. Chen, T., Cheung, S., Yiu, S.: Metamorphic Testing: A New Approach for Generating Next Test Cases (1998)
2. Chen, T., Feng, J., Tse, T.: Metamorphic testing of programs on partial differential equations: a case study. In: Proceedings of the 26th Annual International Computer Software and Applications Conference (COMPSAC 2002), pp. 327–333. IEEE Computer Society, Los Alamitos, CA (2002)
3. Christopher S. Gray, Roxane Koitz, S.P., Wotawa, F.: An abductive diagnosis and modeling concept for wind power plants. In: 9th IFAC Symposium on Fault Detection, Supervision and Safety of Technical Processes (2015)
4. Davis, M., Logemann, G., Loveland, D.: A machine program for theorem-proving. Commun. ACM **5**(7), 394–397 (1962). https://doi.org/10.1145/368273.368557
5. Felfernig, A., Friedrich, G., Jannach, D., Zanker, M.: An integrated environment for the development of knowledge-based recommender applications. Int. J. Electr. Commer. (IJEC) **11**(2), 11–34 (2006)
6. Felfernig, A., Friedrich, G., Jannach, D., Stumptner, M.: An integrated development environment for the design and maintenance of large configuration knowledge bases. In: Proceedings Artificial Intelligence in Design. Kluwer Academic Publishers, Worcester MA (2000)
7. de Kleer, J.: An assumption-based TMS. Artif. Intell. **28**, 127–162 (1986)
8. Kuhn, D.R., Bryce, R., Duan, F., Ghandehari, L.S., Lei, Y., Kacker, R.N.: Combinatorial testing: theory and practice. In: Advances in Computers, vol. 99, pp. 1–66 (2015)
9. Kuhn, D., Kacker, R., Lei, Y.: Introduction to Combinatorial Testing. Chapman & Hall/CRC Innovations in Software Engineering and Software Development Series, Taylor & Francis (2013)
10. Minoux, M.: LTUR: a simplified linear-time unit resolution algorithm for horn formulae and computer implementation. Inf. Process. Lett. **29**, 1–12 (1988)
11. Plant, R.T.: Expert system development and testing: a knowledge engineer's perspective. J. Syst. Softw. **19**(2), 141–146 (1992)
12. Reiter, R.: A theory of diagnosis from first principles. Artif. Intell. **32**(1), 57–95 (1987)
13. Wotawa, F.: Combining combinatorial testing and metamorphic testing for testing a logic-based non-monotonic reasoning system. In: Proceedings of the International Workshop on Combinatorial Testing (IWCT) (2018)

AI-based Techniques

Creation of Human-friendly Videos for Debugging Automated GUI-Tests

Jianwei Shi[✉][iD] and Kurt Schneider[iD]

Software Engineering, Leibniz University Hannover, 30167 Hannover, Germany
{jianwei.shi,kurt.schneider}@inf.uni-hannover.de

Abstract. Test automation can save time and identify failed test cases instantly. However, these test cases run like a robot over Graphical User Interface (GUI). Hence, it is difficult for test engineers to locate defects precisely and quickly by using test automation software.

The following disadvantages of robot-like replay are observed in automated GUI-tests: (1) The mouse-pointer does not move continually; (2) Interactions of certain GUI elements are not triggered; (3) The user view changes abruptly without smooth transition. All this may distract human attention and make debugging a time-consuming task.

For tackling this problem, this paper proposes to create human-friendly videos for replaying automated tests. In these videos, the GUI elements in interaction are highlighted. Our tool provides an intuitive GUI to replay a video step by step. We believe that this automated video creation and playback technique can make defect identification easier than manual replay of original test cases.

Keywords: Video · GUI test · Debugging

1 Introduction

Testing is vital for successful software projects. Software testing has been discussed as a software engineering principle since the NATO Science Conference [9]. Tests detect defects before customers find them. In failed tests, the identification and removal of faults reduce the risk of low customer acceptance.

In recent years, GUI testing and test automation have become popular topics in the academy and industry. According to a literature review of Banerjee et al. [1], three articles about GUI Testing have been published every three years on average from 2003 to 2011. Furthermore, Kasurinen et al. [3] have interviewed organisations and concluded that test automation was most widely used in quality control and quality assurance.

However, there have been challenges in GUI testing. Back to 1997, a workshop on software testing was organised by Kaner [2]. He has summarised that (1) one reason for failures of automation roll-out plan is using capture/playback for creating test cases; (2) straight replay of test cases can only cover a low range

© IFIP International Federation for Information Processing 2022
Published by Springer Nature Switzerland AG 2022
D. Clark et al. (Eds.): ICTSS 2021, LNCS 13045, pp. 141–147, 2022.
https://doi.org/10.1007/978-3-031-04673-5_11

of defects; (3) the ability of logging the test execution is needed. For (3), there are similar opinions in the new century. Memon [4] has suggested to generate expected output which includes screen snapshots, window positions and titles. In a bug reporting context, Zimmermann et al. [12] have claimed that steps to reproduce errors are important.

Sadly, these challenges are still not completely solved, to our best knowledge. In our previous work [10,11], we have proposed video as a documentation for logging automated GUI tests. This paper updates our approach in video creation and makes contribution for replay.

The structure of this paper is as follows. Technical disadvantages in replay are investigated in state-of-the-art test automation tools in Sect. 2. The next section lists relevant literature for advanced capture and replay. Section 4 proposes our approach of video creation and replay techniques. The last section concludes and ends with outlook.

2   Investigation of Robot-Like Replay

In order to investigate replay behaviours of automated GUI-Test, test cases are designed and run on a web application SynchroPC. It is a platform for reviewing papers in context of an online Program Committee meeting. Two test cases are designed: select timezone and create agenda.

For the proposed test cases, two test automation tools (Selenium and UiPath) are chosen. Selenium is an open source software for test automation in browsers. We chose two variants for investigation: Selenium IDE[1] and Selenium WebDriver[2]. UiPath is a Robotic Process Automation (RPA) software suite. RPA means that the robot can interact with digital systems just as human being. According to reports for RPA[3], UiPath is one of the leading software in the industry. The product suite contains Task Capture, Studio, Orchestrator, etc. For our context, UiPath Studio[4] is investigated, which can automate interactions with browser.

Test scripts are generated by recording test steps, according to the descriptions of test cases. After that, test scripts are adapted on chosen test automation tools.

The following three aspects have been observed by executing test cases: (1) If the mouse pointer moves continually; (2) If interaction of a drop down menu is shown; (3) If the view is continually changed during test run. Table 1 gives a summary of results. We describe and discuss results for aspects 1 and 3 in detail.

Aspect 1: In test automation software, the position of the mouse-pointer can be set, e.g., by using function moveToElement in Selenium. In the real test case development, this extra setting does not have to be implemented for finding

---

[1] Version 3.17.0, as Google Chrome extension.

[2] Version 3.141.0, as pip package.

[3] Reports are available upon request on https://www.uipath.com/resources/automa tion-analyst-reports, last accessed 06-Jan-2021.

[4] Version 2020.10.2: Enterprise Trial License, as Windows application.

Table 1. Results for replay in test automation tools

	Selenium IDE	Selenium WebDriver	UiPath Studio
(1) continuation of mouse movement	No	No	Partly
(2) drop-down interaction	No	Yes	Yes
(3) continuation of view changes	No	No	No

faults. Hence, we have investigated aspect 1 without explicitly setting mouse position. On UiPath Studio, mouse-pointer was partly moved in test run, but it is not exactly located on the triggered GUI element. Without continuous mouse movement, the triggered GUI element may be difficult to find in replay.

Aspect 3: It is observed that the user view changes suddenly without smooth transaction in test runs. This phenomena can be observed clearly by replaying test case 2. In test case 2, there are three subsequent actions: (1) Selecting papers from paper list, (2) Entering values in enter fields and (3) Clicking a button. All these actions are run on a web page, which contains a long paper list. The button in action 3 is not visible on the first view and can be reached by scrolling down. In automated test run, the view was firstly on the top part of the page and then suddenly moved to position where the button is very near to the bottom edge of the visible web page. The observed abrupt view change cannot tell test engineers necessary context information, i.e., the selected papers in test case 2.

3   Related Work

To solve the mentioned issues in testing, possible solutions using videos have been proposed. For finding causes of failures in test script, our previous work [10] provides a solution: video as a documentation for GUI tests. An approach for creating videos based on test execution has been introduced. During execution of a test case, actions were recorded only if there was change in visible screen, which is called output-driven screen capturing. In parallel, a matching relationship between test code and action was created. This capturing method requires less memory resource over traditional screen capturing method. Lastly, a side-by-side viewer was used to replay the actions and corresponding line in test code. In this work [10], we have concluded that tailored video-documentation helps to debug GUI tests by applying this approach in a company and conducting a subsequent survey.

Similar to video-medium for replaying test cases, Nass et al. [8] have defined Augmented Testing (AT) as "testing the System Under Test (SUT) through an Augmented GUI, which contains superimposed information on top of the SUT GUI." Text-boxes and rectangles have been augmented on the real GUI. These additional information can give hints for current action (Superimposing) and suggestions for next action (Observing), which are two core concepts of AT.

In an earlier paper from Nass et al. [7], they have explained technical details about this AT tool. Test actions are firstly conducted by tester and captured. By replaying test sessions, the tool highlights possible next actions. These next actions can be automatically triggered or selected from the tester. Comments, such as textual information, can be added by the tester any time to make test step more understandable.

In comparison with the tool from Nass et al. [7], our work has the following novelties: (1) Our tool can capture test by replaying already existing test cases, without extra human labour; (2) While Nass et al. focus on designing and capturing GUI tests, we will investigate how to replay GUI tests for efficient debugging; (3) In AT, human interactions (e.g., choose manual or automatic mode, add comment) are required [7]. Our replay tool provides simpler interaction possibilities: go to next or previous action, move to a certain action, play, and pause. These interactions are intuitive, just as the ones in a video replay tool.

4   Approach

We have updated our tool ScreenTracer, which has been introduced in our previous work [10]. We have enhanced video creation and replay techniques. The workflow is illustrated in Fig. 1 as an UML activity diagram. In comparison with the workflow in our previous versions of ScreenTracer [11], we have used asynchronous programming to ensure live capturing and added a mechanism to make replay human-friendly.

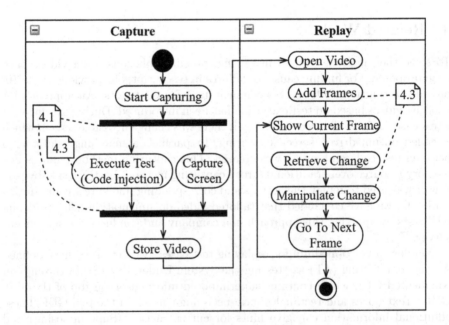

Fig. 1. The novel workflow in the new version of ScreenTracer

Our previous work [11] found some screen changes were not exactly synchronised with code tracing. This is in line with our current observation by using the former `ScreenTracer`: screen was not captured in time when a change happened. The reason of this delay is that capturing and handling of screen change were performed in strict sequence. To solve this problem, we have used asynchronous programming [6] for capturing screen and executing test in this work.

4.1 Asynchronous Screen Capturing and Test Execution

Firstly, screen capturing task and handling of screen change are run asynchronously, hence a screen change can be captured immediately.

Secondly, we execute test asynchronously in the background. The test was triggered via .Net reflection API. Instead of that, we have created a background thread, i.e., BackgroundWorker [5], for running a test project in the background after screen capturing starts. Using BackgroundWorker, the test automation executes asynchronously in a separate thread, while the screen capture thread is running. These two threads are scheduled by CPU in the same time period. For the perspective of human, screen capturing and test execution run in parallel (see the memo "4.1" in Fig. 1).

After test ends, the captured contents and returned test result (i.e., passed, failed) are stored in a special video file, which can be replayed by `ScreenTracer Viewer`.

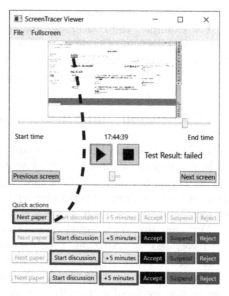

Fig. 2. ScreenTracer viewer and screenshots

4.2 Replay with Highlight

As investigated in Sect. 2, the mouse pointer is not exactly positioned at the GUI element where the interaction is triggered. This problem can be partly solved by highlighting GUI elements, which is realised in our application, as Fig. 2 shows.

We have used two ways for highlighting. The first way is to add JavaScript to test code, so the GUI element in interaction is highlighted in test execution: a red border is added around it. Currently, the JavaScript code is manually added. We plan to conduct automatic code injection in the future. The second way is to manipulate captured screen change. Changes from one video frame to the next one are highlighted. A red rectangle is drawn around the screen change. Tiny or big changes are filtered out and not highlighted, because they are view changes or task bar changes. However, we have observed that there still exist highlights for view changes in real test cases. It is difficult to filter out all changes, which are not relevant for GUI interaction. Hence, we prefer the first approach because the GUI elements can be highlighted precisely.

Highlights can help test engineers to check which GUI element is triggered or examined at a certain time. For example, Fig. 2 (enlarged pictures under GUI) shows highlights chronologically from top to bottom. This test case checks if certain button is clickable or not: after "Next paper" is clicked, "Next paper" should be not clickable, "Start discussion" should be clickable, "+5 min", "Accept", and "Reject" should be not clickable. The test ended by highlighting "+5 min" button with result failed (shown on the right bottom on GUI). A test engineer could then recognise the defect quickly from this information.

4.3   Concept: Code Injection and Frame Manipulation

Based on two approaches of highlighting, a concept for adding human-friendly information to video is proposed, as two "4.3" memos in Fig. 1 show. In capture phase, code injection can be used to adjust behaviours in test execution directly. To adjust behaviours, functions (e.g., JavaScript, Selenium API) are injected into the test code. In replay phase, video frames can be manipulated. Frames can be added, and the changes from one frame to the next one can be modified.

For example, the continuous mouse movement could be simulated in two steps: (1) Injection of code using Selenium API which controls the position of the mouse pointer; (2) Adding continuous frames between two captured frames where the mouse pointer is on different positions.

5   Conclusion and Future Work

Test automation has been widely applied, but there are still challenges that make debugging difficult. We have investigated and listed these challenges in this paper. Trying to overcome these challenges, we updated our tool `ScreenTracer`. This tool creates and replays video with highlights as a documentation for automated GUI test execution.

Our contribution to previous work [11] is a minor but important increment. We have used asynchronous programming to fix capture delay issue (cf. [11]). Moreover, we have tried two approaches to highlight GUI elements in video: JavaScript code injection in capture and frame manipulation in replay. Both approaches are feasible, and the concept can be used in further development to make video more human-friendly. A user study will be conducted to check if the video with additional information helps to debug tests faster than manual replay.

In summary, to help test engineers with debugging, we have proposed an easy video creation method for documenting automated GUI-tests and a replay concept. By creating human-friendly videos in GUI-test automation, debugging will become more efficient.

Acknowledgement. Thank Ms. Banik and Mr. Fahrmeier for implementing SynchroPC. Thank Mr. Holzmann for implementing ScreenTracer in 2011. Thank anonymous reviewers, Ms. Vercelli, Mr. Cai, and Mr. Kortum for their help and comments.

References

1. Banerjee, I., Nguyen, B., Garousi, V., Memon, A.: Graphical user interface (GUI) testing: systematic mapping and repository. Inf. Softw. Technol. **55**(10), 1679–1694 (2013). https://doi.org/10.1016/j.infsof.2013.03.004
2. Kaner, C.: Improving the Maintainability of Automated Test Suites (1997). http://www.kaner.com/pdfs/autosqa.pdf
3. Kasurinen, J., Taipale, O., Smolander, K.: Software test automation in practice: empirical observations. Adv. Softw. Eng. (2010). https://doi.org/10.1155/2010/620836
4. Memon, A.M.: GUI testing: pitfalls and process. Computer **35**(8), 87–88 (2002). https://doi.org/10.1109/MC.2002.1023795
5. Microsoft: Asynchronous programming with async and await (2020). https://docs.microsoft.com/en-us/dotnet/csharp/programming-guide/concepts/async/. Accessed 20 Aug 2021
6. Microsoft: BackgroundWorker Class (2021). https://docs.microsoft.com/en-us/dotnet/api/system.componentmodel.backgroundworker?view=netframework-4.5. Accessed 20 Aug 2021
7. Nass, M., Alegroth, E., Feldt, R.: Augmented testing: industry feedback to shape a new testing technology. In: 2019 IEEE International Conference on Software Testing, Verification and Validation Workshops (ICSTW), pp. 176–183. IEEE, April 2019. https://doi.org/10.1109/ICSTW.2019.00048
8. Nass, M., Alégroth, E., Feldt, R.: On the industrial applicability of augmented testing: an empirical study. In: 2020 IEEE International Conference on Software Testing, Verification and Validation Workshops (ICSTW), pp. 364–371 (2020). https://doi.org/10.1109/ICSTW50294.2020.00065
9. Naur, P., Randell, B.: NATO Software Engineering Conference 1968. Technical Report, Scientific Affairs Division NATO, January 1969. http://homepages.cs.ncl.ac.uk/brian.randell/NATO/nato1968.PDF
10. Pham, R., Holzmann, H., Schneider, K., Brüggemann, C.: Beyond plain video recording of GUI tests: linking test case instructions with visual response documentation. In: 2012 7th International Workshop on Automation of Software Test (AST), pp. 103–109. IEEE, Zurich, Switzerland, June 2012. https://doi.org/10.1109/IWAST.2012.6228977
11. Pham, R., Holzmann, H., Schneider, K., Brüggemann, C.: Tailoring video recording to support efficient GUI testing and debugging. Softw. Qual. J. **22**(2), 273–292 (2013). https://doi.org/10.1007/s11219-013-9206-2
12. Zimmermann, T., Premraj, R., Bettenburg, N., Just, S., Schroter, A., Weiss, C.: What makes a good bug report? IEEE Trans. Softw. Eng. **36**(5), 618–643 (2010). https://doi.org/10.1109/TSE.2010.63

Combining Holistic Source Code Representation with Siamese Neural Networks for Detecting Code Clones

Smit Patel[1]([⊠])[iD] and Roopak Sinha[2][iD]

[1] Indian Institute of Technology Indore, Indore, India
smitpatel2360@gmail.com
[2] IT & Software Engineering, Auckland University of Technology,
Auckland, New Zealand
rsinha@aut.ac.nz

Abstract. Code clones can be defined as two identical pieces of code having the same or similar functionality. Code clone detection is critical to improve and sustain code quality. Current methods are unable to extract semantic and syntactic features and classify code bases satisfactorily. We propose a novel two-stage machine-learning approach towards code clone detection. Firstly, multiple intermediate representations of source code are extracted and combined to generate a holistic embedding based on a recently proposed technique. Next, we use these embeddings to train an Intermediate Merge Siamese Neural Network to detect functional code clones. Siamese Neural Networks are a state-of-the-art machine learning architecture particularly suited to code clone detection. This novel combination allows for learning subtle syntactic and semantic features and identifying previously undetectable similarities. Our solution shows a significant improvement in code clone detection, as shown by experimental evaluation over the OJClone C++ dataset.

Keywords: Functional code clones · Abstract Syntax Tree (AST) · Control Flow Graph (CFG) · Deep learning · Siamese Neural Network

1 Introduction

There is increasing interest in detecting duplicate code. Duplicate code or *code clones* are quite prevalent in software engineering, since engineers often encounter situations where a snippet of code has to be replicated and used in some other part of the program. They can either wrap the code to a module or duplicate the code snippet directly [10]. However, due to time pressure, developers often just create code duplicates.

Even though many code clones are potentially harmless [5], they can affect software maintainability [22] and increase bug propagation [9]. Code duplication increases software maintenance costs that already account for a majority of expenditure in software development [13]. Manual code clone detection is impractical, and so automatic code clone detection has become a widely studied problem [23].

© IFIP International Federation for Information Processing 2022
Published by Springer Nature Switzerland AG 2022
D. Clark et al. (Eds.): ICTSS 2021, LNCS 13045, pp. 148–159, 2022.
https://doi.org/10.1007/978-3-031-04673-5_12

Code clones are segregated into 4 types according to the kind and level of syntactic and/or semantic similarity [24]. Type 1 or *exact clones* are identical copies except for whitespaces, blanks, and comments. Type 2 *renamed clones* are syntactically similar except that they may use different names of variables, types, literals, and functions. Type 3 *gapped clones* are similar but with modifications such as added or removed statements, and the use of different identifiers, literals, types, whitespaces, layouts, and comments. Types 1–3 imply textual/syntactic similarity. Finally, type 4 *semantic clones* are functionally similar, without being syntactically similar. An example of type 4 clones is a pair of for and while loops that have the same functionality but use different loop structures [24].

In this paper, we focus on two key problems in using machine learning to detect code clones, represented by the following research questions:

RQ1: Which techniques are best suited for extracting syntactic and semantic features from source code for training classifiers for code clone detection?

RQ2: Which existing Artificial Neural Network types are well-suited to classify code clones from source code representations selected in answering RQ1?

For RQ1, we reviewed existing code representation methods, categorised as string-based, token-based, syntax-based and semantics-based. The first two are useful only for detecting type 1 and type 2 (renamed) clones. Syntax based approaches use structures like suffix tree [12] or, predominantly, Abstract Syntax Tree (AST) for syntactic feature extraction [4]. ASTs convey the structure of the source code and capture the syntax of every program statement. On the other hand, semantics-based approaches use Program Dependency Graph (PDG) [7] or Control Flow Graph (CFG) [14]. A PDG represents control and data dependencies in a program. PDG is computationally expensive to compute and so often a more efficient semantic representation like CFG is considered. Unfortunately, neither ASTs or PDGs can individually capture all syntactic and semantic features of code. A few hybrid approaches exist that combine AST and CFG representations, but these have been shown to have limitations like the inability to consider inter-code dependencies like in Fig. 1. Inter-function calls have become increasingly important since software engineers constantly update their code to adopt reusability and follow best practices.

For RQ2, we surveyed existing literature to compare existing classifiers for code clone detection [23]. Using distance-based metrics like Cosine Similarity is prone to errors as it requires manually reading vector representations of source code and then choosing threshold values [20]. Bayesian Networks [21] fail to determine the relative importance of various source code features, thereby producing biased or skewed results. Deep Learning overcomes this limitation by updating weights at every step through backpropagation. Nonetheless, challenges like overfitting, vanishing gradient, etc., have also restricted the accuracy of deep learning methods. *Siamese Neural Networks* (SNNs) are a variation of ANN's that use the same weights while working in tandem on two different input vectors to compute comparable output vectors. They have also proved highly effective in capturing similarity between code pairs [17,30] and other applications like

```
                                      int fib (int n)
                                      {
                                        int a=0, b =1;
  int fib (int n)                       if(n==0){ return a;}
  {                                     return calc(a, b, n);
    int a=0, b =1, c;                 }
    if(n==0){ return a;}              int calc(int a, int b, int n
    for(int i=1; i<n; i++)            {
    {                                   for(int i=1; i<n; i++)
      c = a+b;                          {
      a = b;                              int c = a+b;
      b = c;                              a = b;
    }                                     b = c;
    return b;                           }
  }                                     return b;
                                      }
```

(a) Without inter-functional calls   (b) With inter-functional calls

Fig. 1. Code Clones (Nth Fibonacci number) having different functionalities

recognising handwritten checks [11] and face recognition [17]. Xie et al. [30] used Word2vec [3] to represent code and SNNs for calculating code similarity. Mahajan et al. [16] used AST and SNNs for the same purpose. We propose and prototype a solution combining the representation approach in [4] and SNNs (Sect. 2). We evaluated this prototype to show that this novel combination significantly outperforms several existing approaches, including other SNN-based solutions like [30] (Sect. 3). The primary contributions of our research are:

1. A novel conceptual design of our solution combining the representation approach from [4] and Intermediate-Merge Fusional Siamese Neural Networks and its prototype implementation.
2. Experimental validation, including a quantitative comparison between the proposed approach and other Siamese architecture models as well as a no-Siamese model using the OJClone dataset [18].

2   Conceptual Design

The overall solution includes two primary components: *code representation* and *duplicate code detection*. Our entire work has been made publicly available for future reference work.[1]

2.1   Code Representation

Figure 2 shows the conversion of pairs of source methods (step 1) into representations used to train the duplicate code detection component (step 5) through intermediate steps 2–4. This method is adopted from [4].

---

[1] All implementation artefacts are available from https://github.com/smit25/Code-Clone-Detection-Using-Intermediate-Merge-Siamese-Network.

Initially, in step 1, the functionality of the source code is identified by extracting its call graph and analysing the relevant caller-callee relationships. The call graph represents the calling relationships between functions in the code. Each node is a function and every edge (a, b) indicates that function **a** (caller) calls function **b** (callee). Every statement in the entire dataset is marked with a globally unique identifier, regarded as the call identifier. The caller-callee relationship is expressed as a triplet ⟨`callerId, statementid, calleeId`⟩. The `callerId` and `calleeId` are the statement identifiers of the caller and the callee methods, respectively. `statementId` represents the statement from id where the call to the callee function is made. Using the call graph expression as a reference, all connected methods are regarded and procured as a functionality. If a function does not call any other function, it is regarded as a single standalone functionality.

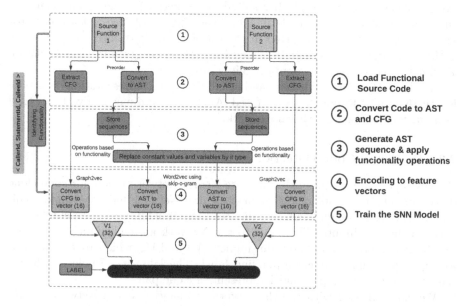

Fig. 2. Capturing syntactic and semantic information in source method pairs

In step 2, we extract comprehensive syntactic and semantic information from the methods in the form of AST and CFG, respectively. The Abstract Syntax Tree representation of the source code snippet is generated. A traversal of the tree in preorder is performed and the corresponding elements in each node are stored in a identifier sequence.

$$\texttt{Identifier Sequence} = [node_1, node_2, node_3, ..., node_n]$$

This sequence captures symbols and variable names (identifiers), which are preprocessed to eliminate distortion due to differing variable names; constants and variables are replaced by their data types. The sequences of all ASTs in the dataset are acquired and the sequences capturing function calls are inserted in a set to represent a singular functionality (step 3).

The source code is also transformed into its CFG representation which holds comprehensive semantic information. Connection rules for functionalities have been established in [4] corresponding to the structure of caller-callee relationship. Since the representations obtained from step 2 and 3 have different structures, we apply word embedding and graph embedding techniques to obtain fixed-length vectors in step 4.

We use Word2vec with skip-o-gram [3] to encode the normalised sequences of syntactic features into vectors. Word2vec uses a corpus of its training model, which is obtained by putting together all sequence identifiers. A graph embedding technique called Graph2vec [19] has been used to encode the CFG of every method into feature vector. Graph2vec model generates vectors that reflect the overall structure of the graph. It resulted in the best F1 value [4] and hence, is the most suitable choice. For both Word2vec and Graph2vec, a feature vector length of 16 is used. As reported in [4], the F1 scores attained stability when both the feature vectors had 16 dimensions. Moreover, training the model on 16-dimensional vector is computationally optimal.

Lastly, in step 5 the syntactic and semantic vector representation vectors of length 16 obtained from step 4 are fused. A 32 (16+16) dimension vector is used as input for the Siamese Neural Network.

2.2   Duplicate Code Detection

We developed and prototyped a Siamese Neural Network model for code clone detection. The two arms of the Siamese Neural Network have the same architecture and share weights, which enhances their capability to learn similarities between the two inputs. The input to the Network are embeddings of dimension length 32 (16+16) of two code snippets, $V1$ and $V2$, which are be classified as duplicates, and their corresponding label. The label is a Boolean value; 0 represents a non-clone pair and 1 represents a clone pair.

We experimented with the three types of Siamese Neural Network (SNN) architectures as shown in Fig. 3 for duplicate code detection. Our choices for various operations in the models are currently supported empirically by experimentation. An early-merge SNN has an architecture that is very similar to a Deep Neural Network having CNN [2]. We use a No-Siamese network to represent early merge SNN. The input vectors $V1$ and $V2$ from Fig. 2 were concatenated and fed into a No-Siamese model with the same layers. This setup uses Cross-Entropy Loss function for updating the weights of the model.

In late-merge, the vectors $V1$ and $V2$ are processed independently by the two arms of the SNN that produce distinct outputs $O1$ and $O2$, respectively. We apply Contrastive loss function takes $V1$ and $V2$ as input and equates the Euclidean distance between them if the code pairs are clones. Otherwise, it behaves like the Hinge Loss Function.

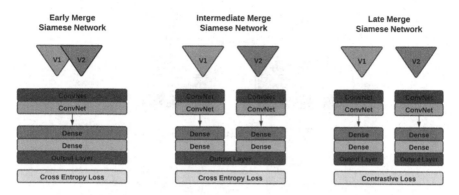

Fig. 3. Different types of Siamese architectures

As discussed later in Sect. 3, we achieved the best performance from an intermediate-merge SNN, illustrated in Sect. 4 and described in detail in subsequent paragraphs. The two inputs are given separately to the two identical arms of the SNN. Each arms consists of two linked networks: **ConvNet** and **Dense**. The arms share the same architectures and weights up until the penultimate layer in **Dense**. The absolute difference of the two internal vectors is calculated and then fed to the final output layer. A difference approach performed better than a summation approach empirically. Since the output is a single vector, this architecture also uses Cross-Entropy Loss for training.

ConvNet comprises Convolutional Neural Network (CNN) and Max Pooling layers. CNNs have relatively higher feature compatibility compared to alternatives like Recurrent Neural Networks (RNNs). Moreover, CNNs consider the local coherence in the input [1] while RNNs process input data sequentially. Detecting type 4 functional code clones requires considering the coherent spatial relationship between statements, which CNNs provide. We trained an architecture with Max Pooling and one without Max Pooling on 10 epochs, while retaining all other hyperparameters. The architecture with Max Pooling performed better, especially for extracting sharp features and providing translation invariance to the internal representation.

Choosing the correct activation function was also crucial. We trained our model using three widely-used activation functions, `Tanh`, `ReLU` (Rectified Linear Unit) and `Leaky-ReLU`, while keeping rest of the configuration the same. The results concluded that ReLU performs better than Leaky-ReLU and Tanh. ReLU's gradient does not get saturated, and therefore the model does not suffer from vanishing gradient. Also, this property accelerates the convergence gradient descent as compared to Tanh [15] and induces regularisation. Compared to Leaky-ReLU, ReLU performs better in our model due to the presence of sparse activations. Leaky-ReLU and Tanh have comparable performances on our model (Fig. 4).

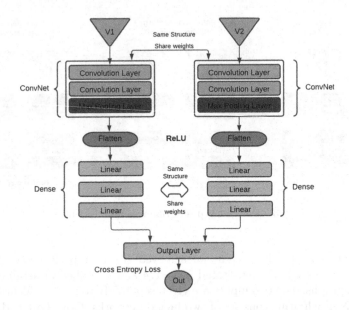

Fig. 4. Duplicate code detection configured using an Intermediate-Merge SNN

Dense receives the flattened output generated by **ConvNet**. All the parameters of the model are optimized. For applying the model to detect code twins, the source code snippets should be preprocessed, converted to embeddings and fed into the model for classification. An output of 1 denotes clones and 0 denotes non-clones.

3   Experimental Evaluation

We benchmarked our solution over the real-world OJClone dataset. OJClone contains answers to a set of problems in a prominent online programming judge. Since different entries submitted by students execute the same logic, we consider all the codes for a problem statement as functional clones. We chose 15 problems from the dataset, each with 100 C++ source code files.

300201 code clone pairs were generated and divided equally into 150100 clone pairs and 150101 non-clone pairs using undersampling. We conducted experiments with 10 epochs to choose the best performing *train-validation-test* split for our approach. A 70-20-10 split exhibited overfitting [6], which affected the trained model's generalizing capability. Therefore we settled on 70-15-15 configuration.

The architecture of an arm is divided into two networks, **ConvNet** and **Dense**. **ConvNet** has two convolution layers with 32 and 64 kernels, respectively, and a Max-Pooling layer of size 2. We experimented with various kernel sizes and found 3 to be the optimal size for our model. The input representation is flattened and then fed to the **Dense** network with 3 hidden layers with dimensions 512, 256, 128 and an output layer. This network remained unchanged while we compared the three SNN types. We use Adam Optimizer (learning rate of 0.0001) and a batch size of 100 for the dataset. We notice saturation during training at around 25 iterations; hence we fix the number of epochs to 30 and train the model on a Tesla K80 GPU.

Table 1. Comparing our solution for different SNN configurations

SNN type	Precision	Recall	F1 score
No Siamese	0.959	0.852	0.901
Intermediate-Merge	0.902	0.933	0.917
Late-Merge	0.437	0.831	0.595

Table 1 shows the Precision (P), Recall (R) and (F1) scores for comparing the three SNN types for clone detection.

It can be observed that Intermediate Merge Siamese Network is the best performing model with R and P scores of 0.933 and 0.902, respectively. We believe this is because combining at an intermediate position enables the model to capture patch-level variability and allows harnessing the capability of Cross-Entropy Loss function. The Early-Merge or No Siamese architecture exhibits results close to Intermediate-Merge SNN whereas Late-Merge SNN performs poorly on the dataset with P and R scores 0.437 and 0.831, respectively.

We compare our results with several prominent approaches that have been tested on the OJClone dataset. The work in [27] proposes a few baselines for comparison. An AST based approach, Deckard [8], uses Euclidean distance for detecting similarity. DLC [29] is a deep-learning approach where code is converted into defined binary trees, and recursive neural networks are used to represent them. SourcererCC [25] is a token-based clone detector for large codebases. We also compare our model with CDLH [27] and CDPU [28]. CDLH is a deep feature learning framework that detects duplicates by formulating them as supervised learning to hash problem. CDPU is an unsupervised learning approach that formulates code clone detection as Positive-Unlabeled (PU) learning problem.

Table 2 shows a comparison of our approach (last row) with several existing code clone detection approaches. The existing approaches include other SNN-based approaches and employ a variety of encoding techniques. Our approach outperforms most existing approaches that have been benchmarked on the OJClone dataset. Our approach also provides a significant improvement over other SNN-based methods such as [30]. The gains in our approach can be explained through the holistic encoding of source code (Sect. 2.1) and a carefully configured Intermediate-Merge SNN for classification (Sect. 2.2).

The deep fusion approach presented in [4] shows slightly better performance than our approach on the OJClone dataset. We carried out a deeper qualitative comparison between our approach and the deep fusion approach to investigate

Table 2. Comparison of various approaches (SNN and non-SNN) benchmarked over the OJClone dataset

Model	Source	Precision	Recall	F1 score
Word2vec	[30]	0.79	0.42	0.55
Code2vec	[30]	0.69	0.56	0.62
N-gram	[30]	0.71	0.59	0.63
WICE-SNN	[30]	0.67	0.83	0.74
Deckard	[8]	0.99	0.05	0.10
DLC	[29]	0.71	0.00	0.00
SourcererCC	[25]	0.07	0.74	0.14
CDLH	[27]	0.47	0.73	0.57
CDPU	[28]	0.19	0.17	0.18
Deep fusion model	[4]	0.97	0.95	0.96
Our approach	–	**0.90**	**0.93**	**0.92**

this. It is important to note that our encoding technique is identical to the method proposed in [4], indicating that the difference in performance comes from the classification phase. Our SNN model is significantly more efficient in terms of the number of epochs used for training. Our model required only 30 epochs to train, while the deep fusion network used in [4] required 10000 epochs to train. In other words, our model achieves very similar performance while requiring only 0.3% of epochs. In terms of time, our model required 337 s while the deep fusion network in [4] took 8043 s, indicating that our approach exhibits a speedup of 23.87. Figure 5 shows that our model approaches saturation with 30 epochs. Another probable reason for the lower performance of our approach can be the lack of pre-training parameter tuning, which remains an interesting future direction for our research.

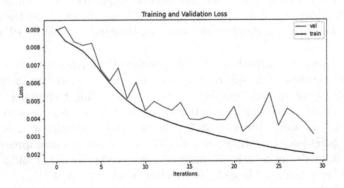

Fig. 5. Train-validation loss plot for Intermediate-Merge SNN

As evident in Table 3, our model performs better in capturing hidden features and predicting similarity between code snippets than other machine learning techniques. LSTM and Bi-LSTM networks have much better recall, but they have poor precision, and consequently, an overall lower F1 score.

Table 3. Comparison with standard ML techniques

Model	Precision	Recall	F1 score
SVM	0.62	0.81	0.70
Logistic regression	0.66	0.71	0.68
LSTM	0.19	0.95	0.31
Bi-LSTM	0.68	0.97	0.32
Our approach	**0.90**	**0.93**	**0.92**

4 Conclusions, Limitations and Future Work

We presented an approach that first encodes syntactic and semantic information from source code using a recently published approach [4] and then employs Siamese Neural Networks to identify functional code clones. We have evaluated our approach on popular C++ solutions from the OJClone dataset. The evaluation metrics indicate that this approach can even detect Type-3 and Type-4 clones with great accuracy. A prototype of our solution shows a significant improvement over existing methods, highlighting the benefits of this novel combination.

A key limitation of this work is using a single benchmark (OJClone) and exploring only a restricted number of SNN configurations. We have not incorporated other datasets such as BigCloneBench in our model. Moreover, we do not tune model parameters before training which may result in a local optimum [26] and affect overall performance.

Future directions include evaluating this solution over other benchmarks such as BigCloneBench to incorporate Java and envisioning modifications in the proposed model. Applying the transfer-learning technique and fine-tuning the parameters for detecting code clones remains a viable future direction.

References

1. Albawi, S., Mohammed, T.A., Al-Zawi, S.: Understanding of a convolutional neural network. In: 2017 International Conference on Engineering and Technology (ICET), pp. 1–6. IEEE (2017)
2. Chicco, D.: Siamese neural networks: an overview. In: Cartwright, H. (ed.) Artificial Neural Networks. MMB, vol. 2190, pp. 73–94. Springer, New York (2021). https://doi.org/10.1007/978-1-0716-0826-5_3
3. Church, K.W.: Word2Vec. Nat. Lang. Eng. **23**(1), 155–162 (2017)

4. Fang, C., Liu, Z., Shi, Y., Huang, J., Shi, Q.: Functional code clone detection with syntax and semantics fusion learning. In: Proceedings of the 29th ACM SIGSOFT International Symposium on Software Testing and Analysis, pp. 516–527 (2020)
5. Göde, N., Koschke, R.: Frequency and risks of changes to clones. In: Proceedings of the 33rd International Conference on Software Engineering, pp. 311–320 (2011)
6. Hawkins, D.M.: The problem of overfitting. J. Chem. Inf. Comput. Sci. **44**(1), 1–12 (2004)
7. Higo, Y., Kusumoto, S.: Enhancing quality of code clone detection with program dependency graph. In: 2009 16th Working Conference on Reverse Engineering, pp. 315–316. IEEE (2009)
8. Jiang, L., Misherghi, G., Su, Z., Glondu, S.: DECKARD: scalable and accurate tree-based detection of code clones. In: 29th International Conference on Software Engineering (ICSE 2007), pp. 96–105. IEEE (2007)
9. Kapser, C.J., Godfrey, M.W.: "Cloning considered harmful" considered harmful: patterns of cloning in software. Empir. Softw. Eng. **13**(6) (2008). https://doi.org/10.1007/s10664-008-9076-6
10. Kim, M., Bergman, L., Lau, T., Notkin, D.: An ethnographic study of copy and paste programming practices in OOPL. In: Proceedings 2004 International Symposium on Empirical Software Engineering, ISESE 2004, pp. 83–92. IEEE (2004)
11. Koch, G., Zemel, R., Salakhutdinov, R.: Siamese neural networks for one-shot image recognition. In: ICML Deep Learning Workshop, Lille, vol. 2 (2015)
12. Koschke, R., Falke, R., Frenzel, P.: Clone detection using abstract syntax suffix trees. In: 2006 13th Working Conference on Reverse Engineering, pp. 253–262. IEEE (2006)
13. Krasner, H.: The cost of poor software quality in the US: a 2020 report. In: Proceedings of the Consortium For Information & Software Quality^{TM} (CISQ^{TM}) (2021)
14. Krinke, J.: Identifying similar code with program dependence graphs. In: Proceedings Eighth Working Conference on Reverse Engineering, pp. 301–309. IEEE (2001)
15. Krizhevsky, A., Sutskever, I., Hinton, G.E.: ImageNet classification with deep convolutional neural networks. In: Advances in Neural Information Processing Systems, vol. 25, pp. 1097–1105 (2012)
16. Mahajan, S., Abolhassani, N., Prasad, M.R.: Recommending stack overflow posts for fixing runtime exceptions using failure scenario matching. In: Proceedings of the 28th ACM Joint Meeting on European Software Engineering Conference and Symposium on the Foundations of Software Engineering, ESEC/FSE 2020, pp. 1052–1064. Association for Computing Machinery, New York (2020). https://doi.org/10.1145/3368089.3409764
17. Melekhov, I., Kannala, J., Rahtu, E.: Siamese network features for image matching. In: 2016 23rd International Conference on Pattern Recognition (ICPR), pp. 378–383. IEEE (2016)
18. Mou, L., Li, G., Zhang, L., Wang, T., Jin, Z.: Convolutional neural networks over tree structures for programming language processing. In: Proceedings of the Thirtieth AAAI Conference on Artificial Intelligence, AAAI 2016, pp. 1287–1293. AAAI Press (2016)
19. Narayanan, A., Chandramohan, M., Venkatesan, R., Chen, L., Liu, Y., Jaiswal, S.: graph2vec: learning distributed representations of graphs. arXiv preprint arXiv:1707.05005 (2017)

20. Nguyen, H.V., Bai, L.: Cosine similarity metric learning for face verification. In: Kimmel, R., Klette, R., Sugimoto, A. (eds.) ACCV 2010. LNCS, vol. 6493, pp. 709–720. Springer, Heidelberg (2011). https://doi.org/10.1007/978-3-642-19309-5_55

21. Pearl, J.: Bayesian Networks, pp. 149–153. MIT Press, Cambridge (1998)

22. Roy, C.K., Cordy, J.R.: A mutation/injection-based automatic framework for evaluating code clone detection tools. In: 2009 International Conference on Software Testing, Verification, and Validation Workshops, pp. 157–166. IEEE (2009)

23. Roy, C.K., Cordy, J.R.: A survey on software clone detection research. Queen's School of Computing TR **541**(115), 64–68 (2007)

24. Saini, V., Sajnani, H., Kim, J., Lopes, C.: SourcererCC and sourcererCC-I: tools to detect clones in batch mode and during software development. In: Proceedings of the 38th International Conference on Software Engineering Companion (2016)

25. Sajnani, H., Saini, V., Svajlenko, J., Roy, C.K., Lopes, C.V.: SourcererCC: scaling code clone detection to big-code. In: Proceedings of the 38th International Conference on Software Engineering, pp. 1157–1168 (2016)

26. Severyn, A., Moschitti, A.: Twitter sentiment analysis with deep convolutional neural networks. In: Proceedings of the 38th International ACM SIGIR Conference on Research and Development in Information Retrieval, pp. 959–962 (2015)

27. Wei, H., Li, M.: Supervised deep features for software functional clone detection by exploiting lexical and syntactical information in source code. In: IJCAI, pp. 3034–3040 (2017)

28. Wei, H., Li, M.: Positive and unlabeled learning for detecting software functional clones with adversarial training. In: IJCAI, pp. 2840–2846 (2018)

29. White, M., Tufano, M., Vendome, C., Poshyvanyk, D.: Deep learning code fragments for code clone detection. In: 2016 31st IEEE/ACM International Conference on Automated Software Engineering (ASE), pp. 87–98. IEEE (2016)

30. Xie, C., Wang, X., Qian, C., Wang, M.: A source code similarity based on Siamese neural network. Appl. Sci. **10**(21), 7519 (2020)

Robustness Analysis of Deep Learning Frameworks on Mobile Platforms

Amin Eslami Abyane[✉] and Hadi Hemmati

Department of Electrical and Software Engineering, University of Calgary,
Calgary, Canada
{amin.eslamiabyane,hadi.hemmati}@ucalgary.ca

Abstract. With the recent increase in the computational power of modern mobile devices, machine learning-based heavy tasks such as face detection and speech recognition are now integral parts of such devices. This requires frameworks to execute machine learning models (e.g., Deep Neural Networks) on mobile devices. Although there exist studies on the accuracy and performance of these frameworks, the quality of on-device deep learning frameworks, in terms of their robustness, has not been systematically studied yet. In this paper, we empirically compare two on-device deep learning frameworks with three adversarial attacks on three different model architectures. We also use both the quantized and unquantized variants for each architecture. The results show that, in general, neither of the deep learning frameworks is better than the other in terms of robustness, and there is not a significant difference between the PC and mobile frameworks either. However, in cases like Boundary attack, mobile version is more robust than PC. In addition, quantization improves robustness in all cases when moving from PC to mobile.

Keywords: Robustness · On-device learning · Deep learning frameworks

1 Introduction

In recent years, advancements in hardware resources and demands from many application domains have led to the growth and success of deep learning (DL) approaches. Consequently, several deep learning frameworks, such as TensorFlow [14] and PyTorch [29], have been introduced to improve DL developers productivity. These powerful frameworks have gained massive success and popularity in academia and industry and are being used on a large scale every day. Among the many application domains of DL systems, one particular domain that has seen much interest is applying DL techniques on mobile devices (i.e., on-device learning). In general, mobile devices' collected or observed data are potentially of great interest for many DL applications such as speech recognition, face detection, and next-word prediction. There are two generic solutions to utilize these data. The first approach is to send the data from the mobile devices to a server

© IFIP International Federation for Information Processing 2022
Published by Springer Nature Switzerland AG 2022
D. Clark et al. (Eds.): ICTSS 2021, LNCS 13045, pp. 160–177, 2022.
https://doi.org/10.1007/978-3-031-04673-5_13

to run the DL task (training or testing) and return the results. This approach has some significant drawbacks. The first one is that in this communication with the server, the user's privacy might be threatened, and the second one is that we are adding a network overhead and delay to the system. This overhead might get very noticeable if the task is frequent, such as image classification using a camera to process lots of images in a second.

The second approach is called on-device machine learning, which does not have the privacy concerns and is the context of this paper. In an on-device machine learning approach, the inference is made on the user's device, and no network communication is required. However, the mobile device's computational power (no matter how powerful the mobile device is) is much less than a server or even a regular GPU-based PC, which is an obstacle for training in this fashion. To help DL models inference possible on a mobile device, libraries such as TensorFlow Lite [9] and PyTorch Mobile [2] have been proposed.

From the software engineering perspective, an important quality aspect of DL-based software systems is their robustness, which is usually tested and analyzed against adversarial attacks [16,18,33]. Robustness is especially significant in mobile apps given the amount of personal information that can be exploited from cell phones, if an adversary gets access to the app. For instance, DL-based face detection is a standard access control measure for cell phones these days. Suppose an adversarial attack on the underlying DL model can misclassify a specific image created by the adversary as the trusted class. In that case, the attacker gets access to the mobile device.

There have been some limited studies in the recent literature that evaluate DL frameworks both on PC and mobile [20,24,27], but only in terms of their accuracy (effectiveness) and performance (efficiency). This has motivated us to conduct this study with a software testing and analysis lens, on mobile and PC DL frameworks in terms of their robustness.

We study two main on-device DL frameworks, TensorFlow Lite and PyTorch Mobile, from Google and Facebook, respectively. We use image classification as a common DL task to evaluate the robustness of the frameworks. Our controlled experiment is designed to study the effect of the models, the adversarial attacks, the quantization process [25], and the framework on robustness. We compare two deep learning frameworks (TensorFlow and PyTorch) with three adversarial attacks (both white-box and black-box) on three different model architectures, both quantized and unquantized. This results in 36 configurations on mobile devices and 18 configurations on PC, as our comparison baseline.

The results show that neither of the mobile deep learning frameworks is better than the other in terms of robustness, and the robustness depends on the model type and other factors, which is the case on PC as well. Moreover, there is no significant difference in robustness between PC and mobile frameworks either. However, cases like the Boundary attack on PyTorch, we see that the mobile version is significantly more robust than the PC version (12.5% decrease in attack success rate). Finally, we see that quantization improves the robustness of both TensorFlow and PyTorch on all models and attacks when moving from

PC to mobile (with median improvements between 2.4% to 23.8%, per attack type). Note that all data and scripts are available for replication purposes[1].

2   Background

2.1   Deep Neural Network (DNN)

A DNN is an artificial neural network consisting of many layers, and each layer has multiple neurons. Each neuron performs a simple task, takes an input, and gives an output based on a function. A simple combination of these layers is often called multi-layer perceptron (MLP). However, DNNs are not limited to MLPs. One of the most popular kinds of neural networks is called Convolutional Neural Networks (CNNs). A convolutional layer is typically used in tasks that work with images. A convolutional layer's objective is to extract features from a picture and reduce the problem's dimensionality. Another group of neural networks is called Recurrent Neural Networks (RNNs). This type of network has units that act as memory. Thus they are often used in tasks that deal with language and speech. Like a human being, DNN learns patterns in the training phase and can be used for the designed task. DNNs are extremely powerful and are widely used for image classification, face recognition, and speech recognition.

In the image classification domain, which is a common application domain of DNNs and is the domain of our experiment, some very well-known models have proven to be very effective:

MobileNetV2 [31]: This model is specially designed for mobile devices and is more light-weight than the other models. It contains 32 convolutional filters and 19 layers of residual bottleneck. The overall size of this model is around 14 MB. This model takes images of size 224 × 224 as input for classification.

ResNet50 [21]: This is one of the most influential models in the image classification domain. It is much heavier than MobileNetV2 (it is close to 100 MB), but it is more accurate than MobileNetV2.

InceptionV3 [34]: Much like ResNet50, this model is another complex model (close to 100 MB). It consists of inception blocks; Unlike the other two models, which used 224 × 224 images, this one takes images of size 299 × 299, which is one reason it is more complex than the previous ones.

2.2   Robustness and Adversarial Attacks

DNNs are known to be sensitive to corner case data (e.g., data items that are close to decision boundaries). That means it is possible that a slight change in the input can result in a corner case sample where the DNN will not perform accurately (e.g., the item is misclassified if the task is classification). Suppose this slight change of input is deliberate to fool the model. In that case, it is called an adversarial attack, and the robustness of a DNN model is the extent that the model can defend itself from such attacks (i.e., still generate correct outputs).

---

[1] https://github.com/aminesi/robustness-on-device.

Adversarial attacks were first introduced in the image processing tasks, where images are easily manipulable, and the tasks (e.g., classification) are pretty sensitive. However, these attacks have gone beyond the image domain and are now being studied in other learning tasks, such as text and audio analysis domains.

Adversarial attacks can be categorized from several perspectives. Most commonly, they are categorized into two groups, based on their level of access to the model details, which are white-box and black-box attacks. White-box attacks require knowledge about the internals of the models they are attacking. For instance, some attacks need the models' gradient after the backpropagation step to generate adversarial samples, whereas black-box attacks do not need such information and are model-agnostic. Another standard categorization of attacks is grouping them into targeted and untargeted attacks. Targeted attacks try to fool the model into misclassifying data into a particular class. In contrast, untargeted attacks just try to force the model to misclassify, no matter the wrong output. Since most of the popular and well-known attacks are defined as untargeted [19,26,28], in this study we focus on the following untargeted attacks both from white-box and black-box categories.

Fast Gradient Sign Method (FGSM) [19] is perhaps the most famous adversarial attack amongst these attacks. FGSM is a gradient-based white-box attack, and it works by adding perturbations into the image following the formula presented in Eq. 1. Where x and y are the input image and label respectively, Θ represents model parameters, ∇ is gradient, J is the loss function, and ϵ is the amount of perturbation.

$$adv = x + \epsilon.sign(\nabla(J(\theta, x, y))) \tag{1}$$

Basic Iterative Method (BIM) [26] is an extension of FGSM attack, so it is also a white-box attack. As its name suggests, it is iterative, and it does the FGSM attack multiple times and updates the input in each iteration.

Boundary Attack [15] is a decision-based (it only uses the final decision of model to create samples) black-box attack. It starts from an adversarial point, and in each step makes a move randomly orthogonal to the image and a move towards the image. Since it uses a small step size to get closest to the image (while staying on the adversarial side), it requires many iterations.

2.3 DL Frameworks

Neural networks use complex mathematical equations that need to be implemented in Libraries like TensorFlow and PyTorch that provide a set of simple Application Programming Interfaces (APIs) for the machine learning developers. Both these frameworks are implemented in python language for their high-level APIs, and they use C++ for their low-level implementation to gain higher speeds.

With the advances in on-device learning, these frameworks are now coming with mobile versions, making programming DL on mobile devices easier.

TensorFlow's mobile variant called "TensorFlow Lite" is a cross-platform (Android, iOS, and edge devices) library and supports languages such as Java and Swift, which is based on a cross-platform serialization library called Flat-Buffers. In addition, it supports multiple quantization configurations and different hardware such as CPU and GPU with various options, and on Android, it supports Android Neural Networks API (NNAPI).

"PyTorch Mobile" is the other on-device DL library, which is similar to TensorFlow Lite in terms of functionalities. It works on the same platforms that TensorFlow Lite does and supports quantization but is less flexible in this aspect. At the time of doing this experiment, PyTorch Mobile only supports CPU without any additional options (e.g., thread count).

However, like any other software program, these implementations are not flawless. There are also quite many different design choices and implementation differences between various frameworks. Especially, given the hardware and operating systems differences, there might be many variations in terms of effectiveness, efficiency, and robustness of the same model implemented on PC vs. mobile in different frameworks.

2.4 Quantization

Quantization is the process of compressing a DNN implementation to speed up the model execution, at the cost of its precision [8]. As we know, DNN models' implementations in DL frameworks include many matrices/tensors and thus many matrix/tensor operations. The motivation behind quantization is to reduce the complexity of matrix operations to be able to run more operations with fewer resources [35]. Typically, all DNN model parameters, like weights and activations, use a 32-bit floating-point precision. Since mobile devices have fewer resources than PCs, the quantization idea has been proposed to slightly reduce the model's precision to make models smaller and infer faster. The quantization target may be an 8-bit integer, or 16-bit floating-point, or any other precision for the numerical data types.

Integer quantization is explored in [25]. In this work, they introduce a formula for quantization to 8-bit integer, which is shown in Eq. 2. Key parameters here are zero_point and scale, which should be selected in a way that every possible normal_value can be mapped to an 8-bit fixed-point value.

$$normal\_value = (int8\_value - zero\_point) \times scale \tag{2}$$

Although TensorFlow currently supports multiple precisions, PyTorch only supports an 8-bit integer at the moment. There are different ways of quantization, and we will briefly describe them in this section.

Post-training dynamic range quantization: This type of quantization [5], as the name suggests, is done after the model is trained. A quantizer quantizes all statically defined parameters, like weights using a formula like Eq. 2. So in this approach, the activations are intact. According to [5], this approach works best for language models. The name dynamic is used since the activation values are quantized on the fly when the model is running.

Post-training static range quantization: This quantization approach [5], like the previous one, is applied on a trained model. The difference is that activations are pre quantized as well, making the model more compact and faster. To find the best quantization, the quantizer should find the best scale and zero_point to ensure successful mapping to the target (e.g., int8), which is not possible for something that is not statically defined like activations.

The solution is to calibrate the model with some image samples in the quantization step so that quantizer can see various possible dynamic values (activation values in this case) and calculate appropriate scale and zero_points for them. This approach is more appropriate for image models compared to the previous one as suggested by the literature [5].

Quantization aware training: This approach [5] is distinct from the other two in that it tries to learn the effect of quantization in the training phase. It is a more robust approach but costs more.

3 Experiments

Our objective is to quantitatively and systematically evaluate the robustness of DL learning frameworks on mobile. To address this objective, we answer the following research questions:

- **RQ1: How robust DL frameworks are on mobile?** This RQ aims to compare TensorFlow Lite and PyTorch Mobile when running on mobile by assessing their robustness against well-known adversarial attacks.
- **RQ2: How does mobile DL frameworks' robustness compare to their PC equivalent?** In this RQ, we compare the robustness results of DL frameworks on PC vs. mobile platforms.
- **RQ3: What is the effect of quantization on the robustness of models?** In this RQ, we will study the quantization's effect by repeating the experiment designed for RQ1, but this time with the quantized models.

3.1 Experiment Design

Models Under Study and the Datasets: Image classification is one of the main application domains of DL models these days. Especially in the mobile application domain, some use cases such as access control, as discussed earlier, are critical and can be heavily dependant on the trustworthiness of the underlying classification models. Therefore, in this study, we focus on image classification and use the three well-known image classification models explained in Sect. 2.1: MobileNetV2, ResNet50, and InceptionV3. These models have been selected to cover various models in terms of power and complexity (MobileNetV2: lightweight, ResNet50: resource-demanding, and InceptionV3: the heaviest).

For TensorFlow models, we use pre-trained models on ImageNet from Keras applications [6]. PyTorch models are all from torchvision [11] models packages (for the sake of quantization, models are selected from quantization packages as regular models are not quantizable).

For quantization, we use the second approach explained in Sect. 2.4, post-training static range quantization, which is a decent fit for image data and still

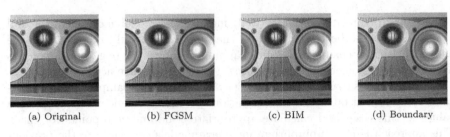

(a) Original   (b) FGSM   (c) BIM   (d) Boundary

Fig. 1. A sample generated for TensorFlow MobileNetV2 model.

not very costly. For calibration of the models in the quantization mode, we use 1,000 random samples from our dataset.

We use ImageNet [3] as our main dataset. ImageNet is one of the biggest and most well-known datasets in the image domain, and it uses WordNet [13] for its label hierarchy. It consists of 1,281,167 training images and 50,000 validation images with a total of 1,000 image classes. It is around 150 gigabytes in size.

Since our robustness analysis heavily depends on the ground truth for classification, we need to make sure that the original test set samples are correctly classified. By doing this, we ensure that if an adversarial sample is misclassified, it is due to perturbations and not intrinsic model errors.

To achieve this goal, we use the intersection of correctly classified validation samples by all the models on all of our frameworks. Then we choose 3,000 samples from these, randomly, to ensure we have enough unbiased samples.

Model Deployment and Inference: The procedure to deploy and test our models on mobile frameworks is as follows:

1. Create a trained model on PC (by creating a new model or using a pre-trained model or fine-tune a pre-trained models with transfer learning)
2. Convert the models into their mobile variant, using TensorFlow Lite and PyTorch Mobile (optionally quantize the model (only in RQ2)).
3. Load the model and samples into memory and run the inference on mobile to calculate the robustness.

Recall that this procedure is divided between PC (model training) and mobile (model inference), since mobile devices alone are not powerful enough to do heavy tasks such as training an extremely resource-intensive neural network.

Adversarial Attacks: As discussed in Sect. 2.2, we use the following three famous untargeted attacks in this study: FGSM, BIM, and Boundary attack. We utilize a python package for creating adversarial attacks called Foolbox [30]. For FGSM and BIM attacks, we use an ϵ of 0.005. For BIM attack, we choose ten iterations which is the default value in Foolbox. For Boundary attack, both orthogonal and towards steps are set to 0.01 (which are again the default values in Foolbox), and the number of steps is set to 5000. A small number of steps results in a very perturbed image, and a huge one is highly time-consuming and does not always result in a better sample.

To generate adversarial samples, we follow these steps that produces visually acceptable images (see Fig. 1):

Table 1. Input image normalization in preprocessing. (values are according to image channels (B, G, R) for ResNet50 in TF and (R, G, B) for other configurations)

Framework	model	mean (μ)	std (σ)
	MobileNetV2	(127.5, 127.5, 127.5)	(127.5, 127.5, 127.5)
TensorFlow	ResNet50	(103.939, 116.779, 123.68)	(1, 1, 1)
	InceptionV3	(127.5, 127.5, 127.5)	(127.5, 127.5, 127.5)
	MobileNetV2	(0.485, 0.456, 0.406)	(0.229, 0.224, 0.225)
PyTorch	ResNet50	(0.485, 0.456, 0.406)	(0.229, 0.224, 0.225)
	InceptionV3	(0.485, 0.456, 0.406)	(0.229, 0.224, 0.225)

1. Preprocess our carefully selected samples according to the model requirements, as follows: First Resize the image's smallest dimension to 256 (299 in case of InceptionV3) (This is the choice of both TensorFlow, and PyTorch [4,12]). Then center crop the resized image according to input size of the model. Afterwards for PyTorch, divide image pixel values by 255 to map the values to [0, 1] range (TensorFlow uses (0, 255) range). For ResNet50 only in TensorFlow, change image format from RGB to BGR. Finally normalize the image channels based on the mean and standard deviation, in Table 1, which is from TensorFlow and PyTorch documentations [7,12].
2. Pass the model and samples to an attacker to generate adversarial samples.
3. Convert adversarial samples to PNG images to use in mobile devices.

Note that we do not generate the adversarial samples on mobile for two reasons: (a) the computation intensity of this task, and (b) models on mobile do not provide essential information for white-box attacks. Another point is that we convert images to PNG format, which is a lossless format. This format is crucial since we want our image to be the same as one on PC to be able to get reliable results. Also, note that for the Boundary attack, we may need to rerun the algorithm several times until all adversarial samples are successfully generated (in our case, we had to rerun three times).

Evaluation Metrics: To evaluate robustness, we use success rate, which measures the proportion of samples that could successfully fool the models. Since our originally selected test set samples are all classified correctly on all configurations on PC, the success rate of an attack has an inverse correlation with the model's robustness.

In RQ2, to better assess the differences between results, when comparing success rates of quantized vs unquantized models, we run a non-parametric statistical significant test (Wilcoxon signed-rank) and report the effect size measure (Vargha and Delaney A Measure), as well.

Execution Environment: We run our PC DL frameworks on a node from the Compute Canada cluster with 32 gigabytes of RAM, an Nvidia V100 GPU, and an Intel Gold 6148 Skylake @ 2.4 GHz CPU. We use a physical device for our mobile device, an HTC U11 with a Qualcomm Snapdragon 835 chipset and 6 gigabytes of RAM, running Android 9. We did not use multiple devices since model robustness is independent of device type, given that implementations are using the same library. It is worth noting that we do not use an emulator as our mobile system. We started the project by testing TensorFlow with an emulator, but surprisingly, we found that quantized models ran slower than regular models in the emulator. It turned out that TensorFlow's quantized kernel is only optimized for mobile CPU. Thus quantized versions ran poorly on an emulator. Therefore, we used a real device, as discussed before. We developed a prototype mobile app (on both frameworks) that takes configuration and images as input and calculates the success rate.

3.2 Results and Discussions

In this section, we present and discuss the results of RQ1 to RQ3.

RQ1 Results (TensorFlow Lite vs. PyTorch Mobile Robustness on Mobile Platforms): Figure 2 reports the results for this RQ. The first observation is that in MobileNetV2 and ResNet50 models, TensorFlow Lite was more robust against FGSM and BIM attacks (Fig. 2a and Fig. 2b). However, in the Boundary attack, PyTorch Mobile was more robust. Also, Fig. 2c shows that, for InceptionV3, PyTorch Mobile is more robust against FGSM and BIM attacks. However, TensorFlow Lite is more robustness against the Boundary attack.

Thus, in mobile DL frameworks, the robustness depends on configurations, and no learning framework among TensorFlow Lite and PyTorch Mobile dominates the other one in terms of robustness.

It can also be seen that the more complex the model gets, the more robust it will be against adversarial samples. For instance, In TensorFlow Lite, the success rate of the FGSM attack on MobileNetV2, ResNet50, and InceptionV3 is 77%, 74.27%, and 55.8%, respectively.

Furthermore, both FGSM and BIM attacks are much more effective than the Boundary attack. In addition, BIM attack always performs better than FGSM as it tries to improve an FGSM sample iteratively.

Moreover, we can see that Boundary attack is less successful than FGSM and BIM in all cases with a very low success rate. This seems contradictory with the definition of Boundary attack, which was supposed to generate samples always on the adversarial side. In other words, the success rate should have always been 100%. The reason for lower success rates is that images are in 8-bit unsigned integer (UINT8) format, but the neural networks work with 32-bit floating-points (FP32). Therefore, when a sample is generated, it is in FP32 format and is always adversarial. However, the reduction of precision to UINT8, in conversion to the image format, makes some samples cross the boundary, and the success rate significantly drops.

Besides the attack success rate, another important factor is performance. Table 2 shows the inference time for the mobile platform when running unquantized models. As the table shows in terms of performance (run-time cost), TensorFlow Lite is much faster in all configurations (the slower framework is high-

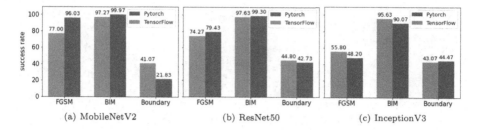

(a) MobileNetV2   (b) ResNet50   (c) InceptionV3

Fig. 2. Success rate of adversarial attacks on mobile device

Table 2. Inference time in the mobile device for the entire test set (3,000 samples).
The bold cells represent the framework with faster inferences.

Model	Attack	Inference time (s)	
		TensorFlow Lite	PyTorch Mobile
MobileNetV2	FGSM	**157**	276
	BIM	**174**	301
	Boundary	**187**	302
ResNet50	FGSM	**1003**	1583
	BIM	**1036**	1504
	Boundary	**1093**	1460
InceptionV3	FGSM	**1617**	1774
	BIM	**1626**	1841
	Boundary	**1516**	1820

lighted in the table) for regular models. This might be because PyTorch Mobile
uses fewer threads as the number of workers cannot be set on PyTorch.

Answer to RQ1: Neither PyTorch Mobile nor TensorFlow Lite is significantly more robust than the other, in all cases. The choice of a more robustness
mobile framework depends on the model architecture and the attack itself. In
terms of performance, however, TensorFlow Lite is consistently faster!

**RQ2 Results (TensorFlow and PyTorch Robustness on PC vs.
Mobile):** To answer this RQ, we start by analyzing robustness on PC DL
frameworks as our baseline. Figure 3 report the success rates of three adversarial
attacks (FGSM, BIM, and Boundary) on three models (MobileNetV2, ReNet50,
and InceptionV3) over two PC frameworks (TensorFlow and PyTorch).

As it can be seen in Fig. 3a and Fig. 3b on MobileNetV2 and ResNet50 architectures TensorFlow is more robust against white-box attacks, while on Boundary attack which is black-box, PyTorch is more robust. However, in InceptionV3
(Fig. 3c), it is the exact opposite, and TensorFlow is more robust against the
black-box attack. Also, PyTorch is more robust against white-box attacks. These
patterns were seen in our experiments on the mobile device (RQ1), as well.

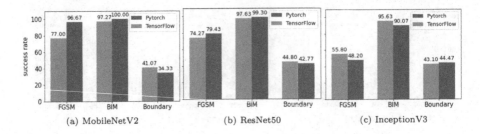

Fig. 3. Success rate of adversarial attacks on PC

Table 3. Adversarial generation time for the entire test sets (3,000 samples) reported in hours:minutes:seconds.

Model	Framework	Generation time (s)		
		FGSM	BIM	Boundary
MobileNetV2	TensorFlow	00:02:20	00:04:13	01:01:46
	PyTorch	00:03:35	00:04:16	01:26:04
ResNet50	TensorFlow	00:02:01	00:03:38	04:31:17
	PyTorch	00:02:30	00:05:37	04:56:24
InceptionV3	TensorFlow	00:03:06	00:03:45	05:54:14
	PyTorch	00:01:36	00:05:18	07:25:36

Table 3 reports adversarial sample generation cost on PC. As it can be seen, the Boundary attack takes a significantly longer time to finish, with a much lower success rate in the end. While white-box attacks finish in minutes, the Boundary attack takes a couple of hours to complete, even in a high-end system, such as Compute Canada cluster. This perfectly illustrates why it is almost impossible to create samples using black-box techniques on mobile devices. Moreover, white-box attacks need gradient, which is unavailable on mobile frameworks at the moment. Thus they too cannot be run on mobile. Consequently, currently, there is no easy way to generate adversarial samples on mobile devices. Finally, we can see that TensorFlow is slightly faster than PyTorch, in most cases.

To better compare mobile and PC platforms, Fig. 4 reports the same raw data as Figs. 2 and 3, but grouped by platforms. As Fig. 4a, 4b, and 4c show, robustness is almost the same in all cases except on the Boundary attack on InceptionV3, where we see a slight increase in robustness on mobile. We also see similar patterns in Fig. 4d, 4e, and 4f, between mobile and PC for PyTorch where the robustness on mobile is either the same or very close to the PC version in all configurations. The exception is the Boundary attack on MobileNetV2, where we see a sudden drop in success rate in PyTorch Mobile. This shows PyTorch's mobile version of MobileNetV2 is more robust against the Boundary attack.

Answer to RQ2: In most cases, switching platforms between PC and mobile does not change the robustness drastically. This means that the implementation

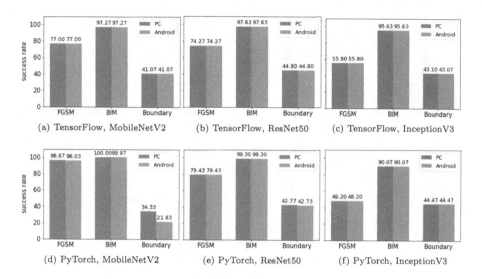

Fig. 4. Different attacks' success rates on different platforms.

of models on both hardware and languages perform similarly, and they are almost equivalent. However, in some cases, like on PyTorch when using Boundary attack on MobileNetV2, we might get much higher robustness on mobile platforms.

RQ3 results (the quantization effect): To answer this RQ, we report the results in Fig. 5. The results show that the attacks lose their initial effectiveness in all cases and their success rate decreases. This shows that quantization can increase the robustness of the model against attacks. In some cases, robustness increases slightly, whereas in a case like a Boundary attack (which is trying to create samples closest to the boundary), the slightest effect like quantization can massively improve the robustness. In other words, these attacks are very dependent on the model's specifications. If model parameters change (as quantization does), the attack will not be as effective as it was.

The median decrease of success rates per attack is 3.55% (FGSM), 2.43% (BIM), and 23.77% (Boundary), with a minimum of 0.47% (for BIM om PyTorch-ResNet50) and a maximum of 37.5% (For Boundary on PyTorch-InceptionV3). This difference between the unquantized and quantized models' robustness is statistically significant with a p-value less than 0.001 when running a non-parametric statistical significant test (Paired Wilcoxon Signed-Rank test), with the effect size measure (Paired Vargha and Delaney A Measure) is 0.608.

In terms of model performance, as Table 4 shows, quantization closes the model inference time gap between the two frameworks, and in some models like MobileNetV2, PyTorch Mobile even runs faster than TensorFlow Lite. As expected, the speedup after quantization is significant, and it goes up to 2.87 times in some cases (e.g., MobileNetV2 in PyTorch).

Answer to RQ3: In addition to the speed and size reduction that quantization provides, it can be a very low-cost and straightforward defense mechanism

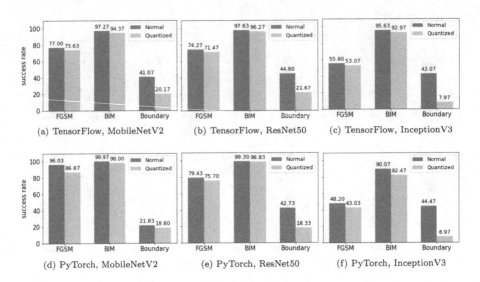

Fig. 5. Effect of quantization on success rate

against adversarial attacks. Quantization increases the robustness with a median up to 37.5% for some attacks (Boundary) over a distribution of three models and two DL frameworks per attack.

3.3 Threats to Validity

In terms of the construct validity, the key to our success rate measure is knowing the ground truth. However, we are only relying on the original classification models to come up with the ground truth. That is, there might be cases where the model is misclassifying, but the adversarial sample is correctly classified. As discussed, we take the intersection of the three models' correctly classified samples to reduce the probability of having a misclassified ground truth.

In terms of the internal validity, our study design is pretty simple, with evaluating the robustness of models using attacks success rate. We are using predefined classification models and existing libraries to create attacks. Therefore, we are not introducing confounding factors in our implementation or design.

In terms of conclusion validity and to address the randomness of the results, we ran a non-parametric paired statistical significant test (Paired Wilcoxon Signed-Rank test) and reported the effect size measure (Paired Vargha and Delaney A Measure) when comparing the success rates in RQ3. In RQ1 and RQ2, the results were mainly the same when comparing frameworks and platforms. Therefore, our conclusions were the differences are practically insignificant anyways, so there was no need to run any statistical significance tests.

Finally, regarding the external validity and generalizability of the study, one potential validity threat is having limited datasets and models, which results in

Table 4. Effect of quantization on mobile inference time

Model	Attack	Framework	Inference time (s)	
			Regular	Quantized
MobileNetV2	FGSM	TensorFlow Lite	157	133
		PyTorch Mobile	276	96
	BIM	TensorFlow Lite	174	128
		PyTorch Mobile	301	105
	Boundary	TensorFlow Lite	187	132
		PyTorch Mobile	302	112
ResNet50	FGSM	TensorFlow Lite	1003	534
		PyTorch Mobile	1583	616
	BIM	TensorFlow Lite	1036	531
		PyTorch Mobile	1504	622
	Boundary	TensorFlow Lite	1093	559
		PyTorch Mobile	1460	554
InceptionV3	FGSM	TensorFlow Lite	1617	798
		PyTorch Mobile	1774	942
	BIM	TensorFlow Lite	1626	804
		PyTorch Mobile	1841	982
	Boundary	TensorFlow Lite	1516	808
		PyTorch Mobile	1820	993

biased conclusions. We mitigate this threat by choosing one of the most extensive datasets in the image domain. Furthermore, we used three state-of-the-art models with different complexities to help generalize our results. Finally, we used both white-box and black-box attacks, and all the attacks were some of the best in their categories. However, still, all of these datasets and models are from the domain of the image. Thus the results might not be generalizable to other domains such as natural language processing. In addition, we only used Android as our mobile platform. Therefore, the results might not be representative of iOS.

4   Related Work

Luo et al. [27] made a comparison for classifiers between different mobile frameworks like TensorFlow Lite PyTorch Mobile and Caffe 2 [1], which is now part of PyTorch. They used many models such as ResNet50, InceptionV3, DenseNet121 [22], and compared all the models on all the mentioned frameworks. They also compared the neural inference power of different mobile devices. Some of the results were as follows: none of the platforms had a noticeable advantage in all cases, TensorFlow Lite had a much faster model loading time compared to the others, the same AI model on the different platform had different accuracy, and Android Neural Networks API (NNAPI) did not constantly improve the inference time. This study was mainly focused on accuracy and performance but did not have any robustness assessments, which our study covers.

Ignatov et al. [24] made a benchmark consisting of multiple tests such as image recognition, face recognition, image deblurring, image semantic segmentation, image enhancement, and memory limitations. Then they compared the performance of DNN models on different mobile phones. This paper's main idea was to measure the power of the CPU chipset; thus, there was no other comparison in this work. They only used TensorFlow Lite as the DL framework, and there was no comprehensive study on the impact of different models.

Guo et al. [20] presented a study on PyTorch Mobile, TensorFlow Lite and TensorFlow.js [10], CNTK [32], MXnet [17]. The paper made a comparison on PC and found that PyTorch and MXnet were more vulnerable in adversarial attacks. It compared browsers using TensorFlow.js with PC for MNIST and CIFAR-10 datasets using different models and found that TensorFlow.js suffered from high memory usage and had meaningful lower accuracy ResNet model. Android devices were faster in small models in inference time, whereas IOS devices were better at large models. It used TensorFlow Lite to compare Android and iOS devices with PC and found similar accuracy to PC. Finally, they found that quantization did not affect accuracy much, and it made inference faster on Android devices. Although there was some robustness analysis in this work, the models were very simple and unrealistic, and evaluation was only on PC.

Huang et al. [23] made some interesting experiments on the robustness of models on Android devices. They used TensorFlow Lite as the framework for their study. Their approach had some key points. They extracted TensorFlow Lite models from the Google Play store. Then based on some criteria, They found similar pre-trained PC models available online and implemented the attacks on similar models. Their results showed that their approach was more effective in fooling the models than blind attacks (attacks without knowing the model). However, this study was only focused on attacking a specific model on mobile, and It did not look at different frameworks and the effect of platforms.

Given the related work, we see a gap in the literature for assessing the robustness of mobile DL frameworks, which our study covers.

5   Conclusion and Future Works

In this paper, we conduct a comprehensive study on deep learning mobile frameworks' robustness with different configurations. We compare the two major mobile frameworks (TensorFlow Lite and PyTorch Mobile), using 18 configurations (36 configurations considering quantization): two frameworks, three models, and three adversarial attack techniques. Our results show that frameworks are not necessarily superior in terms of robustness on the mobile platform, and the more robust framework varies by model architecture and attack type. Furthermore, changing the platform to mobile usually does not affect robustness but in some cases results in a slight increase in robustness which is not significant. However, we also show that quantization is a very effective approach in reducing the cost of model inference and making it more robust toward attacks in DL frameworks, consistently improving the robustness of Mobile DL frameworks (even up to 37.5% improvement when compared to regular models). In the future, we plan to extend this study to other application domains (such as textual data) and study other frameworks and platforms such as TensorFlow.js and iOS devices.

Acknowledgement. This work was enabled in part by support from WestGrid (www.westgrid.ca) and Compute Canada (www.computecanada.ca) and the Natural Sciences and Engineering Research Council of Canada [RGPIN/04552-2020].

References

1. Caffe2—a new lightweight, modular, and scalable deep learning framework. https://caffe2.ai/
2. Home—pytorch. https://pytorch.org/mobile/home/
3. Imagenet. http://www.image-net.org/
4. Inception_v3—pytorch. https://pytorch.org/hub/pytorch_vision_inception_v3/
5. Introduction to quantization on pytorch—pytorch. https://pytorch.org/blog/introduction-to-quantization-on-pytorch/
6. Keras applications. https://keras.io/api/applications/
7. keras-applications/imagenet_utils.py at 1.0.8. https://github.com/keras-team/keras-applications/blob/1.0.8/keras_applications/imagenet_utils.py
8. Model optimization—tensorflow lite. https://www.tensorflow.org/lite/performance/model_optimization
9. Tensorflow lite—ml for mobile and edge devices. https://www.tensorflow.org/lite
10. Tensorflow.js—machine learning for javascript developers. https://www.tensorflow.org/js
11. torchvision—pytorch 1.7.0 documentation. https://pytorch.org/docs/stable/torchvision/index.html
12. torchvision.models—torchvision master documentation. https://pytorch.org/vision/stable/models.html
13. Wordnet—a lexical database for English. https://wordnet.princeton.edu/
14. Abadi, M., et al.: TensorFlow: a system for large-scale machine learning. In: Proceedings of the 12th USENIX Conference on Operating Systems Design and Implementation, pp. 265–283. OSDI 2016, USENIX Association, USA (2016)
15. Brendel, W., Rauber, J., Bethge, M.: Decision-based adversarial attacks: reliable attacks against black-box machine learning models (2018)
16. Carlini, N., Wagner, D.: Towards evaluating the robustness of neural networks. In: 2017 IEEE Symposium on Security and Privacy (SP), pp. 39–57 (2017). https://doi.org/10.1109/SP.2017.49
17. Chen, T., et al.: Mxnet: a flexible and efficient machine learning library for heterogeneous distributed systems (2015)
18. Fawzi, A., Moosavi-Dezfooli, S.M., Frossard, P.: Robustness of classifiers: from adversarial to random noise. In: Proceedings of the 30th International Conference on Neural Information Processing Systems, pp. 1632–1640. NIPS 2016, Curran Associates Inc., Red Hook, NY, USA (2016)

19. Goodfellow, I.J., Shlens, J., Szegedy, C.: Explaining and harnessing adversarial examples. In: Bengio, Y., LeCun, Y. (eds.) 3rd International Conference on Learning Representations, ICLR 2015, 7–9 May 2015, Conference Track Proceedings, San Diego, CA, USA (2015). http://arxiv.org/abs/1412.6572

20. Guo, Q., et al.: An empirical study towards characterizing deep learning development and deployment across different frameworks and platforms. In: 34th IEEE/ACM International Conference on Automated Software Engineering, ASE 2019, 11–15 Nov 2019, pp. 810–822. IEEE, San Diego, CA, USA (2019). https://doi.org/10.1109/ASE.2019.00080

21. He, K., Zhang, X., Ren, S., Sun, J.: Deep residual learning for image recognition. In: 2016 IEEE Conference on Computer Vision and Pattern Recognition, CVPR 2016, 27–30 June 2016, pp. 770–778. IEEE Computer Society, Las Vegas, NV, USA (2016). https://doi.org/10.1109/CVPR.2016.90

22. Huang, G., Liu, Z., van der Maaten, L., Weinberger, K.Q.: Densely connected convolutional networks (2018)

23. Huang, Y., Hu, H., Chen, C.: Robustness of on-device models: adversarial attack to deep learning models on android apps (2021)

24. Ignatov, A., et al.: AI benchmark: running deep neural networks on android smartphones. In: Leal-Taixé, L., Roth, S. (eds.) ECCV 2018. LNCS, vol. 11133, pp. 288–314. Springer, Cham (2019). https://doi.org/10.1007/978-3-030-11021-5_19

25. Jacob, B., et al.: Quantization and training of neural networks for efficient integer-arithmetic-only inference (2017)

26. Kurakin, A., Goodfellow, I., Bengio, S.: Adversarial examples in the physical world (2017)

27. Luo, C., He, X., Zhan, J., Wang, L., Gao, W., Dai, J.: Comparison and benchmarking of AI models and frameworks on mobile devices (2020)

28. Moosavi-Dezfooli, S.M., Fawzi, A., Frossard, P.: DeepFool: a simple and accurate method to fool deep neural networks. In: 2016 IEEE Conference on Computer Vision and Pattern Recognition (CVPR), pp. 2574–2582 (2016). https://doi.org/10.1109/CVPR.2016.282

29. Paszke, A., et al.: Automatic differentiation in pytorch (2017)

30. Rauber, J., Zimmermann, R., Bethge, M., Brendel, W.: Foolbox native: fast adversarial attacks to benchmark the robustness of machine learning models in pytorch, tensorflow, and jax. J. Open Source Softw. 5(53), 2607 (2020). https://doi.org/10.21105/joss.02607

31. Sandler, M., Howard, A.G., Zhu, M., Zhmoginov, A., Chen, L.: MobileNetV2: inverted residuals and linear bottlenecks. In: 2018 IEEE Conference on Computer Vision and Pattern Recognition, CVPR 2018, 18–22 June 2018, pp. 4510–4520. IEEE Computer Society, Salt Lake City, UT, USA (2018). https://doi.org/10.1109/CVPR.2018.00474

32. Seide, F., Agarwal, A.: CNTK: microsoft's open-source deep-learning toolkit. In: Krishnapuram, B., Shah, M., Smola, A.J., Aggarwal, C.C., Shen, D., Rastogi, R. (eds.) Proceedings of the 22nd ACM SIGKDD International Conference on Knowledge Discovery and Data Mining, 13–17 Aug 2016, p. 2135. ACM, San Francisco, CA, USA (2016). https://doi.org/10.1145/2939672.2945397

33. Su, J., Vargas, D.V., Sakurai, K.: One pixel attack for fooling deep neural networks. IEEE Trans. Evol. Comput. 23(5), 828–841 (2019). https://doi.org/10.1109/TEVC.2019.2890858

34. Szegedy, C., Vanhoucke, V., Ioffe, S., Shlens, J., Wojna, Z.: Rethinking the inception architecture for computer vision. In: 2016 IEEE Conference on Computer Vision and Pattern Recognition, CVPR 2016, 27–30 June 2016, pp. 2818–2826. IEEE Computer Society, Las Vegas, NV, USA (2016). https://doi.org/10.1109/CVPR.2016.308
35. Wu, H., Judd, P., Zhang, X., Isaev, M., Micikevicius, P.: Integer quantization for deep learning inference: principles and empirical evaluation (2020)

Use Cases

Specification and Validation of Numerical Algorithms with the Gradual Contracts Pattern

René Fritze[(✉)][iD] and Stephan Rave[iD]

Applied Mathematics Münster, Westfälische Wilhelms-Universität Münster,
48149 Münster, Germany
rene.fritze@wwu.de
https://wwu.de/amm

Abstract. In this contribution we discuss the domain specific problems arising when implementing test suites for numerical algorithms. We propose a design approach based on gradual contracts and a support library to alleviate some of these issues. Gradual contracts do not need to represent a full specification of an algorithm's interface and can include untestable mathematical concepts. This encourages the developer to express their current, possibly incomplete, understanding of the algorithm in code and allows them to use automatic test generation for further insights. We demonstrate the applicability of our approach with the example of the Newton-Raphson method.

1 Introduction

Testing numerical code is widely accepted as necessary to confidently publish generated results, as evidenced by resources from the Software Sustainability Institute [3], and others [7,9,11]. Undiscovered software faults can yield direct consequences ranging from forced article retraction [19], to costly equipment failure [12] and to wasted research effort trying to refine computation models to fit simulation results [13]. Undetected bugs in foundational libraries like Open-BLAS [20] can cause failed computations where a scientist might not even be aware their NumPy-based [15] code is using OpenBLAS.

Despite the importance of extensively testing numerical algorithms, guidance on implementing tests for such algorithms is scarce and often limited to the documentation surrounding a project's test harness or continuous testing infrastructure [1,5,6], or to very basic advice, such as to take round-off errors into account when comparing floating point numbers [2,8] or using fabricated solutions [10] or the empirical convergence order to validate the algorithm.

We claim that this absence of guidance mostly stems from a lack of knowledge about the exact properties of the implemented algorithms: due to the iterative nature of most numerical algorithms, the influence of numerical round-off errors and the high-dimensionality of the input space, is often hard to predict. Even

© IFIP International Federation for Information Processing 2022
Published by Springer Nature Switzerland AG 2022
D. Clark et al. (Eds.): ICTSS 2021, LNCS 13045, pp. 181–188, 2022.
https://doi.org/10.1007/978-3-031-04673-5_14

in exact arithmetic, the set of inputs for which an algorithm converges to the desired solution is, in many cases, only partially known. Overall, writing "good" tests for numerical software is a daunting, murky task. In this contribution we hope to start to remedy this by proposing an improved development paradigm for numerical algorithms which we call "Gradual Contracts Pattern". This paradigm encourages developers to formally express their partial knowledge of the algorithm specification and shows how refining the implementation feeds back into more complete tests and vice-versa.

In Sect. 2 we will explain the difficulties for writing new tests using the example of a Python implementation of the Newton-Raphson algorithm. That algorithm we will then gradually document and test using our proposed approach in Sect. 3.

2 Testing a Newton-Raphson Algorithm

The well-known Newton-Raphson algorithm iteratively seeks a root of a given differentiable function:

Definition 1 (Newton-Raphson algorithm). *Let* $f : (x_l, x_r) \mapsto \mathbb{R}$, *be a differentiable function and* $x_0 \in \mathbb{R}$. *Then, under some conditions, the sequence*

$$x_{n+1} = x_n - \frac{f(x_n)}{f'(x_n)} \tag{1}$$

is well-defined (i.e. $x_n \in (x_l, x_r)$ *for all n) and converges to a root of f.*

We will call this the mathematical language definition (**MLD**). A naive implementation in Python might be

```
def newton_raphson(func, derivative, x0, maxit, tolerance):
    for it in itertools.count():
        residual = f(x0)
        if abs(residual) < tolerance:
            return x0
        if it == maxit:
            raise NewtonError(x0, it, residual)
        x0 -= residual*derivative(residual)
```

We will call this the programming code definition (**PCD**). We can then consider what it means for this PCD to be a "correct" implementation of the MLD.

This PCD has 5 inputs and one output. The output is either a root of f (of return value of **func** type) to within tolerance and after at most **maxit** iterations, or an exception. The inputs however are not clearly defined. Following the duck typing principle, **func** and **derivative** are only mandated to be callable. There are no bounds checks for **tolerance**, **x0** or **maxit**. To define a full contract for the PCD, we would have to check for all inputs if they match the prerequisites of the MLD. However, while using numerical differentiation we could try to verify that `derivative` matches f' in a number of sampling points, it is not clear to which accuracy this should be checked. We also have no means of verifying that x0 lies within the domain of `func` (checking if evaluating (func(x0)) produces a number, does not tell us, whether x0 is really within the domain or if the implementation of `func` just produced a random number).

For any valid input, checking whether the output is correct seems straightforward for the case where a root was found. Simply evaluate `func` at point y and compare if that is within tolerance range of 0. Yet this does not signify that we correctly implemented the algorithm described by the MLD. For instance, the actual implementation might be that of a completely different mathematical method with, for instance, a slower convergence speed. For the case that an error was returned, checking whether that is correct is also not simple. If any other exception than `NewtonError` was raised, the input might have been invalid. The `func` and `derivative` might not have been callable, or they might not accept x0 for the evaluation. Maybe the `tolerance` was of a data type that could not be compared with the residual. These error conditions, while tedious, are easy to check. If a `NewtonError` was raised deciding its correctness is more difficult. Needing more iterations than allowed could be a sign of numerical instability stemming from suboptimal implementation, which needs fixing. If the initial guess was not in the convergence ball or f has no roots at all, then getting an error is correct and expected.

It is obvious that the test implementer needs to input varying data into the function to properly test the algorithm. But how many different `func` instances should they run the test with? After all, C^1 is infinite dimensional. It needs to be sampled. What should the strategy be? How to ensure the most "impactful" representatives get chosen? How then to determine what the initial guess should be? Do they need to check the same function and initial guess combination with different tolerances?

These challenges for writing tests for the present PCD, and many more similar ones, are ubiquitous for all test writing in numerical software. In [16] Kanewala and Bieman have cataloged and categorized them by means of a systematic literature review. The number of interdependent, sometimes conflicting, choices and considerations can appear so large and complex for a scientist-developer they feel no test strategy will be good enough and as a consequence might not test at all. A flexible testing methodology is required that encourages and rewards incorporation of incrementally increasing knowledge about an algorithm. It also needs to be able to express mathematical concepts and properties which might not be checkable, but which are profoundly useful as documentation and for domain specific test-input generation tools.

3   Gradual Contracts

3.1   General Considerations

In this section then we explain how the Gradual Contracts Pattern helps implementers of numerical algorithms to document and test the properties of their

```
@GCP.pre('func: Function(Interval, float, diff=1)',
         'derivative: func.diff()',
         'x0: float', 'maxit: int', 'tolerance: float')
@GCP.pre('maxit > 0', 'tolerance > 0')
@GCP.post('abs(func(ret)) < tolerance')
@GCP.raises(NewtonError, when='derivative(err.x0) == 0')
@GCP.implies(GCP.args(lambda x: 1, lambda x: 0, 1, 100, 1e-3),
             GCP.post('almost_equal(ret, 0, 1e-15)'))
@GCP.implies(GCP.pre('func: Function(Interval, float, diff=2)',
                     'kantorovich(func, derivative, x0, maxit, tolerance, '
                     '            func.domain, func.diff(2).sup_norm))',
             GCP.no_error)
def newton_raphson(func, derivative, x0, maxit, tolerance):
    ...
```

Listing 1. Final contract specification for the Newton-Raphson algorithm

codes. Our approach is founded on the classical design-by-contract (DbC) [18] with special considerations for the numerical code writing space.

Following the Newton-Raphson PDC example from Sect. 2, we demonstrate how incrementally refining contracts and better testing form a feedback loop to produce easier to reason about and more robust code.

We will pretend to have a support library called GCP available that provides decorators to define pre and post conditions, can infer types and generate test inputs from contracts. Our decorators will generally be using a domain specific language to better express concerns and concepts, without using too many implementation-language specifics. As the first step we set type annotations for our inputs and outputs.

3.2 Library Primitives

The GCP library has a collection of primitives available to make this more concise. For instance, we are using the Interval primitive here to denote that func is a function of a real number, which might only be defined on a certain interval.

```
@GCP.pre('func: Function(Interval, float)',
         'derivative: Function(Interval, float)',
         'x0: float', 'maxit: int', 'tolerance: float')
@GCP.post('ret: float')
def newton_raphson(func, derivative, x0, maxit, tolerance):
    ...
```

The library provides a method to exercise a PCD in a test harness. Specifically GCP.test can introspect a given function object and its decorators to generate tests with varying inputs.

```
GCP.test(newton_raphson)
```

Since we did not define any more input properties `GCP.test` might generate this call

```
newton_raphson(lambda x:x, lambda x:0, 1, -1, -1)
```

which will raise a `NewtonError` right in the first iteration. Obviously we should evolve our contract to describe reasonable input bounds and check if the return value satisfies the convergence criterion.

```
@GCP.pre('maxit > 0', 'tolerance > 0')
@GCP.post('abs(func(ret)) < tolerance')
def newton_raphson(func, derivative, x0, maxit, tolerance):
    ...
```

Now a test call might instead be

```
newton_raphson(lambda x:x, lambda x:0, 1, 100, 1e-3)
```

which will result in a `ZeroDivisionError` because we did not consider the $f'(x) = 0$ case yet. Let us handle this case explicitly in the PDC and raise a `NewtonError` if it occurs. We can then use the `GCP.raises` mechanism to express when receiving an exception `err` is expected. In traditional DbC, reaching this error state might be prevented using a pre-condition like $f'(x) \neq 0$. In the context of numerical codes it is sometimes impossible to evaluate such a condition due to dimensionality of the input space. So while the function here is unable to fulfill its contract and raises an exception, if the `when` clause evaluates to `True` the test harness will still mark this test a success. This way we do not violate the second law of exception handling (Section 1.7.2, [18]).

```
@GCP.raises(NewtonError, when='derivative(err.x0) == 0')
def newton_raphson(func, derivative, x0, maxit, tolerance):
    ...
```

Now `GCP.test` recognizes that the input set results in a "correct" error and continue to generate more inputs. Take

```
newton_raphson(lambda x:x, lambda x:-1, 1, 100, 1e-3)
```

as our next example. This function call will terminate unsuccessfully after 100 iterations. Clearly we need to generate an input for `derivative` that is actually the derivative of `func`. Thankfully GCP includes primitives to describe relationships between arguments:

```
@GCP.pre('func: Function(Interval, float, diff=1)',
         'derivative: func.diff()',
         'x0: float', 'maxit: int', 'tolerance: float')
def newton_raphson(func, derivative, x0, maxit, tolerance):
    ...
```

Here, `diff=1` and `func.diff()` will not be used for runtime checking, but are strictly for documentation and test input generation purposes. Similarly, GCP includes primitives to specify matrices with given properties such as shape or condition number. This description now allows GCP to generate a matching pair of input functions:

```
newton_raphson(lambda x:x, lambda x:1, 1, 100, 1e-3)
```

3.3   Contingent Pre-/post-conditions

Another important feature of GCP is the ability to define output conditions which only need to match when certain input conditions are satisfied. In particular, we can use this to check the algorithm for explicit examples for which the correct output of the algorithm is known:

```
@GCP.implies(GCP.args(lambda x: 1, lambda x: 0, 1, 100, 1e-3),
             GCP.post('almost_equal(ret, 0, atol=1e-15)'))
def newton_raphson(func, derivative, x0, maxit, tolerance):
    ...
```

The final feature of GCP is the ability to encode knowledge of the algorithms behavior in an input dependent function. For the Newton-Raphson algorithm Kantorovich's theorem [14] guarantees convergence of the algorithm, if certain conditions on the input are satisfied. First we define a utility function to represent the criterion and then use it to express that if our preconditions satisfy it we expect no error (meaning the previously defined post-condition to be fulfilled). We note that our primitives (`Function`) are designed such that their properties (`func.domain`, `func.diff()`) can be referenced in the DSL.

```
def kantorovich(func, derivative, x0, maxit, tolerance, domain, L):
    h_0 = -1/derivative(x0)*func(x0)
    alpha_0 = L * abs(1 / derivative(x0)) * h_0
    x_1 = x_0 - h_0
    if alpha_0 > 0.5 or x_1 - h0 not in domain:
        return False
    max_residual = abs(func(x0)) * (0.25) ** maxit
    return max_residual < tolerance

@GCP.implies(GCP.pre('func: Function(Interval, float, diff=2)',
                     'kantorovich(func, derivative, x0, maxit, tolerance, '
             '                    func.domain, func.diff(2).sup_norm))',
                GCP.no_error)
def newton_raphson(func, derivative, x0, maxit, tolerance):
    ...
```

We emphasize, that the conditions of Kantorovich's theorem are restrictive, and the algorithm converges in many cases where these conditions are not met. As such, the final contract specification we have developed in this section (Listing 1) is still incomplete yet already gives extensive insights into the algorithm.

When generating random input data from these contracts, we may encounter test failures due to insufficient numerical accuracy. From these failing examples, we will then have to decide whether our implementation is flawed or whether we need to add further restrictions on the input, further extending our understanding of the algorithm.

4   Conclusion and Outlook

In this contribution we have shown how to gradually improve an algorithm's specification using GCP, after explaining the domain-specific challenges for testing numerical codes by non-experts. A prototype implementation of the GCP library for Python is currently work in progress. There we are leveraging the capabilities of the existing `icontract` [4] library to setup the contracts framework, while we use `hypothesis` [17] to generate test inputs from the primitives' specification. Critical to community adoption of approach and library will be a sufficiently large set of primitives and ease of adding new ones.

Acknowledgment. Funded by the Deutsche Forschungsgemeinschaft (DFG, German Research Foundation) under Germany's Excellence Strategy EXC 2044 - 390685587, Mathematics Münster: Dynamics-Geometry-Structure and under RA 3055/1-1: pyMOR – Nachhaltige Software zur Modell-Ordnungs-Reduktion.

References

1. Astropy testing guidelines. https://web.archive.org/web/20210610143923/https://docs.astropy.org/en/latest/development/testguide.html. Accessed 10 June 2021
2. The Boost Test documentation. http://go.wwu.de/5femy. Accessed 11 June 2021
3. How to write code like a scientist. http://go.wwu.de/xo8eu. Accessed 10 June 2021
4. icontract - design-by-contract in Python3 with informative violation messages and inheritance. http://go.wwu.de/b2ws6. Accessed 19 Aug 2021
5. Numpy testing guidelines. http://go.wwu.de/9fzha. Accessed 10 June 2021
6. Petsc testing system. http://go.wwu.de/2mnad. Accessed 10 June 2021
7. Pragmatic unit testing for scientific codes. http://go.wwu.de/4o1tl. Accessed 10 June 2021
8. Stan's user guide. http://go.wwu.de/mui45. Accessed 11 June 2021
9. Unit testing in R. http://go.wwu.de/qw4fl. Accessed 10 June 2021
10. Verify simulations with the method of manufactured solutions. http://go.wwu.de/f7dzl. Accessed 11 June 2021
11. Writing tests for scientific code. http://go.wwu.de/qzi0t. Accessed 10 June 2021
12. Mishap Investigation Board: Mars climate orbiter mishap investigation board phase I report (1999)
13. Dubois, P.F.: Testing scientific programs. Comput. Sci. Eng. **14**(4), 69–73 (2012)
14. Gragg, W., Tapia, R.: Optimal error bounds for the Newton-Kantorovich theorem. SIAM J. Numer. Anal. **11**(1), 10–13 (1974)
15. Harris, C.R., Millman, K.J., et al.: Array programming with NumPy. Nature **585**(7825), 357–362 (2020)

16. Kanewala, U., Bieman, J.M.: Testing scientific software: a systematic literature review. Inf. Softw. Technol. **56**(10), 1219–1232 (2014)
17. MacIver, D.R., Hatfield-Dodds, Z., Contributors, M.O.: Hypothesis: a new approach to property-based testing. J. Open Source Softw. **4**(43), 1891 (2019)
18. Meyer, B.: Applying "design by contract". Computer **25**(10), 40–51 (1992)
19. Miller, G.: A scientist's nightmare: software problem leads to five retractions (2006)
20. Wang, Q., Zhang, X., Zhang, Y., Yi, Q.: AUGEM: automatically generate high performance dense linear algebra kernels on x86 CPUs. In: SC 2013: Proceedings of the International Conference on High Performance Computing, Networking, Storage and Analysis, pp. 1–12 (2013)

Solving the Instance Identification Problem in Micro-service Testing

Theofanis Vassiliou-Gioles[✉][iD]

Weizenbaum Institute, Technische Universität Berlin, Berlin, Germany
vassiliou-gioles@tu-berlin.de

Abstract. Micro-service architecture has become a standard software architecture style, with loosely coupled, specified, and implemented services owned by small teams and independently deployable. In particular, with the emergence of managed services, deployment aspects have to be addressed explicitly. While tools and frameworks support micro-service developers in developing and unit-testing their services, less attention has been given to higher testing levels, particularly to the integration testing phase. This paper identifies aspects that limit the expressiveness of integration testing in the context of managed micros-services and function as a service. We propose the introduction of instance identification to overcome these limitations and illustrate how instance identification can be used to enhance integration testing's expressiveness.

Keywords: Software testing · Integration testing · Micro-service · Web service · Functions as a service · TTCN-3

1 Introduction

Today's standard way of using various IT resources is the availability over the internet, collectively called cloud computing. From "classical" service-oriented architecture (SOA) based application, using WSDL [16] and SOAP[15], this has been extended to microservice-based software architectures based on RESTful APIs (or REST API for short) [8] and HTTP [11] as transport protocol, in more recent times. Testing and testing methodologies have to be adopted to facilitate the delivery of high-quality applications and services in highly distributed service-oriented applications [4].

Canfora and Di Penta [5] identify five key issues that limit the testability of service-centric systems. Addressing different challenges various approaches have been proposed for testing service-centric software systems [6], as well as testing micro-services based software systems [1,12,14].

In the context of serverless architectures with Functions as a Service (FaaS) being their most prominent recent representative, two of the five key issues identified by Canfora, namely "lack of control" and "dynamicity and adaptiveness", limits the expressiveness of integration and regression testing. Lack of control

© IFIP International Federation for Information Processing 2022
Published by Springer Nature Switzerland AG 2022
D. Clark et al. (Eds.): ICTSS 2021, LNCS 13045, pp. 189–195, 2022.
https://doi.org/10.1007/978-3-031-04673-5_15

because the services or functions are running on independently managed infrastructure, which limits the ability of testers to determine which services, or to be more precise which concrete instance of service is being invoked.

This paper would like to close the gap and proposes the introduction of *instance identification* for micro-services via HTTP header fields in Sect. 2. We will discuss the relation to approaches like request-ids in Sect. 3 and reflect the limitations of our proposal in Sect. 4. Finally, in Sect. 5 we will present some lessons learned and gives a short outlook on future work.

2   Instance Identification and Integration Testing

2.1   Integration Testing

One of the testing phases is the integration testing phase. This phase tests whether groups of components operate together as intended in the technical system design or specification [10].

So we speak of integration testing if, in a generic web-service architecture as shown in Fig. 1, we integrate, for example, μSC with μSA and test them as a group. The emphasis of the integration test is the successful communication between them, as we assume that all services have been thoroughly unit tested.

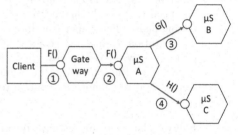

Fig. 1. Generic, abstract web-service architecture with three micro services μSA - μSC accessible via a Gateway

Integration testing of a group of components is typically done via stimulation of service-group at the edges, thus triggering interaction between the grouped components under test. In our case, we use F at μSA (via the *Gateway*) and evaluate the response to F to conclude successful integration[1].

A managed environment limits tester's control on which instance of a service will be used. The platform is under complete control, which deployed service is used and when. Therefore a tester has to observe or infer the information whether a deployed service under test has been used, or not.

If provided, this information can be retrieved by the tester directly from the tested components. Alternatively, the tester could try to correlate generated trace information with the test events to demonstrate successful integration.

We propose introducing an instance identification identifier in the communication of micro-services, thus enriching the communication between services for testing purposes.

---

[1] In this paper, we are not discussing test case generation or test case evaluation strategies but concentrate on the minimum requirements that any testing strategy implies, interacting with a group of components at the edges and evaluating observations.

2.2 Identification of Micro-services as Software Components

Micro-services have to be identified on different levels, first on the service level, defining which service to use and how to reach the named service. Second, we identify a given service by the API version, defining which capability set is offered by the named service. API versioning is typically but not necessarily defined and documented in machine-processable formats like WSDL or OpenAPI specifications. Major or incompatible versions updates are often reflected on resource level, i.e., as part of the URL. Last but not least, a service is identified by the concrete implementation version, specified by build-version, or other means if multiple instances of different implementation versions are accessible. While the first two levels are well and understood and practiced, identifying concrete instances, i.e., the precise identification of the communicating software components at execution time, is heavily neglected. Still, the information is particularly crucial in the testing of a micro-service-based application.

2.3 Micro-service Instance Identification

We propose the introduction of a micro-service *instance identification* (IID) as an additional request and response header field in HTTP to increase their testability, in particular, their observability aspects as defined by Binder [3][2].

The primary purpose of our IID is to relate the result of an operation to the contributing micro-services. Thus we define the following requirements for the instance identification of micro-services

R1 The micro-service should be identifiable by name
R2 The micro-service's version number should be exposed, which identifies the version of the micro-service. This version is not related to the API version the micro-service is exposing.
R3 Optionally, version control information that unambiguously identifies the source file status of the build
R4 Information that describes the up-time of a service
R5 A returned IID should include the IIDs of micro-services that have been called to implement the response to a request.
R6 To limit exposure of internal information, IIDs should be disclosed only on request by the caller.
R7 Optionally, to request IIDs might require authorization

Figure 2a shows the proposed request header for HTTP. A client requests the disclosure of the identity of the used services by sending the X-Instance-Id header field with the value "empty" (R6) or, if authorization is being implemented (see Sect. 4) <IIDkey>, with <IIDkey> as authorization key (R7)[3].

---

[2] While we do not limit the application of IIDs in different protocols, we are focusing here on the HTTP.
[3] The assignment and communication of authorization keys is outside the scope of this paper and will be discussed in the future.

<pre>
                                    CIID := MIID [„(" UIDs+ „)"]
                                    UIDs := CIID [„+" CIID]+
X-Instance-ID: empty | key=<IIDKey> MIID := <sN>„/"<vN>[„/"<vA>]„%"<t>„s"
</pre>

(a) Structure of an HTTP IID request   X-Instance-ID: CIID
header
                                    (b) Structure of an HTTP IID response
                                    header

Fig. 2. HTTP header fields

A micro-service responding to a request which contains a valid
X-Instance-Id header field shall respond with the response header field
X-Instance-Id with a complete IID (CIID) containing its own micro-service iden-
tifier (MIID) and a structured list of contributing MIIDs as shown in Fig 2b (R5).

A micro-service's MIID shall contain the following elements

- <sN> representing the service name (R1)
- <vN> representing the version number of the microservice sN (R2)
- optionally, <vA> representing additional information like, for example, the
  branch name used in the version control system and/or a commit identification, for example, a potentially shortened git commit ID (R3)
- <t> the epoch time of the service, in seconds (R4)

```
1 X-Instance-Id: msA/1.1.3/src%12s(msB/3.0/dev-9987efa%12s+
    msC/2.1.1%4071s(msD/5.2.x/main-unknown%12s))
```

Listing 1.1. Example of IIDs returned by the the called micro-service msA to the
tester client

As a result, if the IID request is forwarded to all contributing micro-services
and they respond with their IID, the resulting CIID describes the complete
micro-service graph for this request. Listing 1.1 shows a complete CIID with
various MIIDs as returned by μSA using micro-services μSB-μSD from Fig. 1.

3   Comparison with Other External Purpose Header Fields

The requirement to expose and transfer internal server information to a requesting client is not uncommon with web services. Standard response header fields
like Server [7] or framework-specific header fields like Microsoft's .NET framework X-AspNet-Version are widely being used to communicate internal information. We call this type of information external purpose header fields as they
carry information neither required for the remote API's protocol implementation
nor required for the remote API.

Other examples of external purpose header fields are trace-id as
used by Amazon's AWS X-Ray (X-Amzn-Trace-Id) [2] or Google Trace
(X-Cloud-Trace-Context) [9].

The trace-ids have in common that they offer a proprietary way to trace individual calls through the contributing services in a managed platform. The primary purpose of these services is to support *operations* to log and monitor distributed applications.

They also have in common that they do not contain any instance information as defined above by default. While every platform supports the addition of the necessary information, this must be performed individually and platform-specific. Integration testing, performed via the edges, relying on trace-ids requires additional integration efforts with the managed platforms to access and evaluate logs or retrieve the correlated information per request.

4   Limitations and Other Considerations of the Presented Approach

By using the presented IID approach, some limitations have to be taken into account, which will be discussed in the following.

While not limited by the HTTP protocol, in practice servers might restrict the length of header fields. Assuming a minimum header field length of 8190 bytes and an average IID size of 50–100 bytes, 80–160 IIDs could be carried by a response header field which we consider sufficient in practical setups.

In asynchronous communication, where the result of an operation is communicated to the requesting client via other channels than the request, only the request delivery is acknowledged in the response. Therefore, a response including a CIID would typically contain the first contacted service only, which in general is not sufficient. Depending on the selected method, different strategies are currently being analyzed to coherently correlate the operation request, the result, and the participating services.

Exposing detailed internal information of software components, like version numbers, is often considered bad practice from a security perspective. Attackers could exploit this knowledge by creating precise attack vectors for specific versions of the software component. Thus we introduce the possibility to authorize legitimate receivers only, by including authorization keys (`key=<IIDkey>`) when requesting IIDs[4].

Further, we consider the case where a micro-service-based application uses authorization at the boundaries and no authorization inside. In this case, the *Gateway* would validate a received IIDkey. After successful validation, it would rewrite the header field indicating "no authorization" to the used services. This centralization simplifies key management and concentrates it at the *Gateway*. Also, it reduces the overhead by removing the necessity to validate the IIDkey at every micro-service.

---

[4] The assignment and communication of authorization keys is outside the scope of this paper and will be discussed in the future.

5   Lessons Learned and Outlook

We have embedded instance identification capabilities into our services primarily to facilitate integration testing. The overhead to support instance identification was very low, both from an implementation and run-time perspective.

By implementing instance identification into our service as a standard pattern, developers profit most from the continuous presence of this additional information when developing each service. In particular, the epoch information embedded in the services' MIID reduced the round-trip time (developing, deploying, unit testing) by giving easy-to-access instance information. Furthermore, it helped avoid situations where interacting with the wrong instance of a given service happened due to wrong or incomplete deployment configurations - for example, starting an updated version of a service while a previous service was still alive. In such cases, experimenting (in the development phase) or testing was done against the unexpected, previous service version, running, for example, on the default port. In contrast, the updated service version has used a different, dynamically allocated port. With the presence of the IID and its availability, the impact of these situations could be minimized.

In the debugging phase, the CIID, more precisely the embedded call graph, provided invaluable omnipresent information on the interactions of the services. Omnipresent, as the X-Instance-Id header is visible immediately in various tools that are being used to trigger and debug services. From simple tools like curl to more visual tools like Postman.

For the integration testing phase in our CI/CD pipeline, we implemented IID support in our TTCN-3 based test environment [13]. As <vA> element of the IID, we have been using a combination of the current VCS-branch name and a (short) commit-id, in the form master-60c74ad. General assertions on the epoch time of the micro-services under test, as well as additional information within the <vA> element, have added value to the test results, as we managed to automatically assert that the latest committed version was interacting in the integration test scenario.

While hiding the information contained in IIDs from end-users or clients in production, embedding it and making it available at hand in the development and testing phase reduces the development round-trip times. We are currently investigating in a fintech environment how IIDs can be used in professionally developed, large scale-microservice applications and extend the applicability to asynchronous communication paradigms.

Acknowledgment. Funded by the Federal Ministry of Education and Research of Germany (BMBF) under grant no. 16DII113. We are also grateful to the anonymous reviewers for their valuable suggestions to improve the presented ideas in this paper.

References

1. Ashikhmin, N., Radchenko, G., Tchernykh, A.: RAML-based mock service generator for microservice applications testing. In: Voevodin, V., Sobolev, S. (eds.) Supercomputing. RuSCDays 2017. CCIS, vol. 793, pp. 456–467. Springer, Cham (2017). https://doi.org/10.1007/978-3-319-71255-0_37
2. AWS: AWS X-Ray concepts - AWS X-Ray. https://docs.amazonaws.cn/en_us/xray/latest/devguide/xray-concepts.html
3. Binder, R.V.: Design for testability in object-oriented systems. Commun. ACM **37**(9), 87–101 (1994). https://doi.org/10.1145/182987.184077
4. Bucchiarone, A., Severoni, F.: Testing service composition. In: ASSE: Proceedings of the 8th Argentine Symposium on Software Engineering (2007)
5. Canfora, G., Di Penta, M.: Service-oriented architectures testing: a survey. In: De Lucia, A., Ferrucci, F. (eds.) ISSSE 2006–2008. LNCS, vol. 5413, pp. 78–105. Springer, Heidelberg (2009). https://doi.org/10.1007/978-3-540-95888-8_4
6. Canfora, G., Penta, M.D.: SOA: testing and self-checking. In: Bertolino, A. (ed.) Proceedings of International Workshop on Web Services - Modeling and Testing (WS-MaTE), Palermo, Italy, pp. 3–11, June 2006
7. Fielding, R., Reschke, J.: Hypertext transfer protocol (HTTP/1.1): Semantics and Content - RFC 7231, June 2014. https://tools.ietf.org/html/rfc7231. Library Catalog: tools.ietf.org
8. Fielding, R.T.: Architectural styles and the design of network-based software architectures. Doctoral thesis. University of California, Irvine (2000). https://www.ics.uci.edu/~fielding/pubs/dissertation/top.htm
9. Google Cloud: Cloud Trace documentation—Google Cloud. https://cloud.google.com/trace/docs
10. ISTQB.International Software Testing Qualifications Board: ISTQB Glossary. https://glossary.istqb.org/en/search/
11. Reschke, J.F., Fielding, R.T.: Hypertext Transfer Protocol (HTTP/1.1): Message Syntax and Routing - RFC 7230. https://tools.ietf.org/html/rfc7230#page-26
12. Savchenko, D., Radchenko, G.: Microservices validation: methodology and implementation. In: CEUR Workshop Proceedings. CEUR Workshop Proceedings, Yekaterinburg, Russia, vol. 1513, pp. 21–28 (2015). iSSN: 16130073
13. Vassiliou-Gioles, T.: A simple, lightweight framework for testing RESTful services with TTCN-3. In: 2020 IEEE 20th International Conference on Software Quality, Reliability and Security Companion (QRS-C), QRS-C 2020, Macao, China, pp. 498–505. IEEE, October 2020. https://doi.org/10.1109/QRS-C51114.2020.00089. https://qrs20.techconf.org/QRSC2020_FULL/pdfs/QRS-C2020-4QOuHkY3M10ZUl1MoEzYvg/891500a498/891500a498.pdf
14. Viglianisi, E., Dallago, M., Ceccato, M.: RESTTESTGEN: automated black-box testing of restful APIs. In: 2020 IEEE 13th International Conference on Software Testing, Validation and Verification (ICST), pp. 142–152, October 2020. https://doi.org/10.1109/ICST46399.2020.00024. iSSN: 2159-4848
15. W3C: Simple Object Access Protocol (SOAP) 1.1 (2000). https://www.w3.org/TR/2000/NOTE-SOAP-20000508/
16. W3C: Web Services Description Language (WSDL) Version 2.0 Part 1: Core Language (2007). https://www.w3.org/TR/wsdl20/

On the Quality of Network Flow Records for IDS Evaluation: A Collaborative Filtering Approach

Marta Catillo[(✉)], Andrea Del Vecchio, Antonio Pecchia, and Umberto Villano

Dipartimento di Ingegneria, Università degli Studi del Sannio, Benevento, Italy
{marta.catillo,andrea.delvecchio,antonio.pecchia,villano}@unisannio.it

Abstract. Network flow records consist of categorical and numerical features that provide context data and summary statistics computed from the raw packets exchanged between pairs of nodes in a network. Flow records labeled by human experts are typically used in high speed networks to design and evaluate intrusion detection systems. In spite of the ever-increasing body of literature on flow-based intrusion detection, there is no contribution that investigates the accuracy of flow records at rendering the class of traffic of the original aggregation of packets.

This paper proposes a collaborative filtering approach to compute sanitized labels for a given set of flow records. Sanitized labels are compared with the labels assigned by human experts. Experiments are done with CICIDS2017, i.e., an intrusion detection dataset that provides raw packets and labeled flow records obtained from benign operations and attack conditions. Results indicate that around 3.61% flow records might fail to render benign aggregations of packets; surprisingly, the percentage of flow records, which fail to render aggregations of packets pertaining to attacks, ranges from 5.39% to 27.18% depending on the type of attack. These findings indicate the need for improving the features collected or potential imperfections while computing the flow records.

Keywords: Network flows · Research datasets · Intrusion detection systems · Collaborative filtering

1 Introduction

A **network flow** is an aggregation of packets exchanged between a *source* computer and a *destination* across a network; a flow of packets is logically equivalent to a "call" or a "connection" according to the RFC 2722[1]. Network flows are a common abstraction for analyzing network traffic. Network flows are conveniently represented by **network flow records**, which consist of categorical and numeric features that provide context data and summary statistics computed

---

[1] https://datatracker.ietf.org/doc/html/rfc2722.

© IFIP International Federation for Information Processing 2022
Published by Springer Nature Switzerland AG 2022
D. Clark et al. (Eds.): ICTSS 2021, LNCS 13045, pp. 196–209, 2022.
https://doi.org/10.1007/978-3-031-04673-5_16

from the headers of the packets pertaining to a flow. Commonly-used features include, but are not limited to, source-destination IP address and port, duration, number and length of packets, flag counts, min, max, mean, and standard deviation of the packet inter-arrival time. There exist many products –either commercial or developed by the academic community– supporting the abstraction of flow and to compute flow records, such as Netflow[2], CICFlowMeter[3] and Tranalyzer[4]. For example, CICFlowMeter generates fixed-length flow records (83 values per record, not including the label). It is worth noting that flow records are used in high speed networks to overcome the limitations of payload inspection-based methods [21]. Moreover, many existing public datasets are based on the notion of flow records [16].

Nowadays, the research community leverages network flow records to develop modern intrusion detection techniques. In fact, many detectors have spread in the literature [5,8,13]. In this domain, intrusion detection consists in identifying the flow records that point to aggregations of packets related to attack conditions. In spite of the ever-increasing body of literature on the design and evaluation of flow-based intrusion detection systems, to the best of our knowledge there is no contribution that investigates the *quality* of flow records. By **quality** we mean the accuracy of the flow records at *rendering* the class of traffic, i.e., benign or attack, of the original aggregation of packets. It should be noted that there is an information gap between the packets that pertain to a given flow and the high-level –and occasionally aggregated– statistics of the corresponding flow record. More importantly, many existing attacks rely on forging malicious headers and packets: this bears the risk that flows and, in turn, the corresponding records are misled by inherently corrupted data.

This paper proposes an approach to measure the quality of network flow records. Our measurement study is based on publicly-available flow records that pertain to both benign operations and Denial of Service (DoS) attacks from CICIDS2017, i.e., a widely-used dataset for designing and evaluating IDS techniques. The reference CICIDS2017 paper [17] is rapidly approaching 900+ Google scholar citations at the time of this writing; given the increasing attention by the community, this dataset is strongly relevant in the context of our work. Flow records were obtained with CICFlowMeter, i.e., a software tool developed by the same research team proposing CICIDS2017.

Our approach is based on **collaborative filtering**. The approach relies on the availability of two disjoint sets of labeled flow records, i.e., **target set** (R, L_R) and **control set** (C, L_C): R and C are matrices of values, where rows represent flow records, while L_R and L_C are column vectors providing the *expert labels* of the records. **Expert labels** represent the "intended" class of traffic, i.e., BENIGN or ATTACK (encoded with 0 and 1, respectively), of the packets summarized by the flow records. As for CICIDS2017 –collected in a controlled environment

---

[2] https://www.cisco.com/c/en/us/products/ios-nx-os-software/ios-netflow/index.html.

[3] https://github.com/ahlashkari/CICFlowMeter.

[4] https://tranalyzer.com/.

by means of simulated attacks– *expert labels* were manually established by the domain experts based on the precise knowledge of attackers and victims nodes, and the time the attacks were conducted. In this respect, *expert labels* represent the true class of traffic of the records. We aim to measure whether the records, consisting of summary features in lieu of the raw packets, do render the intended class of traffic. Our approach is twofold: for each record/row r in R, we (i) determine its *top-N* closest neighbor rows in C based on the cosine similarity and (ii) compute a supplementary label for r, i.e., the **sanitized label**, based on the expert labels of the closest neighbors. Overall, we compute a supplement column vector of labels for R, i.e., L'_R, aimed to assessing experts' choices. By comparing L_R and L'_R we note that around 3.61% flow records might fail to render benign aggregations of packets; surprisingly, the percentage of flow records, which fail to render aggregations of packets related to attacks, ranges from 5.39% to 27.18% depending on the type of DoS attack. Moreover, we also note that UDP flow records are less prone to errors when compared to TCP. These findings indicate the need for improving the features collected, potential imperfections while computing the flows, or specific behaviors of the attacks that distort the computation of the flow records.

The rest of the paper is organized as follows. Section 2 presents related work in the area. Section 3 describes our collaborative filtering approach to compute the sanitized labels. Section 4 presents the results of our study, while Sect. 5 concludes the paper and provides future perspectives of our work.

2   Related Work

Nowadays intrusion detection datasets have become ubiquitous among researchers and practitioners. They aim –at least in theory– to represent real-world data, and sophistication and volume of security threats along with regular network traffic behaviors. Customarily, network traffic is generated in synthetic environments and captured in either packet-based or flow-based format. Packet-based data encompass complete payload information, whereas flow-based data, collected only from the packet headers, provide records of aggregate and summary statistics on the top of corresponding flows. It is worth pointing out that traffic classification by using flow records is often proposed as an alternative to payload inspection-based methods [21]. As a matter of fact, most intrusion detection datasets are distributed as labeled network flow records, organized in comma-separated values files specially crafted to apply modern machine learning techniques. In particular, each record is the representation of a flow and the label states if it relates to benign or attack packets.

An example of flow-based intrusion detection dataset widely used in the literature is certainly CICIDS2017 [17]. Released by the Canadian Institute for Cybersecurity (CIC) in 2017, it simulates real-world network data and uses the tool CICFlowMeter to produce labeled flow records. The authors provide benign traces to create profiles for synthetically generating HTTP, SMTP, SSH, IMAP, POP3 (email), and FTP traffic, for 25 users. The range of threats includes:

Brute Force FTP, Brute Force SSH, DoS, Heartbleed, Web Attack, Infiltration, Botnet and DDoS. Another popular public intrusion detection dataset is **UGR'16**[5] [14], proposed by the University of Granada. It contains netflow records spanning more than four months of network traffic from an Internet Service Provider (ISP) and comprises 16900 million unidirectional flow records. An important feature of this dataset is that the background traffic was captured from sensors located in an ISP network, which normally models heterogeneous profiles of clients. A recent dataset is **USB-IDS-1**[6] [3]. It provides ready-to-use labeled normal and abnormal network flow records and considers both network traffic and application-level facets, such as defense modules of the victim server under attack [6]. Other known flow-based intrusion datasets are **CTU-13**[7] [9], **TUIDS**[8] [2,10] and **ISCX 2012**[9] [18]. It is worth noting that in the last few years papers that look more critically at these datasets have spread. For example in [4] the authors analyze the representativeness of the data contained in public intrusion detection datasets. They observe that public datasets do not fit real-life conditions, and therefore the value of analysis performed against them may be of questionable value.

Network flow records play a key role in many machine-learning based intrusion detection systems. As mentioned above, thanks to the *granularity* of flow records, distinguishing accurately and timely between normative and attack traffic is a trivial task. Traditional network anomaly detection involves developing models based on packet inspection [19]. However, the massive use of encrypted protocols makes packet-based inspection unsuited for today's networks. Therefore, flow-based intrusion detection is an active research topic [7]. A detailed review of flow-based detection is proposed by Sperotto et al. [20]. They focus on NetFlow data and provide a detailed discussion of detection techniques. Umer et al. [21], instead, summarize current available flow-based datasets used for evaluation of intrusion detection methods and survey flow-based intrusion detection methods.

Typically, many intrusion detectors are implemented with well-known classifiers, which are able to detect almost all the anomalous records contained in the dataset used for the training phase. For example, a comparative analysis between different classifiers is reported in [1]. All algorithms are evaluated by means of the CICIDS2017 dataset. In [11], instead, the authors describe a feature reduction approach based on the combination of filter-based algorithms, namely Information Gain Ratio (IGR), Correlation (CR), and ReliefF (ReF). In particular, they aim to reduce the number of features and exploit a rule-based classifier called Projective Adaptive Resonance Theory (PART) in order to detect DoS attacks. The classifier is evaluated on CICIDS2017 and achieves 99.95% accuracy. The detector proposed in [22] is specifically focused on DoS detection; a neural-network based approach relying on the implementation of a simple

---

[5] https://nesg.ugr.es/nesg-ugr16/.

[6] http://idsdata.ding.unisannio.it.

[7] https://www.stratosphereips.org/datasets-ctu13.

[8] http://agnigarh.tezu.ernet.in/~dkb/resources.html.

[9] http://www.unb.ca/cic/datasets/ids.html.

Multi-Layer Perceptron is compared to the Random Forest technique. Again focused on DoS detection is the paper [12], where well-known machine learning approaches (e.g., Naïve Bayes and Logistic Regression) are used to distinguish normative conditions from malicious ones.

3   Proposed Approach

3.1   Collaborative Filtering

Our approach is based on a technique called **collaborative filtering**. This technique is typically leveraged in the context of *recommendation systems*, which aim to suggest items (e.g., books, movies, articles) to customers. These systems attempt to compute the **rating** a user A would give to a certain item, based on the ratings given to the same item by users deemed "similar" to A. Similar users are selected among those who rated more or less analogously the same items rated by A. The approach is composed by two steps:

- in the first step, users similar to A (also called **neighbors**) are identified by computing a *distance metric* between A and the pool of users who rated some items. The selected **distance metric** may be computed for all the users; however, only the users whose distance from A is lower than a specific threshold will be considered close enough to be deemed *neighbors*.
- given the closest neighbors, the rating for the item to be recommended to A is computed based on the ratings provided by the closest neighbors. For instance, the rating is computed as the mean of the ratings. If the rating is higher than a certain threshold, then the item is recommended (there is a high probability that A will like the item, just like his/her similar users); on the contrary, if the rating is lower than the threshold, the item will not be recommended.

The steps above are common for every collaborative filtering approach. However, distinct implementations may differ in some factors, such as the distance (or similarity) metric, the threshold computation and, consequently, the way the neighbors are identified. As for the latter, beside the aforementioned threshold strategy, closest neighbors can be identified by sorting them according to the computed distance/similarity metric and by selecting the *top-N* ones[10].

Although our study does not pertain to recommendations, we adopt a similar approach to compute the **sanitized label** (i.e., the "rating" in the recommendation terminology) for a given flow record; computation is done by relying on the closest neighbor flow records based on a certain distance metric. This concept is further elaborated in Sect. 3.3.

---

[10] If a distance metric is adopted, the computed distances need to be sorted in ascending order; on the other hand, sorting needs to be in descending order in case of similarity metrics.

3.2   Neighbors Selection Metrics

In spite of the variety of available metrics, these can be grouped into two categories: *euclidean metrics* and *non-euclidean metrics*. While the latter needs to be used, for instance, when the observations encompass also categorical features, the former is adopted when the observations belong to an $\mathbb{R}^n$ vector space, i.e., each observation can be shaped as a vector of n dimensions, each of which varies in a range of real numbers.

One of the most known distance metric is the L_2 distance, better known as euclidean distance, which can be computed as:

$$L_2(x, y) = \sqrt{\sum_{i}^{n} (x_i - y_i)^2} \tag{1}$$

where x and y represent the vectors between which the metric is computed. The value computed by (1) represents the length of the difference vector obtained by subtracting x from y (or viceversa), which is basically the vector that joins the data points related to the vectors used for the calculation. This metric is widely used because its underlying distance concept is simple and intuitive: two points can be considered similar if they lie close to each other in the observation space, i.e., the value of the metric is small.

On the other hand, an important similarity metric –although slightly more difficult to grasp– is the *cosine similarity*. Just like the previously described one, the *cosine similarity* can be leveraged in a euclidean space to estimate how similar two data points are. The similarity can be computed as:

$$cosine\ similarity(x, y) = \frac{x \cdot y}{\|x\|\|y\|} \tag{2}$$

As for (2), the metric is equal to the cosine of the angle θ formed by the two vectors, which can be computed as the ratio between the *dot* product of x and y and the product of their norms. This means that the narrower θ, the more similar x and y. It is worth noting that according to this metric, indeed, two data points will appear closer to each other than the rest of the data observations, if their vectors show a similar pattern in terms of relationship between features.

Because of this peculiarity and the specific structure of the dataset in hand, we decided to adopt the **cosine similarity** for our experiments.

3.3   Computation of the Sanitized Labels

Collaborative filtering in our domain is applied as follows. We rely on two disjoint sets of flow records labeled by domain experts: (i) the former contains the flow records to be assessed, i.e., **TARGET SET**, and (ii) the latter provides the pool of potential neighbors, i.e., **CONTROL SET**. We use two sets in order to avoid any possible bias that could arise from computing a similarity metric between instances included in the same set. The flow records (i.e., vectors of features) are used to compute the similarity, while the labels are 0 or 1.

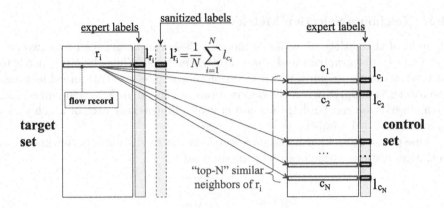

Fig. 1. Representation of the proposed approach.

Data: TARGET SET, CONTROL SET
Result: Sanitized labels for the flow records in the TARGET SET
for *each flow record in TARGET SET* **do**
| determine the top-15 similar neighbors from the CONTROL SET;
| compute the sanitized label of the flow record as the mean of the labels of
| the similar neighbors;
end

Algorithm 1: Computation of the sanitized labels

Algorithm 1 formalizes the computation of the sanitized labels. For each flow record in the *TARGET SET*, we determine its *top*-15 most similar neighbors. We rely on 15 neighbors because this is a good trade-off between flexibility and consistency. Indeed, if we considered too few similar instances, all the records in the *TARGET SET* would appear as perfectly labeled, because neighbors belonging to a different class –which unavoidably lie further in the observation space– would be not taken into account. On the contrary, considering a wider range of neighbors may cause the final score to suffer from the influence of those records which, despite being far from the one under evaluation, were still considered as close. It should be noted that the value of N is in line with other approaches adopted for label sanitization [15].

As represented in Fig. 1, the sanitized label is given by the mean of the expert labels of the *top-N* similar neighbors from the *CONTROL SET*. We leverage the mean because it makes it possible to find out the cases where the expert label is equal to or different from the sanitized label. In fact, when the sanitized label equals 0 or 1 it implies that the batch of neighbors all belong to the same class. We compute the cosine similarity between the records of the *TARGET SET* and every record contained in *CONTROL SET* by means of the Python library SciKit Learn[11].

---

[11] https://scikit-learn.org/stable/.

4   Experimental Results

4.1   Reference Dataset

CICIDS2017[12] is a public dataset created by the Canadian Institute for Cybersecurity (CIC) [17]. It consists of both benign and malicious traffic obtained by means of state-of-the-practice attack tools. The dataset is based on a laboratory environment with attacker and victim nodes; it contains both packet capture files (`pcap`) and bidirectional flow records in the form of comma separated values files (`csv`). Each record –obtained from the network packets by means of CICFlowMeter– is identified by 83 features. Records are accompanied by the labels supplied by domain experts, i.e., either BENIGN or a given attack. The data capture period started at 9 a.m., Monday, July 3, 2017 and ended at 5 p.m., Friday, July 7, 2017, for a total of 5 days. In the context of our study we focus on flow records from Wednesday –named *CICIDS2017-Wednesday* in the following– that pertains to Denial of Service (DoS) attacks in addition to benign traffic. In particular, the attacker was a Kali Linux node and the victim an Ubuntu 16.04 system with an Apache web server.

4.2   Data Preprocessing

We preprocess the CICIDS2017-Wednesday `csv` file to make it suitable for the analysis. First, we remove non-relevant or biasing features, i.e., *timestamp* and *id* of the flow records, *source address* and *port*, *destination address* and *port*, which leads to total 78 remaining features (label included). According to the method described in Sect. 3, flow records referring to different types of attacks are considered as belonging to a generic class named ATTACK – encoded with 1 (one); BENIGN records are assigned the label 0 (zero).

Flow records in the aforementioned CICIDS2017-Wednesday file are split into three **disjoint subsets**, i.e., *model*, *control* and *target*. While splitting the file, we adopt a stratified sampling strategy with no replacement, which means that (i) the ratio between benign and attack classes of the original file is preserved in the output splits and (ii) each record from the original file is assigned to a unique split. The original CICIDS2017-Wednesday file contains 692703 flow records, where 1297 are discarded due to the presence of malformed or unsuitable values (e.g., "Infinity" or "NaN"); moreover, we discard from the analysis the Heartbleed attack class, which consists of only 11 records. The remaining 691395 records are divided as follows:

- **TARGET SET**: *15%* of the total (i.e., 103706), divided into 65952 BENIGN and 37754 ATTACK flow records;
- **CONTROL SET**: *15%* of the total (i.e., 103706), divided into 65952 BENIGN and 37754 ATTACK flow records;
- **MODEL**: *70%* of the total (i.e., 483975) divided into 307778 BENIGN and 176197 ATTACK flow records.

---

[12] https://www.unb.ca/cic/datasets/ids-2017.html.

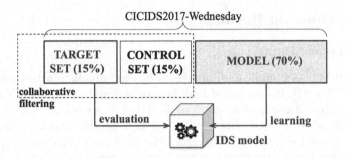

Fig. 2. Evaluation framework.

As a minor note, it can be noted that the three splits sum up to 691387, i.e., 8 records less than the total. Occasionally, the chosen percentages did not return an integer number of flow records to be assigned to a given split; in such cases, the number is rounded down to the highest preceding integer.

Figure 2 provides a representation of the evaluation framework. *TARGET SET* and *CONTROL SET* are used for the collaborative filtering approach in order to gain insight into the quality of flow records at rendering the intended class of traffic. After the application of the approach, for each flow record of the *TARGET SET* we have both the expert label and its "paired" sanitized label. The *MODEL* split is used to learn an IDS model for assessing the impact of the quality of flow records on intrusion detection.

4.3   Quality Assessment and Impact on Intrusion Detection

Table 1 (`all` row) shows the number of flow records of the *TARGET SET* where the expert label is *equal* to or *different* from the sanitized label, i.e., 98848 and 4858, respectively. It is worth noting that the two contributions sum up to 103706, i.e., the total records (`total` column). According to the results, the *percentage* of flow records that *do not* properly render the class of traffic intended by the domain experts is thus $\frac{4858}{103706} \cdot 100$, i.e., 4.68%. Through the rest of this Section, **percentage** quantifies the quality of flow records at rendering the expert label: *the higher percentage, the lower the quality.*

The breakdown of the `all` row by **class of traffic** is shown by `BENIGN` and `ATTACK` rows in Table 1. As for the `BENIGN` records of the *TARGET SET* there are 63574 equal and 2378 different labels, i.e., 3.61% different labels out of total 65952 `BENIGN`. Interestingly, the percentage of different labels increases up to 6.57% for `ATTACK` records, i.e., 2480 out of 37754. The difference can be appreciated in Fig. 3a, where it can be noted that the percentage for `ATTACK` is significantly higher than `BENIGN`. The finding indicates that flow records –mostly computed from packet headers– may suffer from packet forging and specifically-crafted HTTP interactions, such as for DoS attacks, that do not reflect into the numeric features.

Table 1. Breakdown of the collaborative filtering results by class of traffic and protocol.

	equal	**different**	*total*	**percentage**
all	*98848*	*4858*	*103706*	*4.68%*
breakdown by class of traffic				
BENIGN	63574	2378	*65952*	3.61%
ATTACK	35274	2480	*37754*	6.57%
breakdown by protocol				
TCP	68378	4710	*73088*	6.44%
UDP	30431	140	*30571*	0.46%
unspecified	39	8	*47*	17.02%

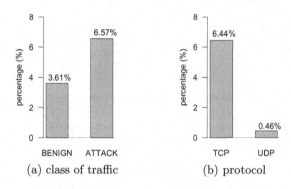

(a) class of traffic   (b) protocol

Fig. 3. Percentage of different flow records by class of traffic and protocol.

Table 1 provides a further breakdown of the `all` row by **protocol**, i.e., TCP and UDP rows[13]. One interesting outcome is that most of the cases where the expert label differs from the sanitized label pertain to TCP, i.e., 6.44%; as for UDP, the percentage is only 0.46%. Percentages are represented also in Fig. 3b. It must be noted that all the attacks considered in this paper capitalize on various weaknesses of TCP and HTTP; in consequence, UDP flow records are obtained only from benign traffic. In spite of the lack of attack instances, it can be reasonably claimed that UDP flow records are less affected by error when compared to TCP, as it can be noted by looking at the percentage of the BENIGN row in Table 1, which encompasses both TCP and UDP. We hypothesize that UDP, which is a stateless protocol, is much more easy to handle –and thus, less prone to errors– when packets are grouped by flows and transformed into records.

Table 2 provides the breakdown of ATTACK flow records. To this aim, the ATTACK row from Table 1 –reproduced in Table 2 as the `all` row– is divided by type of DoS attack available in CICIDS2017-Wednesday. It can be noted that the total number of records, i.e., 37754, is composed of 4 attacks whose

---

[13] For a small number of flow records the protocol field is unspecified.

Table 2. Breakdown of the collaborative filtering results by type of DoS attack.

	equal	**different**	*total*	**percentage**
all	*35274*	*2480*	*37754*	*6.57%*
GoldenEye	1239	304	*1543*	19.70%
Hulk	32656	1862	*34518*	5.39%
Slowhttptest	600	224	*824*	27.18%
Slowloris	779	90	*869*	10.36%

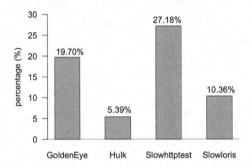

Fig. 4. Percentage of different flow records by type of DoS attack.

cardinality ranges from 824 (`Slowhttptest`) to 34518 (`Hulk`) – *total* column. For each type of attack we determine the number of flow records where the expert label is *equal* to or *different* from the sanitized label; percentages shown in the rightmost column of Table 2 measure the quality of flow records and are given by $\frac{different}{total} \cdot 100$.

The percentage of the `all` row –averaged across all the attacks– is 6.57%. Surprisingly, a closer look at the data reveals that the percentages of individual attacks range from 5.39% (`Hulk`) up to 27.18% (`Slowhttpest`). Figure 4 provides a representation of the percentages, which allows appreciating the difference across the attacks. The percentages of `GoldenEye` and `Slowhttpest` are significantly high (thus low quality of the flow records). In a previous replication study [4], we demonstrate that `Slowhttpest` of CICIDS2017 has a *bursty* nature, which means that it alternates activity and inactivity periods. We hypothesize that the research group that published CICIDS2017, labelled as `ATTACK` all the flow records collected during the progression of `Slowhttpest`, with no awareness of activity and inactivity periods: in consequence, flow records from inactivity periods –although labeled as `ATTACK`– tend to resemble benign operations. As for `GoldenEye`, it aims to consume server-side sockets by means of KeepAlive and Cache-Control options[14]: this subtle behavior does not properly reflect into the numeric features of `ATTACK` flow records.

---

[14] https://allabouttesting.org/golden-eye-ddos-tool-installation-and-tool-usage-with-examples/.

Impact on Intrusion Detection. To gain insights into the impact of low quality flow records on intrusion detection, we develop an IDS on the top of the *MODEL* split presented in Sect. 4.2, which accounts for 70% of records in CICIDS2017-Wednesday. The IDS model is a supervised **deep neural network** consisting of 6 hidden layers –each encompassing 100 neurons– and an output layer consisting of 2 neurons, i.e., one per class (`BENIGN` or `ATTACK`), weighted by means of the *softmax* activation function.

We use the IDS model to classify the flow records of the *TARGET SET*; the performance of the model is measured by the typical metrics of *precision* (P), *recall* (R) and *F-score* (F). Metrics are computed from the total number of true negative (TN), true positive (TP), false negative (FN) and false positive (FP). For instance, a TN is a `BENIGN` record that is classified `BENIGN` by the model; a FN is an `ATTACK` flow record that is deemed `BENIGN` by the model. Metrics are computed as follows:

$$P = \frac{TP}{TP + FP} \quad R = \frac{TP}{TP + FN} \quad F = 2 \cdot \frac{P \cdot R}{P + R} \tag{3}$$

The model achieves high P, R and F on the entire *TARGET SET*, i.e., 0.953, 0.975 and 0.964, respectively. Interestingly, if we narrow the IDS to the *sole* records of the *TARGET SET* where the expert label differs from the sanitized label, i.e., 4858 records – Table 1 (`all` row), P, R and F drop to 0.703, 0.808 and 0.752. This finding suggests that the quality of flow records plays a crucial role for designing and evaluating modern intrusion detection systems.

5   Conclusion

The recent spread of machine learning techniques has boosted significantly the performance of intrusion detection systems. Machine learning models can learn normal and anomalous patterns from training data and generate classifiers that are successively used to detect attacks. In spite of the ever-increasing body of literature on the design and evaluation of flow-based intrusion detection systems, to the best of our knowledge there is no contribution that investigates the quality of flow records. This paper proposed an initial investigation on the topic by analyzing DoS attacks of CICIDS2017. Most notably, we observe that while quality issues of flow records are negligible for benign traffic, there exist major issues with attack-related records. Our results are extremely relevant both for the release of new datasets, automated data labeling and the implementation IDS models.

In our future work, we will extend the analysis to other attack types, datasets and existing products to export flow records. Our aim is also to analyze the resilience of *deep learning* techniques with respect to the quality of network records as far as their use on real-world data is concerned, since data may be affected by the issues pointed out in this paper.

Acknowledgment. Andrea Del Vecchio gratefully acknowledges support by the "Orio Carlini" 2020 GARR Consortium Fellowship.

References

1. Ahmim, A., Maglaras, L., Ferrag, M.A., Derdour, M., Janicke, H.: A novel hierarchical intrusion detection system based on decision tree and rules-based models. In: Proceedings of the International Conference on Distributed Computing in Sensor Systems, pp. 228–233 (2019)
2. Bhuyan, M.H., Bhattacharyya, D., Kalita, J.: Towards generating real-life datasets for network intrusion detection. Int. J. Netw. Secur. **17**, 683–701 (2015)
3. Catillo, M., Del Vecchio, A., Ocone, L., Pecchia, A., Villano, U.: USB-IDS-1: a public multilayer dataset of labeled network flows for IDS evaluation. In: 51st Annual IEEE/IFIP International Conference on Dependable Systems and Networks Workshops (DSN-W), pp. 1–6. IEEE (2021)
4. Catillo, M., Pecchia, A., Rak, M., Villano, U.: Demystifying the role of public intrusion datasets: a replication study of DoS network traffic data. Comput. Secur. **108**, 102341 (2021)
5. Catillo, M., Rak, M., Villano, U.: 2L-ZED-IDS: a two-level anomaly detector for multiple attack classes. In: Barolli, L., Amato, F., Moscato, F., Enokido, T., Takizawa, M. (eds.) WAINA 2020. AISC, vol. 1150, pp. 687–696. Springer, Cham (2020). https://doi.org/10.1007/978-3-030-44038-1_63
6. Catillo, M., Pecchia, A., Villano, U.: Measurement-based analysis of a DoS defense module for an open source web server. In: Casola, V., De Benedictis, A., Rak, M. (eds.) ICTSS 2020. LNCS, vol. 12543, pp. 121–134. Springer, Cham (2020). https://doi.org/10.1007/978-3-030-64881-7_8
7. Chandola, V., Banerjee, A., Kumar, V.: Anomaly detection: a survey. ACM Comput. Surv. **41**(3), 1–58 (2009)
8. Cotroneo, D., Paudice, A., Pecchia, A.: Empirical analysis and validation of security alerts filtering techniques. IEEE Trans. Dependable Secure Comput. **16**(5), 856–870 (2019)
9. García, S., Grill, M., Stiborek, J., Zunino, A.: An empirical comparison of botnet detection methods. Comput. Secur **45**, 100–123 (2014)
10. Gogoi, P., Bhuyan, M.H., Bhattacharyya, D.K., Kalita, J.K.: Packet and flow based network intrusion dataset. In: Parashar, M., Kaushik, D., Rana, O.F., Samtaney, R., Yang, Y., Zomaya, A. (eds.) IC3 2012. CCIS, vol. 306, pp. 322–334. Springer, Heidelberg (2012). https://doi.org/10.1007/978-3-642-32129-0_34
11. Kshirsagar, D., Kumar, S.: An efficient feature reduction method for the detection of DoS attack. ICT Express **7**, 371–375 (2021)
12. Lee, J., Kim, J., Kim, I., Han, K.: Cyber threat detection based on artificial neural networks using event profiles. IEEE Access **7**, 165607–165626 (2019)
13. Liu, H., Lang, B.: Machine learning and deep learning methods for intrusion detection systems: a survey. Appl. Sci. **9**(20), 4396 (2019)
14. Maciá-Fernández, G., Camacho, J., Magán-Carrión, R., García-Teodoro, P., Therón, R.: UGR'16: a new dataset for the evaluation of cyclostationarity-based network IDSs. Comput. Secur. **73**, 411–424 (2017)
15. Paudice, A., Muñoz-González, L., Lupu, E.C.: Label sanitization against label flipping poisoning attacks. In: Alzate, C., et al. (eds.) ECML PKDD 2018. LNCS (LNAI), vol. 11329, pp. 5–15. Springer, Cham (2019). https://doi.org/10.1007/978-3-030-13453-2_1
16. Ring, M., Wunderlich, S., Scheuring, D., Landes, D., Hotho, A.: A survey of network-based intrusion detection data sets. Comput. Secur. **86**, 147–167 (2019)

17. Sharafaldin, I., Lashkari, A.H., Ghorbani., A.A.: Toward generating a new intrusion detection dataset and intrusion traffic characterization. In: Proceedings of the International Conference on Information Systems Security and Privacy, pp. 108–116. SciTePress (2018)
18. Shiravi, A., Shiravi, H., Tavallaee, M., Ghorbani, A.: Toward developing a systematic approach to generate benchmark datasets for intrusion detection. Comput. Secur. **31**, 357–374 (2012)
19. Smallwood, D., Vance, A.: Intrusion analysis with deep packet inspection: increasing efficiency of packet based investigations. In: Proceedings of the International Conference on Cloud and Service Computing, pp. 342–347. IEEE (2011)
20. Sperotto, A., Schaffrath, G., Sadre, R., Morariu, C., Pras, A., Stiller, B.: An overview of IP flow-based intrusion detection. IEEE Commun. Surv. Tutor. **12**(3), 343–356 (2010)
21. Umer, M.F., Sher, M., Bi, Y.: Flow-based intrusion detection: techniques and challenges. Comput. Secur. **70**, 238–254 (2017)
22. Wankhede, S., Kshirsagar, D.: DoS attack detection using machine learning and neural network. In: Proceedings of the 4th International Conference on Computing Communication Control and Automation, pp. 1–5 (2018)

GROOT: A GDPR-Based Combinatorial Testing Approach

Said Daoudagh$^{(\boxtimes)}$ and Eda Marchetti

ISTI-CNR, Pisa, Italy
{said.daoudagh,eda.marchetti}@isti.cnr.it

Abstract. For replying to the strict exigencies and rules imposed by the GDPR, ICT systems are currently adopting different means for managing personal data. However, due to their critical and crucial role, effective and efficient validation methods should be applied, taking into account the peculiarity of the reference legal framework (i.e., the GDPR). In this paper, we present GROOT, a generic combinatorial testing methodology specifically conceived for assessing the GDPR compliance and its contextualization in the context of access control domain.

Keywords: Combinatorial testing · Data protection · GDPR

1 Introduction

Nowadays, quality of Information and Communication Technology (ICT) systems and modern applications is strictly tied with the security and privacy. However, most the times, due to the peculiarity of the General Data Protection Regulation (GDPR) [8], effective and efficient validation methods have to be applied for avoiding possible violations. In this paper, we present GROOT, a combinatorial testing methodology specifically conceived for assessing the GDPR compliance of ICT systems in processing Personal Data. We specifically contextualize GROOT into the Access Control (AC) domains, because they are the most promising approach for taking in consideration the peculiarities of the GDPR [5,6]. Indeed, Access Control Systems (ACSs) aim to ensure that only the intended subjects (e.g., Data Subject, Controller and Processor) can access the protected data (e.g., Personal Data or special Categories of Personal Data) and get the permission levels required to accomplish their tasks and no much more.

The testing of ACSs represents a key activity to guarantee the trustworthiness of (personal or sensitive) data and protect information technology systems against inappropriate or undesired user access [4]. However, testing is still a time consuming, error prone activity and a critical step of the development process. Bad choices in each stage of the testing phase may compromise the entire process, with the risk of releasing inadequate security and privacy solutions that allow unauthorized access (*security perspective*) or unlawful processing (*legal perspective*).

© IFIP International Federation for Information Processing 2022
Published by Springer Nature Switzerland AG 2022
D. Clark et al. (Eds.): ICTSS 2021, LNCS 13045, pp. 210–217, 2022.
https://doi.org/10.1007/978-3-031-04673-5_17

Indeed, several strategies for the generation of test cases (i.e., access requests) for access control systems have been defined in scientific literature. They leverage the application of combinatorial approaches to access control policies values for generating test inputs [2]; or exploit data flow for test cases generation starting from policies specification [17]; or are based on the representation of policy implied behavior by means of models [1,9]. However, to the best of our knowledge, there are few proposals for assessing the compliance with the GDPR [7,10], and none targeting the testing access control systems in the context of the GDPR. Therefore, our work aims at advancing the state-of-the-art by providing, for the first time, the GdpR-based cOmbinatOrial Testing (GROOT) strategy, i.e., a general combinatorial strategy for testing systems managing GDPR's concepts (e.g., Data Subject, Personal Data or Controller). To better illustrate the GROOT procedural steps, an application example is also provided.

Outline: Section 2 provides an overview of the main concepts, Sect. 3 illustrates the GROOT methodology and its application. Finally, Sect. 4 concludes the paper and depicts future works.

2   Background

GDPR Concepts. The General Data Protection Regulation (GDPR) is the currently European Regulation for the protection of *Personal Data*. In its Art. 4, the GDPR defines *Personal Data* as "any information relating to an identified or identifiable natural person ('data subject')", whose data are managed by a *Controller*. The *purpose* of the *processing* of Personal Data is determined by the controller, and this "processing shall be lawful only if and to the extent that at least one of the" six legal bases "applies" (Art. 6). In particular, one of those legal bases is the consent given by the data subject "to the processing of his or her Personal Data for one or more specific purposes" (Art. 6.1(a)). The GDPR also sets other fundamental rights of the data subject, such as the right of access (Art. 15) and the right to data portability (Art. 20).

Access Control. *Access Control* (AC), implemented through *Access Control Mechanism* (ACM), provides a decision to an authorization request, typically based on predefined *Access Control Policy* (ACP). This is a specific statement of what is and is not allowed on the basis of a set of rules. For instance, a policy contains a set of rules that specify who (e.g., Controller, Processor or Data Subject) has access to which resources (e.g., Personal Data) and under which circumstances (e.g., based on the Consent and Purpose) [15].

Representing the GDPR. Implementing the GDPR's requirements is a challenging task, and a standardized solution is still missing. The most promising approaches can be divided into: using Semantic Web technologies, i.e., ontologies, using UML representation and using access control policies specification. Concerning the first group, recent proposals are [14], which models the legal concepts through the Privacy Ontology (PrOnto), and the GDPR text extensions [13] where the GDPR is represented as inked data resource. Works in the second group use the UML notation for representing the GDPR's concepts. Among them we refer to [16] where the authors use the UML model for designing automated methods for checking the GDPR compliance, and [11] where the authors use an educational e-platform paradigm for combining the regulation, information privacy and best practices. The third group represents the legal concepts through access control policies. In particular, authors in [6] propose a semantic model to represent the GDPR consent customized for the XACML reference access control architecture, whereas in [3] authors provide a life cycle for the development of access control policies and mechanisms in reference to the GDPR's demands.

Our proposal requires (and exploits) the possibility of having a structured and machine readable specification of the legal concepts. The aim is therefore to provide a methodology independent from any GDPR representation. The adaptation of the methodology to the different GDPR's representations is left and handled during the development stage of the GROOT proposal.

3   GROOT

GROOT is a general combinatorial testing approach, for validating systems managing GDPR's concepts (e.g., Data Subject, Personal Data or Controller). In the following, we first illustrate the GROOT methodology, and then we show its usage in the context of access control.

3.1   GROOT Methodology

In illustrating the GROOT methodology, we use the following definitions:

Definition 1 (GDPR-based SUT Model). *A GDPR-based SUT Model is a tuple $Model_{GDPR}(PAR, V)$, where:*

- *$PAR \subseteq \{DS, PD, DC, DP, C, P, PA, TP\}$ is the set of parameters that affect the GDPR-based SUT, where DS = Data Subject, PD = Personal Data, DC = Controller, DP = Processor, C = Consent, P = Purpose, PA = Processing Activity, TP = Third Party, and*
- *$V = \{V_i \mid i \in PAR$ and V_i is the set of values for the parameter $i\}$ is the set of sets of the values that can be selected for each parameter.*

Definition 2 (GDPR-based Test Case). *Given a GDPR-based SUT Model $Model_{GDPR}(PAR, V)$, a GDPR-based Test Case is a tuple $TC_{GDPR}(ATT)$ where: $ATT = \{ATT_i \mid ATT_i \subseteq V_i, i \in PAR$ and $V_i \in V\}$.*

The GROOT methodology takes as an input a GDPR-based implementation, that is a representation of the GDPR in terms of a specification language. As detailed in Sect. 2, currently, different proposals are available and can be used for the purpose. Under this hypothesis GROOT is composed of three main steps (see Fig. 1): GDPR-based Model Derivation; Test Cases Generation; and Test Cases Translation.

GDPR-Based Model Derivation (Step ①). In line with Definition 1, the GDPR-based SUT Model of the GDPR-based implementation is then derived. For this, the GDPR-based implementation is parsed in order to identify the set of parameters P, and the associated set of sets V. More precisely, for each parameter i, the subset V_i, containing the values used in the GDPR-based implementation, is derived.

Test Cases Generation (Step ②). In this step, the combinatorial testing is performed. Based on the derived parameters' values sets, different combinatorial strategies can be adopted such as: all-combinations, pairwise combinations or t-wise combinations. For instance, in the all-combinations test strategy according to the Definition 2, for each parameter i and its set of value V_i, the power set of V_i ($P(V_i)$) is derived, i.e., all possible subsets of V_i. Then, the obtained power sets $P(V_i)$ are combined so as to derive the test cases i.e., the $TC_{GDPR}(ATT)$ tuples. Because combinatorial testing is a costly activity, the selection of the best combinatorial strategy, that could be adopted, may depend on different testing objectives such as: coverage, effectiveness, reduction or prioritization.

Test Cases Translation (Step ③). According to the domain specific language, each of the obtained $TC_{GDPR}(ATT)$ tuples in Step ② is translated into specific executable test case. In the context of AC, a test case is represented through an AC request that can be evaluated by the ACM.

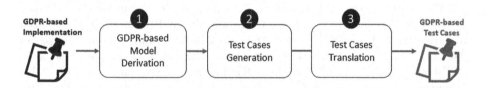

Fig. 1. GROOT methodology.

3.2 Using GROOT

In this section, we illustrate the application of GROOT through a use case scenario based on a realistic fitness environment. More precisely, we consider Alice, a Data Subject, who wants to use a smart fitness application to monitor her daily activities to achieve a predefined training objective. In this case, we suppose that a customized (mobile) application is provided by a generic myFitness company (Controller). To meet Alice's needs, myFitness has so far defined two purposes (MyCholesterol and Untargeted Marketing), each related to a specific data set of Personal Data and achieved by allowing access to perform a specific set of Actions. Specifically, the MyCholesterol purpose is achieved by performing AGGREGATE, DERIVE, and QUERY actions; whereas the Untargeted Marketing purpose is achieved by performing COLLECT, QUERY, and SEND actions. At the time of subscribing to the myFitness application, Alice provided her Personal Data (i.e., e-mail, Age, Gender, and Blood Cholesterol) and gave her consent to process her e-mail and Age for Untargeted Marketing purpose, and her Blood Cholesterol for MyCholesterol purpose. In turn, myFitness gave Alice controller's contacts that include: orgName, address, e-mail, and phone number.

GDPR-Based Implementation. In this application example, the GDPR-based implementation refers to the Art. 6.1(a) of the GDPR. In the context of AC, considering for instance the GDPR formalization proposed by [6], the article is represented through the access control policy (called Alice's policy) reported in the listing below. The policy allows a lawfulness of processing of Personal Data related to Alice and it is composed of two rules (**R1** and **R2**):

Alice's Policy:

R1: permission(data_controller=myFitness,   data_subject=Alice,   personal_data={Blood Cholesterol, Age, Gender}, purpose=MyCholesterol, action={DERIVE, AGGREGATE, QUERY}, consent=TRUE)

R2: permission(data_controller={myFitness, address}, data_subject=Alice, personal_data=Email,   purpose=UntargetedMarketing,   action=SEND, consent=TRUE)

For instance, R1 allows `data_controller` (who) to process `personal_data` (which resources) because of the `consent` (under which circumstances).

GDPR-Based Model Derivation (Step ①). According to the GROOT methodology presented in the previous section, the GDPR-based Model is parsed to derive the PAR, and the associated values of the parameters. In the case of Alice's policy, the identified set of parameters derived from the policy elements is $PAR \subseteq \{DS, PD, DC, C, P, PA\}$. For instance, the values associated with parameter P is $V_P = \{MyCholesterol, UntargetedMarketing\}$. In line with Definition 1, the result of this step is represented in tabular form in Table 1. The first column (labeled PE) reports the related Alice's policy elements, the second column (labeled PAR) reports the derived parameters, and the last column (labeled V_{PAR}) lists the related values.

Test Cases Generation (Step ②). The combination of the parameters' values of Table 1 is computed in order to derive the set of test cases. Different strategies can be adopted in this step. By considering the all-combination, for each parameter $j \in PAR$, the power set of the associated values is derived. For instance, the power set associated with parameter P (i.e., Purpose) is $P_{V_P} = \{\{\}, \{UntargetedMarketing\}, \{MyCholesterol\}, \{UntargetedMarketing, MyCholesterol\} \}$. Possible test cases are $TC_{GDPR}(ATT_1)$ and $TC_{GDPR}(ATT_2)$ where $ATT_1 = \{DC=myFitness, DS=Alice, PD=\{Blood Cholesterol\}, P= MyCholesterol, PA=DERIVE, C=TRUE\}$ and $ATT_2 = \{C=myFitness, DS=Alice, PD=\{Email,Age\}, P=UntargetedMarketing, PA=SEND\}$.

For all-combination the cardinality of the derived test suite is 16.384, because the number of test cases follows exponential growth with the numbers of values'

Table 1. GDPR-based SUT model associated of Alice's policy.

PE	PAR	V_{PAR}
data_subject	DS = Data Subject	Alice
personal_data	PD = Personal Data	Blood Cholesterol, Age, Gender, Email
data_controller	DC = Controller	myFitness, Address
consent	C = Consent	TRUE
purpose	P = Purpose	UntargetedMarketing, MyCholesterol
action	PA = Processing Activity	DERIVE, AGGREGATE, QUERY, SEND

parameters. The number of generated test cases can be reduced by considering different approaches. For instance, by applying the pairwise technique the cardinality of test suite has been reduced to 259 covering the 16.384 variants. However, it is out of the scope of this paper discussing solutions for managing the explosion problem of combinatorial testing. For more details, we refer to [12].

Test Cases Translation (Step ③). Finally, each of the obtained test cases is translated into an executable one. In the context of AC, possible AC requests, associated with $TC_{GDPR}(ATT_1)$ and $TC_{GDPR}(ATT_2)$ respectively, are reported below. For instance, **Req1** states that *myFitness* (who) wants to process *Blood Cholesterol* (which resources) for *MyCholesterol* purpose (under which circumstances).

Example of Access Control Requests using GROOT:

Req1:   request(DC=myFitness,   DS=Alice   PD=Blood   Cholesterol,
          P=MyCholesterol, PA=DERIVE, C=TRUE)
Req2:   request(C=myFitness,   DS=Alice,   PD={Email,Age},
          P=UntargetedMarketing, PA=SEND)

---

4   Conclusions and Future Work

In this paper, we presented GROOT, a combinatorial testing strategy specifically conceived for assessing the compliance with the GDPR of systems managing personal data. We have firstly presented the conceived methodology, which consists of three main steps, then we have exemplified its application by considering a realistic use case scenario coming from fitness environment. In particular, we illustrated how to apply GROOT for testing GDPR-based access control policies. It is part of our work-in-progress the assessment of the GROOT approach by considering real case studies as well as the use of mutation approaches for evaluating its test effectiveness. We are also working on the GROOT implementation in order to automatize the overall proposed process. As a future work, we will customize GROOT approach by considering other technologies such as consent management systems.

Acknowledgement. This work is partially supported by the project BIECO H2020 Grant Agreement No. 952702, and by CyberSec4Europe H2020 Grant Agreement No. 830929.

References

1. Abassi, R., El Fatmi, S.G.: Security policies a formal environment for a test cases generation. In: Artificial Intelligence and Security Challenges in Emerging Networks, pp. 237–264. IGI Global (2019)
2. Daoudagh, S., Lonetti, F., Marchetti, E.: XACMET: XACML testing and modeling. Softw. Qual. J. **28**(1), 249–282 (2020)
3. Daoudagh, S., Marchetti, E.: A life cycle for authorization systems development in the GDPR perspective. In: Proceedings of the 4th Italian Conference on Cyber Security, Ancona, Italy, 4–7 February 2020, vol. 2597, pp. 128–140. CEUR (2020)
4. Daoudagh, S., Marchetti, E.: GRADUATION: a GDPR-based mutation methodology. In: Paiva, A.C.R., Cavalli, A.R., Ventura Martins, P., Pérez-Castillo, R. (eds.) QUATIC 2021. CCIS, vol. 1439, pp. 311–324. Springer, Cham (2021). https://doi.org/10.1007/978-3-030-85347-1_23
5. Daoudagh, S., Marchetti, E., Savarino, V., Bernardo, R.D., Alessi, M.: How to improve the GDPR compliance through consent management and access control. In: Proceedings of the 7th International Conference on Information Systems Security and Privacy, ICISSP 2021, 11–13 February 2021, pp. 534–541. SCITEPRESS (2021)
6. Davari, M., Bertino, E.: Access control model extensions to support data privacy protection based on GDPR. In: IEEE International Conference on Big Data (Big Data), Los Angeles, CA, USA, 9–12 December 2019, pp. 4017–4024. IEEE (2019)
7. Drozdowicz, M., Ganzha, M., Paprzycki, M.: Semantic access control for privacy management of personal sensing in smart cities. IEEE Trans. Emerg. Top. Comput. **10**(1), 199–210 (2022). https://doi.org/10.1109/TETC.2020.2996974
8. Regulation (EU) 2016/679 of the European Parliament and of the Council of 27 April 2016 (General Data Protection Regulation). Official Journal of the European Union L119, 1–88, May 2016. http://eur-lex.europa.eu/legal-content/EN/TXT/?uri=OJ:L:2016:119:TOC
9. Khamaiseh, S., Chapman, P., Xu, D.: Model-based testing of obligatory ABAC systems. In: 2018 IEEE International Conference on QRS 2018, Lisbon, Portugal, 16–20 July 2018, pp. 405–413. IEEE (2018)
10. Mahindrakar, A., Joshi, K.P.: Automating GDPR compliance using policy integrated blockchain. In: 2020 IEEE 6th Intl BigDataSecurity, IEEE International Conference on HPSC and IEEE International Conference on IDS, pp. 86–93 (2020)
11. Mougiakou, E., Virvou, M.: Based on GDPR privacy in UML: case of e-learning program. In: 2017 8th International Conference on Information, Intelligence, Systems Applications (IISA), pp. 1–8 (2017)
12. Nie, C., Leung, H.: A survey of combinatorial testing. ACM Comput. Surv. (CSUR) **43**(2), 1–29 (2011)
13. Pandit, H.J., Fatema, K., O'Sullivan, D., Lewis, D.: GDPRtEXT - GDPR as a linked data resource. In: Gangemi, A., Navigli, R., Vidal, M.-E., Hitzler, P., Troncy, R., Hollink, L., Tordai, A., Alam, M. (eds.) ESWC 2018. LNCS, vol. 10843, pp. 481–495. Springer, Cham (2018). https://doi.org/10.1007/978-3-319-93417-4_31

14. Robaldo, L., Bartolini, C., Palmirani, M., Rossi, A., Martoni, M., Lenzini, G.: Formalizing GDPR provisions in reified I/O logic: the DAPRECO knowledge base. J. Logic, Lang. Inf. **29**(4), 401–449 (2019). https://doi.org/10.1007/s10849-019-09309-z
15. Sandhu, R.S., Samarati, P.: Access control: principle and practice. IEEE Commun. Mag. **32**(9), 40–48 (1994)
16. Torre, D., Soltana, G., Sabetzadeh, M., Briand, L.C., Auffinger, Y., Goes, P.: Using models to enable compliance checking against the GDPR: an experience report. In: 2019 ACM/IEEE 22nd International Conference, MODELS, pp. 1–11. IEEE (2019)
17. Zhang, Y., Zhang, B.: A new testing method for XACML 3.0 policy based on abac and data flow. In: 2017 13th IEEE International Conference on Control Automation (ICCA), pp. 160–164 (2017)

Appendix – Project Reports

H2020 DIGITbrain – Advanced Digital Twins for Manufacturing

Antonio M. Ortiz[1(✉)], Jeanett Bolther[1(✉)], Carolina Salas[1(✉)], Luong Nguyen[2(✉)], and Monika Rakoczy[2(✉)]

[1] PNO Innovation, S.L, Barcelona, Spain
{antonio.ortiz,jeanett.bolther,carolina.salas}
@pnoconsultants.com
[2] Montimage EURL, Paris, France
{luong.nguyen,monika.rakoczy}@montimage.com

Abstract. DIGITbrain presents the Digital Product Brain (DPB) that extends the traditional Digital Twin concept with memorizing capacity. Together with a smart business model called manufacturing as a service (MaaS) to allow the customisation and adaptation of on-demand Data, Models, Algorithms and Resources for industrial products according to individual conditions. MaaS will enable manufacturing SMEs to reach advanced manufacturing facilities within their territories and beyond. DIGITbrain supports the development of advanced digital and manufacturing technologies through more than 20 highly innovative cross-border experiments, in addition to training and assisting Digital Innovation Hubs in the implementation of the Maas model, contributing to their long-term sustainability.

Keywords: Digital Twins · Manufacturing · Validation · Testing · Monitoring

1 DIGITbrain in a Nutshell

The manufacturing industry is in constant evolution; customers have new requirements and want more personalisation; interoperability with new products and technologies is expected; regulations and norms are becoming stricter; the environment calls for more protection; the ageing of the workforce jeopardises the collective know-how. These aspects cause an increasing pressure that the manufacturing industry needs to address. Especially manufacturing SMEs are challenged, because of the limited resources and the difficulty in accessing digital technologies and advanced manufacturing hardware tailored to their needs.

Digital Twins [1] are a way to answer these challenges. However, implementing Digital Twins is yet another challenge for many manufacturing SMEs, since it requires a lot of expertise and a holistic approach ranging from the manufacturing machines to

The DIGITbrain project has received funding from the European Union's Horizon 2020 research and innovation program under grant agreement No 952071. https://digitbrain.eu/.

© IFIP International Federation for Information Processing 2022
D. Clark et al. (Eds.): ICTSS 2021, LNCS 13045, pp. 221–223, 2022.
https://doi.org/10.1007/978-3-031-04673-5

become data resources, to data-driven and/or physically based modelling, to mastering data lakes and compute resources such as HPC, Cloud and Edge Computing.

The DIGITbrain project aims to enable customised industrial products and to facilitate cost-effective distributed and localised production for manufacturing SMEs, by means of leveraging Edge-, Cloud- and HPC-based modelling, simulation, optimisation, analytics, and machine learning tools, and through augmenting the concept of digital twin with a memorising capacity towards: (a) recording the provenance and boosting the cognition of the industrial product over its full lifecycle, and (b) empowering the network of DIHs to implement the smart business model Manufacturing as a Service (MaaS). Figure 1 shows the full digital and physical lifespan covered by DIGITbrain.

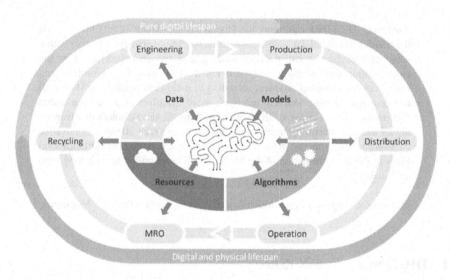

Fig. 1. DIGITbrain conceptual overview.

1.1   DIGITbrain Objectives

The main objectives are:

- To implement the concepts behind the Digital Brain, to orchestrate Data, Models, Algorithms, and Resources available for the Industrial Products.
- To provide the DIGITbrain Solution extending the CloudiFacturing [2] platform with new automated deployment, support for co-simulation, etc.
- To develop feasible business models for MaaS-empowered DIHs to foster a growing community of stakeholders.
- To augment the capabilities of an established market- and workplace technology by supporting the operation of the Digital Brain concept and the nurture of MaaS-empowered DIHs.

- To conduct 3 waves of application experiments (2 of them through funded Open Calls) to validate the project results [3].
- To evangelise the manufacturing community on the benefits of MaaS.

References

1. Boschert, S., Rosen, R.: Digital twin—the simulation aspect. In: Hehenberger, P., Bradley, D. (eds.) Mechatronic Futures, pp. 59–74. Springer, Cham (2016). https://doi.org/10.1007/978-3-319-32156-1_5
2. H2020 CloudiFacturing project. https://www.cloudifacturing.eu/
3. https://digitbrain.eu/experiments

Definition and Assessment of Security and Service Level Agreements (Project Report)

Huu Nghia Nguyen$^{(\boxtimes)}$ and Edgardo Montes de Oca

Montimage, Paris, France
{huunghia.nguyen,edgardo.montesdeoca}@montimage.com

Abstract. The fifth generation of mobile networks relies on a complex, dynamic and heterogeneous environment that implies the emergence of numerous security challenges and testing objectives. In this paper, we propose a framework that we are developing in the context of H2020 INSPIRE-5GPlus project to allow users to formalise and define security and service level agreements (SSLAs). The framework will then be able to assess in realtime the SSLAs and eventually trigger automatic remediation strategies when an SSLA is violated.

Keywords: 5G · SSLAs · Rule-Based assessment · Auto remediation

1 Context: INSPIRE-5GPlus Project

Intelligent Security and Pervasive Trust for 5G and Beyond (INSPIRE-5GPlus) project[1]. It is intended for advancing security of 5G and Beyond networks from different perspectives [1], i.e., overall vision, use cases, architecture, integration to network management, assets, and models. Such advancements of the security vision will be archived for the first time through the adoption of a set of emerging trends and technologies, such as Zero-touch network Service Management (ZSM), Software-Defined Security (SD-SEC) models, AI/ML techniques and Trusted Execution Environments (TEE). New breed of SD-SEC assets and models are being developed to address some of the challenges that remain (e.g., adaptive slice security) or are completely new (e.g., liability and proactive security) to cover the whole cybersecurity spectrum for fulfilling the SSLAs [2]. The project will then ensure that the provided security level is in conformance to the requirements coming from the security-related legalisation, verticals needs, and the standard requirements.

2 SSLAs: Definition and Assessment

The framework concerns the definition of SSLAs for assessing and testing that: 1) the security functions are correctly implemented, 2) the security properties are not violated, and 3) the violations trigger self-healing and -protection strategies.

---

[1] The Horizon 2020 INSPIRE-5GPlus project was started on November 1st, 2019 and lasts 3 years. More details can be found in: https://www.inspire-5gplus.eu/.

© IFIP International Federation for Information Processing 2022
Published by Springer Nature Switzerland AG 2022
D. Clark et al. (Eds.): ICTSS 2021, LNCS 13045, pp. 224–226, 2022.
https://doi.org/10.1007/978-3-031-04673-5

The functional architecture is depicted in Fig. 1. SSLAs are defined in a High-level Security Policy Language (HSPL) for specifying abstract security policies regardless of the underlying technology. This key feature of the framework allows multiple implementations and enforcement points for the same high-level policy. This level of abstraction also provides other important features such as allowing a non-technical end-user to specify general protection requirements without possessing deep knowledge of the lower technical layers of the system.

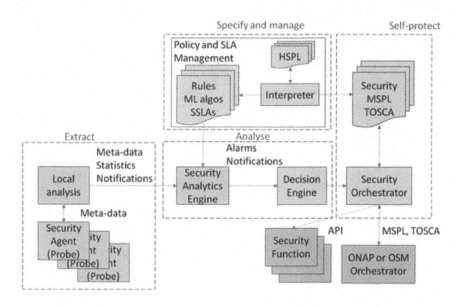

Fig. 1. Functional architecture diagram

The SSLAs are then interpreted into a lower level to perform the assessment. The outcome is used by 1) a Security Orchestrator, e.g., to deploy the probes to collect metadata or to realise the remediation, and 2) the Security Analytic Engine. The interpretation can add or modify specific protocols or data parser plugins so that the probes can capture the needed data and the framework can trigger reactions. The probes provide in realtime the metrics required by the SSLAs and integrate local analysis functions. They should have the ability of analysing the data using specified rules extracted from the SSLAs, and analysing statistics and behaviour using machine learning techniques. The metrics are feed to the Security Analytic Engine to perform the assessment based on the rules and algorithms to detect the non-respected SSLAs. The Decision Engine will trigger the corrective actions that could involve interacting with the Security Orchestrators or directly with the Security Functions and Controllers.

References

1. Murillo, J.O., de Oca, E.M., et al.: INSPIRE-5Gplus: intelligent security and pervasive trust for 5G and beyond networks. In: ARES 2020, pp. 105:1–105:10 (2020)
2. Rios, E., Mallouli, W., Rak, M., Casola, V., Ortiz, A.M.: SLA-driven monitoring of multi-cloud application components using the MUSA framework. In: ICDCS Workshops, pp. 55–60 (2016)

Attack Configuration Engine for 5G Networks

Zujany Salazar$^{(\boxtimes)}$ ⓘ, Huu Nghia Nguyen$^{(\boxtimes)}$ ⓘ, Wissam Mallouli$^{(\boxtimes)}$ ⓘ,
Ana R. Cavalli$^{(\boxtimes)}$ ⓘ, and Edgardo Montes de Oca$^{(\boxtimes)}$ ⓘ

Montimage, Paris, France
{zujany.salazar,huunghia.nguyen,wissam.mallouli,
ana.cavalli,edgardo.montesdeoca}@montimage.com

Abstract. The evolution of 5G mobile networks towards a service-based architecture (SBA) comes with the emergence of numerous new testing challenges and objectives. Regarding security testing, 5G issues have been the subject of numerous studies. Standardization organisms list collections of threats and vulnerabilities, also investigated by academia and industrial researchers. However, there is no specific tool on the market that allows easy 5G security testing to verify if its components are protected against reported security issues. In this paper, we propose AcE which is an attack configuration engine conceived in the context of H2020 SANCUS project dealing with 5G network security.

Keywords: 5G · Traffic engineering · Attack injection · Fuzz testing

1 AcE: Attack Configuration Engine for 5G Networks

1.1 Context: SANCUS Project

Security, Trust and Reliability are crucial issues in mobile 5G networks from both hardware and software perspectives [2]. These issues are of significant importance when considering implementations over distributed environments, i.e., corporate Cloud environment over massively virtualized infrastructures as envisioned in the 5G service provision paradigm. The SANCUS[1] solution intends providing a modular framework integrating different engines in order to enable next-generation 5G system networks to perform automated and intelligent analysis of their firmware images at massive scale, as well as the validation of applications and services. SANCUS also proposes a proactive risk assessment of network applications and services by means of maximising the overall system resilience in terms of security, privacy and reliability.

1.2 Attack Configuration Engine

The proposed AcE engine in SANCUS delivers inclusive solution for modelling and emulating network container services and applications, along with

---

[1] H2020 SANCUS project was started on September 1st, 2020 and lasts 3 years. More details can be found in: https://www.sancus-project.eu/.

© IFIP International Federation for Information Processing 2022
Published by Springer Nature Switzerland AG 2022
D. Clark et al. (Eds.): ICTSS 2021, LNCS 13045, pp. 227–229, 2022.
https://doi.org/10.1007/978-3-031-04673-5

network-wide attacks, forensic investigations, and tests that require a safe environment without the risk of proprietary data loss or adverse impact upon existing networks. It also simulates the main attacks identified by the ENISA [3]. The strength of this engine is that it will allow testing not only large-scale network infrastructures, but also emulating the end-users (IoT, routers, hotspots). One of the main components of this tool is 5Greplay solution designed by Montimage.

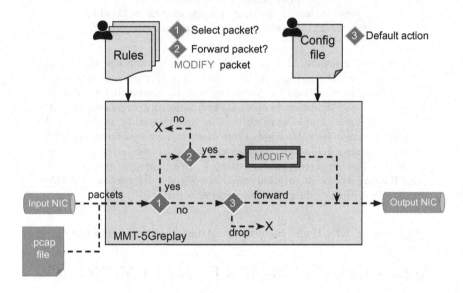

Fig. 1. 5Greplay main architecture

5Greplay[2] is an open-source 5G fuzzer that allows forwarding 5G network packets from one network interface card (NIC) to another with or without modification. 5Greplay's global architecture is depicted in Fig. 1. It can be considered as a one-way bridge between the input NIC and the output one. Its behavior is controlled by user defined rules and completed by a configuration file. The user defined rules allow explicitly indicating which packets can be passed through the bridge and how a packet is to be modified in the bridge. The configuration file allows specifying the default actions to be applied on the packets that are not managed by the rules, i.e., if they should be forwarded or not. 5Greplay address the lack of an open-source tools to perform security testing in 5G networks. Thanks to its ability to create a variety of 5G network traffic scenarios, 5Greplay enables the implementation of cyberattacks, such as those identified by ENISA [3], as well as the security test cases proposed by the 3GPP [1].

---

[2] http://5greplay.org/.

References

1. T. 3rd Generation Partnership Project (3GPP). 3GPP TS 33.117 - catalogue of general security assurance requirements (2020)
2. Ahmad, I., Kumar, T., Liyanage, M., Okwuibe, J., Ylianttila, M., Gurtov, A.: Overview of 5G security challenges and solutions. IEEE Commun. Stand. Mag. **2**(1), 36–43 (2018)
3. ENISA. Enisa threat landscape for 5G networks, February 2021

The BIECO Conceptual Framework Towards Security and Trust in ICT Ecosystems

Ricardo Silva Peres[1,2(✉)], Lilian Adkinson[2], Emilia Cioroaica[2],
Eda Marchetti[2], Enrico Schiavone[2], Sara Matheu[2], Ovidiu Cosma[2],
Radosław Piliszek[2], and José Barata[1,2]

[1] UNINOVA - Centre of Technology and Systems (CTS),
2829 -516 Caparica, Portugal
{ricardo.peres,jab}@uninova.pt
[2] The BIECO Consortium, Caparica, Portugal

Abstract. Modern ICT supply chains are complex, multidimensional and heterogeneous by nature, encompassing varied technologies, actors and interconnected resources. This makes it so that cybersecurity has become a major concern for such ecosystems, particularly given the tremendous velocity cybersecurity threats evolve requiring continuous monitoring, assessment and improvement of these ecosystems to assure their integrity and security. In this regard, BIECO aims to deliver a holistic approach to building and validating methodologies and technologies tailored to foster security and trust within ICT ecosystems across their entire lifecycle, from design to runtime phases. Here we present an initial project report with an overview of the BIECO project, emphasizing its concept, objectives and main building blocks.

1 Introduction

With progressing digitalization and the trend towards autonomous computing, systems tend to form digital ecosystems, where each participant (system or actor) implements its own operational goals. Systems operating within ecosystems can deploy smart agents [1] in the form of software applications, which would enable cooperative behaviour with other ecosystem participants, and achievement of common tactical and strategic goals.

Effective collaboration within these emerging digital ecosystems strongly relies on the assumption that all components of the ecosystem operate as expected, and a level of trust among them is established based on that. BIECO aims to provide mechanisms that ensure the collaboration between ecosystem participants remains trustworthy in case of failures. By making systems resilient in the face of malicious attacks, a trustworthy behaviour is always displayed to the user (which can be an interacting service or a human user). Assessing the trustworthiness of ecosystem participants requires new platforms that enable behaviour evaluation at runtime, with this being one of the main goals of BIECO.

© IFIP International Federation for Information Processing 2022
Published by Springer Nature Switzerland AG 2022
D. Clark et al. (Eds.): ICTSS 2021, LNCS 13045, pp. 230–232, 2022.
https://doi.org/10.1007/978-3-031-04673-5

2   The BIECO Concept

The rationale behind BIECO's concept is to deliver a framework for improving trust and security within ICT supply chains [2]. These are complex ecosystems comprising several heterogeneous technologies, processes, actors (e.g., end-users, software or hardware providers and organizations) and resources, all of which generate or exchange data forming complex information management systems.

Due to this, cybersecurity and integrity are important aspects to take into account in this context, which need to be addressed with an integrative approach that contemplates the entire chain, as opposed to restraining it only to the individual components. BIECO proposes a holistic approach to building and validating methodologies and technologies tailored to foster security [3] and trust [4] within ICT ecosystems, with its building blocks being shown in Fig. 1.

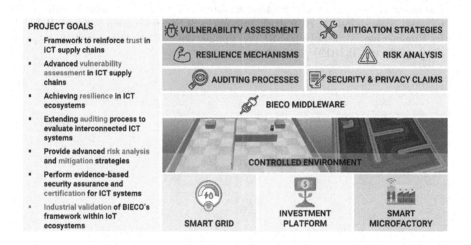

Fig. 1. The main building blocks of the BIECO framework.

The goal is to instantiate the framework iteratively in order to enable a continuous testing and improvement of ICT supply chain's security [5], given the speed at which the cybersecurity landscape evolves with new threats emerging every day. As shown, the methodologies and tools developed or adapted in this context will be evaluated in three use cases from different domains, namely within smart grid/energy, financial and the manufacturing industry sectors.

Acknowledgement. This work was partially supported by the project BIECO (www. bieco.org) that received funding from the European Union's Horizon 2020 research and innovation programme under grant agreement No. 952702.

References

1. Peres, R.S., Jia, X., Lee, J., Sun, K., Colombo, A.W., Barata, J.: Industrial artificial intelligence in industry 4.0-systematic review, challenges and outlook. IEEE Access **8**, 220121–220139 (2020). https://doi.org/10.1109/ACCESS.2020.3042874
2. Deliverable D2.3, "Overall Framework Architecture Design (1st Draft)", BIECO project, February 2021
3. Baldini, G., Skarmeta, A., Fourneret, E., Neisse, R., Legeard, B., Le Gall, F.: Security certification and labelling in internet of things. In: 2016 IEEE 3rd World Forum on Internet of Things (WF-IoT), pp. 627–632. IEEE, December 2016. https://doi.org/10.1109/WF-IoT.2016.7845514
4. Cioroaica, E., Chren, S., Buhnova, B., Kuhn, T., Dimitrov, D.: Reference architecture for trust-based digital ecosystems. In: 2020 IEEE International Conference on Software Architecture Companion (ICSA-C), pp. 266–273. IEEE, March 2020. https://doi.org/10.1109/ICSA-C50368.2020.00051
5. Cioroaica, E., et al.: Towards runtime monitoring for malicious behaviors detection in smart ecosystems. In: 2019 IEEE International Symposium on Software Reliability Engineering Workshops (ISSREW), pp. 200–203. IEEE, October 2019. https://doi.org/10.1109/ISSREW.2019.00072

Industrial Machine Learning for Enterprises (IML4E)

Jürgen Großmann[1]([✉]) and Jukka K. Nurminen[2]

[1] Fraunhofer FOKUS, Berlin, Germany
juergen.grossmann@fokus.fraunhofer.de
[2] University of Helsinki, Helsinki, Finland
jukka.k.nurminen@helsinki.fi

Abstract. Smart software solutions, i.e., software that includes artificial intelligence (AI) and machine learning (ML), have shown a great potential to automate processes that were previously not accessible to automation. These areas include predictive maintenance, the creation of clinical diagnoses, recommendations systems, speech, image and scenario recognition, automated driving etc. Since AI and ML differ from classical software development regarding fundamental activities and processes, it is currently unclear how AI and ML can be integrated into existing industrial-grade software development processes. Addressing the industrialization of ML development and operations, the IML4E project will directly address the specifics of AI and ML by providing interoperability, automation and reusability in the data and the training pipeline. Moreover, IML4E enables continuous quality assurance and supervision for different types of machine learning (supervised learning, unsupervised learning, etc.) throughout the whole life cycle of a smart software solution. In this project presentation, we will focus in particular on the quality assurance and testing research planned in the project.

Keywords: ML · ML-Testing · MLOps

1 IML4E Background

Estimates show that the use of AI-based solutions for business applications will also experience significant growth in Europe over the next five years, with projected revenues worldwide rising from $14.69 billion in 2019 to an expected $126 billion in 2025. However, the high growth rates for AI-based software and services can only be achieved if AI- and ML-based software can be produced, operated and maintained with similar efficiency and quality as classic software. In analogy to classical software, AI-based software must be implemented and validated according to the requirements of the end user and fulfil the established quality characteristics of classical software as well as a number of new quality characteristics (e.g., interpretability, intelligent behavior, non-discrimination, etc.). Their use must be technologically, socially and ethically acceptable and safe. All this must be carefully planned, realized, validated and maintained throughout the software life cycle.

© IFIP International Federation for Information Processing 2022
D. Clark et al. (Eds.): ICTSS 2021, LNCS 13045, pp. 233–234, 2022.
https://doi.org/10.1007/978-3-031-04673-5

2 IML4E Objectives

Against this background, the IML4E project[1] develops a European framework for the development, operation and maintenance of AI-based software, thereby ensuring the development and quality assurance of intelligent services and intelligent software on an industrial scale. The main IML4E objectives are:

- Improving the modularity and reuse of development and data artefacts throughout the development process by (a) providing datasets and metadata that may serve the training of models in different application contexts, (b) pretrained models that are reused as a basis for further training in different application contexts, and (c) test patterns and test procedures that allow for standardized test suites to ensure dedicated ML specific quality attributes like security, robustness, transparency etc.
- Boosting the automation, interoperability and tool support throughout the whole ML lifecycle. In particular, there is currently a lack of tools that allow for (a) automated processing with integrated quality assurance of data in the data preparation pipeline, (b) continuous testing and verification of ML artefacts during development, reuse and deployment, (c) versioning and traceability of development and data artefacts (data sets, models, parameters, test results) in the course of data preparation, training and (d) operations, and systematic surveillance and monitoring of models in the field (monitoring corner cases, model evolution, functional fitness, security etc.) including the ability to intervene in case severe deviations are reported.

It has become clear that a paradigm shift is imminent, especially in the area of quality assurance for AI-supported software. Classical verification approaches are not applicable due to the complexity of deep neural networks. Basic assumptions about the stability of the software and its non-determinism no longer hold, as the well-known problems with adversarial attacks and concept drift show. Quality assurance must become a continuous process that accompanies the entire life cycle of the software. Appropriate methods and tools with the necessary degree of automation as well as a focus on known ML vulnerabilities and stochastic applications are missing.

3 Expected IML4E Results

The IML4E project will develop methods and tools for risk-based quality assurance over the next three years that are specifically adapted to the characteristics of deep neural networks. This includes a catalogue of formalized quality attributes dedicated to data, ML and ML-based software, tools for debugging, testing and safeguarding ML especially in safety critical areas as well as an MLOps methodology that seamlessly integrate ML and data science activities with processes and best practices from software engineering, quality assurance and safety engineering.

---

[1] https://itea4.org/project/iml4e.html.

NLP-based Testing and Monitoring for Security Checking

Andrey Sadovykh$^{1,6(\boxtimes)}$, Zujany Salazar$^{2(\boxtimes)}$, Wissam Mallouli$^{2(\boxtimes)}$,
Ana R. Cavalli$^{2(\boxtimes)}$, Dragos Truscan$^{4(\boxtimes)}$, Eduard Paul Enoiu$^{3(\boxtimes)}$,
Rosa Iglesias$^{5(\boxtimes)}$, and Olga Hendel$^{3(\boxtimes)}$

^{1} Softeam, Paris, France
andrey.sadovykh@softeam.fr
^{2} Montimage EURL, Paris, France
{zujany.salazar,wissam.mallouli,ana.cavalli}@montimage.com
^{3} Mälardalen University, Västerås, Sweden
{eduard.paul.enoiu,olga.hendel}@mdh.se
^{4} Åbo Akademi University, Turku, Finland
dragos.truscan@abo.fi
^{5} Ikerlan Technology Research Centre, Basque Research and Technology Alliance
(BRTA), Gipuzkoa, Spain
riglesias@ikerlan.es
^{6} Innopolis University, Innopolis, Russia
a.sadovykh@innopolis.ru

Abstract. VeriDevOps aims at bringing together fast and cost-effective security verification through formal modelling and verification, as well as test generation, selection, execution and analysis capabilities to enable companies to deliver quality systems with confidence in a fast-paced DevOps environment. Security requirements are intended to be processed using NLP advanced algorithms in order to deliver formal specifications of security properties to be checked during development and operation of a system under test.

Keywords: Model-Driven engineering · Cybersecurity · Test and validation · Runtime analysis · Natural language processing.

1 The VeriDevOps Concept

Figure 1. depicts the overall concept of the project. VeriDevOps intends to advance the state of the art by tailoring formal verification of security requirements to DevOps and real-world CD pipelines. Given an existing system under continuous integration/delivery, security and safety requirements at physical, application and network level [2] come in different forms. These can be standard requirements, such as those from ISA/IEC 62443 standard for control systems or description of vulnerabilities from common repositories, as well as reports

H2020 VeriDevOps project: https://cordis.europa.eu/project/id/957212

from security experts. In all cases, these requirements should be immediately taken into account according to their severity. In this way, the protection mechanisms such as firewalls may be the first to be re-configured in order to avoid an immediate danger and secure the system perimeter. Next, the design of the system should be examined in order to locate the root-cause of the potential security breach and identify the remediation methods on code level as a patch or upgrade, at the design level, as a major redesign.

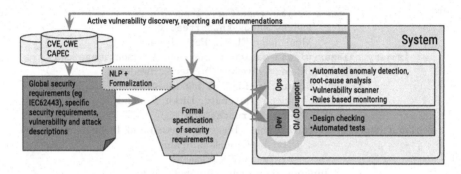

Fig. 1. The VeriDevOps main concept

The use of security requirements for protection and prevention suffers from limited automation support which is mostly limited to vulnerability scanners. There is still a tremendous amount of manual work to configure protection means at operations level and locate and prevent the vulnerabilities at design level, beyond the use of tools for scanning the libraries and tool chains used during the implementation. Despite the large volume of academic research on software testing and verification, there are relatively few commercial and industry-strength tools for security testing that require formal specifications of the system. In addition, the formalization of requirements is still a very human-intensive activity; much information is informally exchanged among the engineers and due to this, most verification activities cannot be automated and need human intervention. We argue that this formalization of security requirements and the creation of environment and system models could increase the product quality, and make the development and operation more efficient and less costly.

Thus, the key challenge of the project is to automatically express and manage security requirements in an effective and unambiguous way, by formalizing them using NLP [1], such that both engineers and stakeholders have a common understanding of their content. Once these security requirements are unambiguously specified and decomposed, one needs to verify the compliance of the realizations to required security behavior by formal verification and testing for both protection and prevention means. In order to save time and lower the effort for adjusting the prevention and protection mechanisms, VeriDevOps automates the specification and analysis of requirements with security relevance, at the system and network levels, testing of system realizations and the integration of these techniques and tools with current VeriDevops practices in industry.

References

1. Garousi, V., Bauer, S., Felderer, M.: NLP-assisted software testing: a systematic mapping of the literature. Inf. Softw. Technol. **126**, 106321 (2020)
2. Khan, R.A., Khan, S.U., Khan, H.U., Ilyas, M.: Systematic mapping study on security approaches in secure software engineering. IEEE Access **9**, 19139–19160 (2021)

Author Index

Printed in the United States
by Baker & Taylor Publisher Services